THE EVOLUTION OF THE PRIVATE
LANGUAGE ARGUMENT

The Evolution of the Private Language Argument presents a continuous view of modern analytical philosophy by telling the history of one of its central strands. It is an in-depth history of this well known philosophical argument, the evolution of Wittgenstein's thoughts and its influence on analytical philosophy of mind and language.

Nielsen looks at early discussions of the private language argument in the Vienna Circle and the influence of Wittgenstein's ideas and examines the relation between the early and later Wittgenstein on this subject. He discusses which influential versions of the private language argument have been presented in the fifty years since *Philosophical Investigations* was published and how they relate to Wittgenstein's thoughts, and considers how the role and the interpretation of the argument, and Wittgenstein's philosophy, changed along with changes in the conception of the nature of analytic philosophy.

D1739475

ASHGATE WITTGENSTEINIAN STUDIES

Series editor: Mario von der Ruhr, University of Wales, Swansea, UK

Ludwig Wittgenstein was one of the greatest philosophers of the twentieth century, his work leading to a variety of differing readings which in turn have had a diverse influence on contemporary philosophy. As well as exploring the more familiar Wittgensteinian themes in the philosophy of language, this series will be a centre of excellence for Wittgensteinian studies in mathematics, aesthetics, religion and philosophy of the mind. Wittgenstein's philosophy has proved extremely fruitful in many contexts and this series will publish not only a variety of readings of Wittgenstein's work, but also work on philosophers and philosophical topics inspired by Wittgensteinian perspectives.

The Evolution of the Private Language Argument

KELD STEHR NIELSEN
University of Copenhagen, Denmark

Routledge
Taylor & Francis Group

LONDON AND NEW YORK

First published 2008 by Ashgate Publishing

2 Park Square, Milton Park, Abingdon, Oxon OX14 4RN
711 Third Avenue, New York, NY 10017, USA

Routledge is an imprint of the Taylor & Francis Group, an informa business

First issued in paperback 2017

British Library Cataloguing in Publication Data
Nielsen, Keld Stehr, 1975–
  The evolution of the private language argument. – (Ashgate Wittgensteinian studies)
  1. Wittgenstein, Ludwig, 1889–1951 2. Private language problem 3. Analysis (Philosophy)
  I. Title
  121.6'8

Library of Congress Cataloging-in-Publication Data
Nielsen, Keld Stehr, 1975-
  The evolution of the private language argument / Keld Stehr Nielsen.
    p. cm. — (Ashgate Wittgensteinian studies)
  Includes bibliographical references.
  ISBN 978-0-7546-5629-6 (hardcover : alk. paper) 1. Private language problem. 2. Analysis
(Philosophy) 3. Wittgenstein, Ludwig, 1889–1951. I. Title.

  B832.3.N54 2007
  121'.68—dc22

                                                        2007007967

ISBN 978-0-7546-5629-6 (hbk)
ISBN 978-1-138-24947-9 (pbk)

Contents

Part III: Language within Philosophy

Acknowledgements

It is a pleasure to acknowledge my debt to my supervisor Jan Riis Flor, who turned my initial tentative enquiries into the evolution of the private language argument into a more detailed and determined study of it. His help with the literature, and his comments along the way, have also been invaluable.

I would also like to thank Dr Paul Robinson, of Quercus Editorial, whose linguistic revisions improved the readability and flow of the manuscript immensely. The preparation of this manuscript was generously supported by grant no. 273–05–0136 from the Danish Research Council for the Humanities.

Jan Faye convinced me that the book was worth publishing, and Leo Catana that Descartes and Cartesianism has little to do with each other. Nikolaj Nottelmann clarified issues concerning Otto Neurath's philosophy and suggested the cover picture.

On a more personal level, I cannot express enough gratitude to my girlfriend, Karina, for enduring the periods when I have become heavily preoccupied with my work, and to Cecilia, Amalia, Liva and Olga Rose for always being grateful no matter how little I had to offer. This book is dedicated to all the girls in my life.

Chapter 1

Introduction

The preoccupation with language that characterized much analytic philosophy after 1900 is distinctive. With a seriousness and determination that had not been witnessed before, twentieth-century philosophers took on the task of exploring the nature of language. In particular, they sought to identify the philosophical consequences, and the consequences for philosophy, of the notion that language is the public manifestation and essential bearer of a person's thoughts. This book focuses on a single, central issue in this task: it traces and explicates the determining factors in the debate over the possibility of a *private language*. This debate has developed over many years. In the late 1920s it was part of the Vienna Circle's struggle to combine a 'scientific world conception' with the experiential basis of observation. Later it featured in discussions about the foundations of normativity in language – discussions that continue to this day.

With the exception of a few unavoidable jumps back and forth in time, the chronological structure of the book is broken only by an examination of Wittgenstein's account of the subject in his *Philosophical Investigations*, published in 1953. This structure represents an acknowledgement that the interpretation of Wittgenstein's work has played, and continues to play, a significant part in discussions of the exact form and consequences of argumentation against a private language. On the basis of the impact of the interpretations, it is fair to conclude that these, rather than Wittgenstein's original text, have played the most decisive part in the argument's history. To some extent this continues to be the case even today, although I think that Chapter 10 presents a fairly accurate picture of what Wittgenstein intended by his 'private language argument'.

Wittgenstein's influence on the debate whose history is considered in this book can hardly be exaggerated.[1] The thoroughness with which he discussed the possibility of a private language and epistemic privacy in general, and the compactness of his remarks in *Philosophical Investigations*, ensured that discussion after 1953 more or less equated the question whether there can be a private language with the question

---

[1]   A few numbers might serve to underline this claim. In their 1990 bibliography of secondary literature on Wittgenstein, Frongia and McGuinness (1990) list 128 entries on 'private language' up to 1987. This makes 'private language' the largest single entry. *The Philosopher's Index* (July, 2002) carries 168 entries for the same period. Of these, 85 also appear in the Frongia and McGuinness list. Of the remaining 83, 42 make explicit reference to Wittgenstein and only 20 refer to other philosophers. In these 20 items, indirect reference to Wittgenstein is common. The philosophers mentioned are: Kripke (5), Frege (1), Castañeda (1), Schlick (1), Anscombe (1), Ryle (1), Winch (1), Quine (2), Hegel (1), Ginet (1), Ayer (3), Zemach (1), Mead (1). A similar picture emerges from a search on the perhaps even more distinctively Wittgensteinian phrase 'private language argument'.

whether Wittgenstein's attack on such language was sound. Even before 1953 Wittgenstein exerted an influence on the debate. Thus his presence is detectable, as I show in Chapter 2, in pre-1950s discussions between Rudolf Carnap and Otto Neurath. In some cases this was unfortunate. His authority as a genius, combined with the difficulty of his thinking and his unorthodox writing style, led to accounts that carried conviction largely because they seemed to respect his thought. On the other hand, these factors encouraged philosophers to speculate about the subject even at times when the prospects of advance in this field seemed dim. There is little doubt that the issue would have received much less attention had it not been for Wittgenstein's treatment. He condensed into it issues of considerable significance in epistemology, the philosophy of mind and the philosophy of language.

This book is therefore not just about the evolution of the private language argument. It is also about the evolution of Wittgenstein's philosophy and, especially, the reception of that philosophy.

It should be made clear from the outset that the label 'the private language argument' is quite misleading. In so far as the promise is to demonstrate the *impossibility* of a private language, it would be more appropriate to speak of the anti-private language argument. At this late hour it would, however, be futile to abandon the conventional name. Another problem is posed by the use of the definite article. Not even within the confines of *Philosophical Investigations* is it merited. A survey of literature of the last hundred years reveals a wide range of different arguments that have been invoked to demonstrate the impossibility of a private language. I have respected this diversity by giving these arguments different names, but I have used the label 'the private language argument' in my title as the prevailing tendency is to speak of a single argument demonstrating the impossibility of a private language. With this label, philosophers will more often than not be referring to whatever is to be found in Wittgenstein's book.

Let me emphasize that one should not be misled by the title into thinking that the book is structured around the evolution of a single argument which gradually improved over the years. It might be possible to base the discussion during some periods on that model, but to see the entire period from the 1920s onwards in this light would be to distort what actually happened. Argumentation against private language cuts through several philosophical genres, and considerable discussion has concentrated on the question what, exactly, this sort of argument targets. So the history is not one in which a clear-cut case against a particular position is developed, but rather one in which several different arguments succeed one another as philosophical currents change.

This also means that I have not attended much to the question whether a certain elaboration by one writer is valid, but rather placed my emphasis on the underlying premises. Consequently, when, in Chapter 6, I criticize certain arguments, I do not do so with the intention of proving them to be invalid. Rather, I am attempting merely to point out that the arguments rest on certain premises that had, at the relevant time, been recognized as problematic. Generally, I think this strategy generates the most authentic picture: most of the arguments that have played a role in the history of the private language argument are valid – or, if that is too technically loaded a term, do not rest on mistaken reasoning. There are, however, cases in which the use of this strategy is less obviously sound. Most notably, perhaps, the arguments described by Norman Malcolm in his review of *Philosophical Investigations* are not obviously valid, given Malcolm's description of the premises. Equally, my account of Anthony Kenny's interpretation of §265 trades on a selective focus; only so does it live up to Kenny's own observations. Still, I think the interpretations in these cases are justified. For the sake of clarity, I have summarized some of the arguments in point-by-point fashion in the appendices.

As mentioned above, there are certain discontinuities in the slice of intellectual history discussed here. I have attempted to register these by dividing the discussion of the book into two parts. Part I concentrates mainly on what went on in the bustling philosophical environment of Vienna in the late 1920s – home, during that period, to both the Vienna Circle and Wittgenstein, though the latter frequently travelled beyond the city. Here, discussion concentrated on problems associated with the apparently commonplace notion that our only experience of the world is derived from what we directly perceive. Once language had moved to the centre of philosophical attention it became clear that a more nuanced picture was needed of the way in which language connects with, and communicates, the contents of experience. To begin with, the revisions placed certain strictures on what could be communicated. Later on, in a radical departure from his contemporaries, Wittgenstein came to think that revision of our conception of the contents of experiences was needed.

Part II begins with the publication of *Philosophical Investigations* in 1953, a book many observers would probably see as marking the beginning of discussions about privacy. The upshot was a remarkably confused discussion with underlying methodological discord. Underlying the various discussions there was often disagreement about the nature and aim of philosophy. Nonetheless, successful and lasting contributions were made to the philosophy of mind, and more specifically to efforts at that time to query Cartesian dualism, which had dominated the field for centuries. So-called 'ordinary language philosophy', for all its problems, proved to be an effective way to direct attention to details in our conception of the mind which had been neglected in the Cartesian drive for a theoretically stringent picture.

Part III covers discussion of the private language argument from the early 1970s until today. Although the debate had all along centred on certain essential features of language, in the early 1970s the discussion liberated itself from the methodological crusades so distinctive of the Vienna Circle and ordinary language philosophy and focused on the mechanisms of language. Philosophers focused their attention, so to speak, on the tool – language – rather than simply using it, as they had in previous decades. This meant that discussion of the private language argument gradually became merged, as a sub-theme, with other discussions about such matters as following a rule and the possibility of a scientific approach to the mental. In so far as there still is a distinctive private language discussion today, it is among Wittgenstein scholars. I enter this debate in Chapter 10.

How, then, do these parts connect? Should we think of these transitions in the discussion as part of an evolution or merely as a superficial change of appearance? We can approach this question by acknowledging the fact that the private language debate shares certain general characteristics with the role that language has played in one branch of twentieth-century philosophy. Two leading reasons why language became central in philosophy in the early twentieth century were that it promised, first, to demarcate the borders of sense, and second, simultaneously to satisfy the striving for objectivity so essential to philosophical progress. Philosophers of the Vienna Circle took these features to provide a powerful tool with which to, as it were, muck out the metaphysical concepts of their contemporaries. It is true that this role of philosophical watchdog was also adopted in the linguistic philosophy emanating from Cambridge and Oxford in the 1950s. Here, however, philosophical aspirations were connected less closely with science, and in particular with a belief in the superiority of scientific language, than they were in the work of members of the Vienna Circle.

The purpose of drawing this crude, one-sided picture of philosophy in Vienna, and Cambridge and Oxford, is to shed light on what was regarded as the primary aim of argument against the possibility of a private language: within a linguistic framework, the private language argument promised to banish ghosts and myths that had haunted philosophy for centuries. These myths were not just found on the periphery: both Carnap, in 1932, and Malcolm, in 1954, saw their private language arguments as proving the impossibility of phenomenalism and Cartesianism. Private language argumentation was, therefore, conceived of as a facilitator of progress, because it was part of modern philosophy distancing itself from its predecessors. The discussion of private language in Part III continues this line, but the ideas that are disposed of there are of more recent origin and have to do with the conception of language inherent in the two earlier parts of the book. Wittgenstein had exposed and confronted not only the demons of his predecessors, but also those of his earlier self. His argument was taken to turn against the idea that ostensive definition is the ultimate meaning-fixing mechanism. It also constituted part of a serious problem for several conceptions of the normativity so essential for language. Since these discussions are still in vogue, the private language argument is still part of a cleansing process.

These remarks are very general and are intended to draw lines that pervade the whole period. Let me conclude by briefly introducing the book's chapters in turn.

Chapter 2 focuses on the protocol sentence debate of the early 1930s involving Carnap and Neurath. This debate addressed the problem of reconciling the scientific demand for inter-subjectivity with the primacy of experience. An important part of it centred on the recognition that private language was unacceptable.

Chapter 3 presents Wittgenstein's struggles in 1929, when he still believed in the necessity of a phenomenological language – a language which directly and non-hypothetically describes what is immediately given in sense experience. His repeated attempts to make sense of this language, and his subsequent abandonment of it, amount essentially to a private language argument.

Chapter 4, like the preceding chapter, draws upon material from Wittgenstein's *Nachlass* that has only recently become available in published form. It examines Wittgenstein's thoughts on privacy as they appear in a text written in 1941. This text outlines more clearly and coherently, but also more superficially than similar passages in *Philosophical Investigations*, the problems Wittgenstein saw here. Although the material is related to the discussion of Chapter 10, I have included it here, because in conjunction with Chapter 3 it brings out an important transition in Wittgenstein's philosophy.

Chapter 5 presents the earliest reactions to the publication of *Philosophical Investigations* in 1953, and to the alleged demonstration, in that work, of the impossibility of a private language. Together, these reactions introduced a variety of topics into the discussion and raised it to the top of the agenda in philosophy. In particular, Malcolm's review proved influential here. Indeed it probably explains why the topic came to enjoy such prominence, since he argued that the idea of a private language was inherently unstable, as opposed to being, merely, irreconcilable with new trends in philosophy. This created an expectation of real progress.

Chapters 6 and 7 look at discussions that occurred during the 1960s. This was the period in which the subject received the greatest attention. Chapter 6 asks whether Malcolm's promise of a *reductio ad absurdum* of the notion of a private language was, or could have been, delivered on during the 1950s and 1960s; in particular it analyzes the alleged neutrality of Malcolm's assumptions.

Chapter 7 focuses on methodological issues that also formed part of the privacy discussion during that period. It describes contributions that bore fruit independently of this methodological agenda, not only as interpretations of Wittgenstein, whose authority greatly influenced the debate, but also within the philosophy of mind. These contributions, however, did not amount to direct arguments against the possibility of a private language; they were located on the perimeter of the argument.

Chapter 8 discusses the important steps in the debate in the early 1970s, a time in which interest in private language had begun to cool as a result of external factors. Previous arguments had usually focused on the use of language as a medium; but philosophers now sought consciously to clarify their conception of this medium. Thus the debate about private language became more distinctively an issue in the philosophy of language. Once located here, the issue was gradually subordinated, during the 1970s, to the problem of rule-following.

Chapter 9 discusses the private language argument in the context of Wittgenstein's rule-following considerations. In fact the conclusions of these considerations are reached before Wittgenstein turns to comment on private language in *Philosophical Investigations*. Hence, the private language argument proves to be relevant to questions about normativity in language and the question whether language is an essentially social phenomenon.

Chapter 10 analyses certain sections in *Philosophical Investigations* whose interpretation has been the focal point of the debate since 1953. I offer my own interpretation of these sections, but I also analyze some interpretations provided by leading Wittgenstein scholars. I show that although Wittgenstein's main target seems to have been the Cartesian private object, his investigations connect thematically with recent applications of the argument. Accordingly, Chapter 11 links his conclusions to issues beyond the scope of Wittgenstein exegesis.

PART I
Between the Wars

Chapter 2

The Dispute between Carnap and Neurath

Our story begins in Vienna in the late 1920s. Since 1923 a loosely associated group of scientifically orientated philosophers, most of them trained in formal and empirical sciences, had met for weekly discussions. This group would soon be referred to as the 'Vienna Circle'. It was internationally renowned in its own time and is a reference point in twentieth-century analytical philosophy. From the very beginning the main topic of discussion was the philosophical understanding of scientific knowledge, and what gradually emerged from these discussions was the substantial convergence in the members' approaches to this question. In due course this convergence was institutionalized. Thus in 1929 the *Verein Ernst Mach* (Ernst Mach Society) was founded and something as exotic as a manifesto, *The Scientific Conception of the World: The Vienna Circle* (Carnap et al, 1929), was published by some of the group's leading members.[1]

Within the group, discussion of the status of private language soon began, and in time it became an important theme in what is commonly referred to as the *Protocol Sentence Debate* between Rudolf Carnap and Otto Neurath, both leading members of the Vienna Circle. The subject of the protocol debate was the nature of empirical knowledge, and when physicalism had an impact on this debate in the early 1930s, two arguments against the possibility of a private language were, in effect, explored.

In this chapter I will present a detailed analysis of Carnap's and Neurath's arguments. This, I hope, will bring out significant differences in their agendas. I shall describe the way in which divergences between Carnap's and Neurath's views were reflected in contrasts in the way they marshalled their opposition to the notion of a private language; only so is it possible to appreciate the role of the relevant arguments vis-à-vis the real concern, namely: how traditional empiricism could survive the strictures of consistent scientism and the verification principle. I will begin by describing the historical setting, in Vienna, in which the possibility of private language became a central issue.

---

[1]   Another programmatic paper was Moritz Schlick's (1930) 'The Turning Point in Philosophy'.

2.1 The Vienna Circle Before 1932

When the Vienna Circle became a recognized group in 1929 the background against which philosophical concerns about privacy would subsequently arise had already been set out in two major works. One was Ludwig Wittgenstein's *Tractatus Logico-Philosophicus*; the other was Rudolf Carnap's *The Logical Structure of the World*. Both are very hard to assess and would ideally receive thorough examination; but since they constitute the background to Carnap's and Neurath's arguments, we must merely extract some elements of immediate relevance here.

One characteristic of all members of the Vienna Circle was a confidence about scientific enquiry: scientific knowledge was not only possible but also actual. Given this, the questions discussed within the Circle were not so much traditional philosophical ones about the possibility of knowledge, but rather enquiries into knowledge's nature. Here the Circle steered clear of strong currents in German philosophy in the 1920s which exhibited growing scepticism about the ability of science to deliver knowledge. In particular, growing acceptance of relativity theory in physics, with its unintuitive account of time and space and its failure to fit the traditional philosophical accounts of knowledge, suggested to many that science employed principles and concepts not univocally supported by empirical evidence. Science had distanced itself from its object of enquiry, the world we confront, and was therefore incapable of producing empirical knowledge. In opposition to this tendency, one of the first tasks of the Vienna Circle was to defend the new theories of physics.

The dissociation with academic philosophy was even more radical. In the clash between science and traditional philosophy, members of the Vienna Circle chose science. Comparing 2000 years of unresolved discussion in philosophy with the advances in the physical sciences since Newton, Circle members thought the choice was simple: if traditional philosophy could not account for scientific rationality, it would have to be replaced. What the nature of the replacement would be was, to be sure, a matter of intense debate among Circle members. But opposition to traditional philosophy was shared: our possession of scientific knowledge was not to be *justified* by metaphysical and epistemological considerations rebutting the sceptic; it was a basic epistemological fact to be *understood* and *explained*. In so far as justifications were provided, they would be accounts of the way in which scientific claims come to be meaningful (Uebel, 1992, pp. 12–13). Carnap's talk of justifications (discussed below) was not therefore an answer to the sceptic who doubts the existence of the outer world or its intelligibility, but an analysis of the nature of scientific claims.

The Logical Structure of the World was Rudolf Carnap's first major contribution to this project. It was written mainly between 1922 and 1925, but not published until three years later. Its stated purpose was to provide a genealogy of concepts, or constructional system, within which there would be 'a step-by-step derivation or "construction" of all concepts from certain fundamental concepts' (Carnap, 1928, p. 5). Carnap believed that this would show how scientific knowledge claims can be understood and justified in principle.

Carnap's approach was paradigmatic of logical empiricism, the methodology generally taken to characterize Vienna Circle philosophy. Carnap embraced logicism.

Formal sciences were considered part of mathematical logic and devoid of empirical content. Because of this, they could be presupposed in the construction of empirical scientific knowledge (Carnap, 1928, §106); they could be employed in the 'translation' or reduction of all scientific concepts to one basic domain. Approaching the matter from the opposite direction, Carnap's thesis was that every scientific concept could be *rationally reconstructed* from elements in that basic domain by exclusively logical means. Remaining faithful to the fundamental tenet of empiricism that all factual knowledge derives from the given, he chose a phenomenalist language as the basic domain for his system. Hence the name 'logical empiricism' – the combination of logicism and empiricism.

The choice of phenomenalist language as the basic currency was made, Carnap said, not in response to any philosophical presuppositions, but in order to reflect what he called the 'epistemic order of objects' (§66): first, auto-psychological objects were constructed, then physical objects, then other minds, and finally cultural objects. To distinguish his own from other philosophical positions he chose 'Methodological Solipsism' as the name for his theory. This term was intended to mark the fact that he had adopted the epistemological position of the solipsist without acknowledging its central thesis that only one subject and its experiences are real (§64).

Translating all scientific knowledge claims into a single basic language amounted, in effect, to defending the 'thesis of the unity of science' – that is, the endeavour to link and harmonize the various fields of science (Carnap et al, 1929, p. 306). In *The Logical Structure of the World*, this was accomplished by showing how all scientific concepts could be rationally reconstructed in a basic universal language. The idea was that all science proceeded analytically from what is given in experience and hence verified directly. But if demonstrating the unity of science was one major goal of Carnap's enquiry, another was to show how scientific knowledge could be objective. He did this by excluding the content of experience, which was subjective, from knowledge claims, which would then only include claims about the structure of immediate experience. Since these claims could be compared, in as much as different structures would result in different judgments, objectivity, in the sense of intersubjectivity, was secured (Carnap, 1928, §66).

The Logical Structure of the World was Carnap's first concerted attempt to establish the unity of science and defend its objectivity. However, soon after its publication in 1928 he realized that his constructional theory needed to be revised: it was better seen as a point of departure than as a conclusion. One of the tensions in the theory was the relation between the intersubjectivity of scientific knowledge and the auto-psychological, phenomenalist domain which he had chosen as the base of his construction. The choice of basic domain was made somewhat tentatively. Carnap had even mentioned the physical domain as another possibility, but epistemological considerations having to do with the order of cognition had been problematic here, since a physical base would have left scientific claims unaccounted for. In Neurath's crude words this choice could be considered a '... weakened left-over from idealistic metaphysics ...' (Neurath, 1932a, p. 540, my translation).

Neurath's remark probably alludes to a problem with Carnap's choice of basic domain that began to surface around 1930. Carnap had to take this problem very seriously, given the apparent implication that his rational reconstruction would not secure the objectivity of scientific knowledge. In *The Logical Structure of the World* objectivity, in the sense of intersubjective agreement of knowledge claims, was secured by restricting science to statements about the structural properties of streams of experience (Carnap, 1928, §66). The thought was that if two subjects receive the same stimulation, they will give the same verdict as long as their conceptual structures are identical. This characterization was given from above, looking down on the system, but that is not a position a subject can occupy. Carnap had given a more suspect explanation of how one subject could compare his construction of concepts to another's. He suggested that one 'constructs' a world containing another subject M. Part of that construction is a construction of the world-of-M, or the world as M experiences it. The intersubjective world is then made up of the 'objects' that generate intersubjective correspondences, i.e. instances where there is a one-to-one correspondence between one's own world and the world-of-M (§146).

The first person to see this failure of Carnap's account to confer genuine intersubjective validity on scientific statements was probably Heinrich Neider, who was at that time a student loosely associated with the Vienna Circle.[2] The problem came to this: Carnap's account of the intersubjectivity of empirical content was artificial in the rather serious sense that it did not require the existence of others. For it was ultimately the experiencing subject's construction of other subjects' worlds that determined which 'objects' generated intersubjective correspondences. From a solipsistic starting position, the acceptance of a statement as objectively valid would, in the end, depend exclusively on the constructing subject, since the world-of-M, which was supposed to be a corrective factor, would be part of the same construction. Carnap saw that the account he had given would need improvement. It simply did not handle the intersubjective element of knowledge acquisition in scientific practice well enough.

Another major problem concerned the status of Carnap's analysis in *The Logical Structure of the World*. The book is to a large extent written in a metaphysically neutral vein; and it is clear from the book's introduction that Carnap himself considered it to be a scientific book, writing within, not beyond and about, the body of science (Carnap, 1928, p. III). The subject of the book is the factual basis of meaning – that is, Carnap is attempting to represent the logical form of empirical statements by translation. However, according to Moritz Schlick, another leading member of the Vienna Circle, exhibiting the meaning of statements was a distinctively philosophical enterprise:

> Philosophy ... is that activity whereby the *meaning* of statements is established or discovered. Philosophy elucidates statements, science verifies them. In the latter we are concerned with the truth of statements, but in the former with what they actually mean. (Schlick, 1930, p. 157)

This statement reflects the powerful influence of Wittgenstein's *Tractatus* on the Vienna Circle, and Schlick in particular, in the late 1920s. Despite being published

---

[2]   Uebel (1992), pp. 89–96. The account I have presented is based on Thomas Uebel's reconstruction of the actual proceedings drawn from a few remarks made by Neider in Haller and Rutte (1977).

in 1921 and incorporating material written a good deal earlier, the *Tractatus* was not intensively discussed in the Vienna Circle before 1926, when Hans Hahn held a seminar on the book at the Circle's Thursday afternoon meetings. Hahn had actually given the same seminar in 1922 with a much impressed Schlick among the audience. But Schlick had to wait four years to meet the *Tractatus'* author, and Carnap did not read the *Tractatus* through until 1926.

This notwithstanding, some of the *Tractatus'* conclusions had found their way into the published edition of *The Logical Structure of the World*. One element extracted by the Vienna Circle from Wittgenstein's dissertation was the Verification Principle, which Schlick formulated in the catch-phrase 'the meaning of a proposition is its method of verification'. Carnap's attitude to this doctrine was never entirely straightforward and would soon become more sceptical, but in *The Logical Structure of the World* he had adopted it without explicit acknowledgement (Carnap, 1928, §161): the logical form of a statement, he claimed, the form revealing which logical operations could be performed on it, was represented by its verification conditions.

What, then, was the obstacle to stating the logical form of a statement or proposition? According to the *Tractatus*, meaningful sentences present pictures of the world, or logically possible state of affairs; and a statement or proposition, as a picture, is made true, or verified, when that which it depicts obtains. Logical form determines what a statement depicts, what it means; it is that which a picture must have in common with what it depicts. However, this means that logical form cannot *itself* be represented by a statement. Wittgenstein held this view for two reasons. First, he drew the lesson from type theory that no statement could talk about itself on pain of paradox. Secondly, the only way that the logical form of a statement *s* could be represented by another statement s$_*$ would be by possessing that logical form itself, and this in turn would mean that it would speak about its own logical form, thereby violating type theory.

It follows that the meaning of statements cannot be given by statements (Schlick, 1930, p. 157). However, the *Tractatus* was itself a series of statement about meaning, so these statements could not be thought of as on a par with scientific statements. They would have to be, strictly speaking, meaningless. According to Wittgenstein, they were at best improper statements or elucidations – ladders which you should throw away once climbed (Wittgenstein, 1921, §p. 6.54). Of course, this sort of philosophy would still distance itself from traditional philosophy in being concerned with form instead of intuitive content, but it would not be science either. Thus the Wittgensteinian challenge to Carnap was that he had misunderstood the nature of his own project: his rational reconstruction was not science, but elucidation, and strictly speaking it was without meaning. This separation of philosophy from science was not something to which Carnap could become reconciled (Schilpp (ed.), 1963, pp. 29–30).

2.2 The Unity of Science

So the problem of intersubjectivity and difficulties over the status of his own analysis were among the challenges Carnap faced in 1929. It was three years before Carnap felt equipped to deal with these problems in published work. The publication in question was in *The Unity of Science*, which appeared in 1932. In the course of this discussion, Carnap introduced both a new conception of philosophy and a strategy for relieving the tension between intersubjectivity of science and the epistemic order of objects. It was in his treatment of the second subject that he rejected of the possibility of a private language.

Proper evaluation of Carnap's private language argument requires consideration of his new conception of philosophy – a conception that might be interpreted as an answer to Schlick. Contra Wittgenstein and Schlick, Carnap now held that philosophy trades, not in elucidations, but real sentences, and can produce knowledge. Like Wittgenstein, he considered philosophical investigation to be an analysis of language: 'a philosophical, i.e. logical, investigation must be an analysis of language' (Carnap, 1932a, pp. 37–8). But influenced by the promising formalist methods developed by David Hilbert and Kurt Gödel, and in particular Gödel's new method of using arithmetic to describe linguistic signs and expressions, he came to the conclusion that language could, after all, speak about itself, in the sense that one part of language could describe another part.[3] This metalinguistic method meant that philosophical analysis should be conducted at a purely formal level and be concerned with translations and the various kinds of interdependence connecting syntactical structures. Carnap's conception was thus that philosophy should proceed according to 'the syntactic method, [which] consists in describing a language together with its rules of deduction by reference only to signs and the order of their occurrence in expressions, thus without reference to meaning' (Schilpp (ed.), 1963, p. 928).

In *The Unity of Science*, Carnap expressed the difference between this new conception and traditional philosophy using the distinction between the *formal* and *material* modes of speech. The formal mode restricted its reference to words and sentences and described relations between these, whereas the material mode spoke of objects and facts. The last mode was tolerated, because it could sometimes be a shorter and more familiar way of expressing oneself, but only under the condition that the material mode expressions could be translated into the formal mode, which, strictly speaking, was the only correct mode: when talking in the material mode, one could be misled to ask, and seek answers to, pseudo-questions. These questions pervaded philosophy. However, translation to the formal mode would disclose such illegitimate uses of language.

Ultimately, this meant that the bridges between language and world were down: philosophy was a purely intra-linguistic investigation. For example, the ostensive definitions (such as pointing to an elephant while saying 'By "elephant" I mean this!') which, according to Schlick, connected language and world were interpreted by Carnap as intra-linguistic. Thus we find him writing: '(e.g. "Elephant" = animal of the same kind as the animal in this or that position in space-time)' (Carnap. 1932a, p. 39).

With this distinction drawn, Carnap was in a position to pursue the governing aim of *The Unity of Science*, namely, to advance *physicalism*. In the formal mode, physicalism amounted to holding that every sentence could be translated into another one containing exclusively physical terms – that is, terms from the vocabulary of the science of physics. Initially, he characterized this language as consisting of sentences

---

[3]   See Uebel (1992), Ch. 5, for a closer examination of this point.

giving five coordinates: three relating to space, one to time, and one to value (Carnap, 1932a, pp. 52–3). However, not wishing to rely on the current state of physics, he stated that the physical language would be constituted so that

> every protocol statement composed entirely of words which can be (quite crudely) described as sensation-, perception-, or thing-words, can be translated into it (Carnap, 1932a, p. 54).

Protocol sentences were characterized as directly acquired and free of 'worked on' words; phrased in the material mode, they describe the immediately given. Thus Carnap remarked that the protocol language also was called the phenomenal language (Carnap, 1932a, p. 44). So 'protocol' was in fact just a new term he had adopted for the observation sentences constituting the auto-psychological basis of scientific justification in *The Logical Structure of the World*. Protocol sentences were merely linguistic reports of the structure of immediate experiences. And essentially repeating the constructional system of *The Logical Structure of the World*, he stated that empirical, scientific sentences were tested in bunches by virtue of the protocol sentences that could be derived from them. He never specified exactly what these would look like, but he did give a tentative example of an original protocol:

> Arrangement of experiment: at such and such positions are objects of such and such kinds ...: here now at 5, simultaneously spark and explosion, then smell of ozone there. (Carnap, 1932a, p. 44)

He did not imagine there being a problem in not being able to frame a genuine protocol sentence; this was a matter for scientific research.

The relationship between these physical and protocol languages was rather complicated and non-symmetrical. From a bundle of physical sentences one could *derive* protocol sentences which a person could then compare with his own protocol to see whether they obtained or not. A protocol sentence could then be *translated* into a bundle of physical sentences. This last claim was the physicalist hypothesis whose defence was Carnap's main project in *The Unity of Science*.

2.3 Carnap's Private Language Argument

To maintain his hypothesis, Carnap had to show how sentences of other sublanguages could be translated into physical language. Aware that this mapping was most likely to be resisted in the case of the psychological and protocol sublanguages, he explained these cases in some detail.[4] It is true that a successful mapping of this sort would refute the possibility of a private language on some interpretations of 'private', but I shall not be concerned with this part of his argument, because it was founded on doubtful empirical evidence, to say the least. His conclusion was nonetheless that the problematic sublanguages could be mapped on to behavioural

---

[4]   The reduction of the psychological was later that year the subject of a whole article, 'Psychology in Physical Language', in which Carnap restated the argument for his claim and considered some objections.

and/or neurophysical language; and since the languages dealing with these domains admitted of physical translations, he took his goal to have been achieved. At the formal level, then, physicalism would be defended if it could be demonstrated that every non-physical statement had a physical translation.

However, before exploring the details of these translations Carnap considered some fundamental ontological objections to physicalism:

> Rain may be a physical event but not my present memory of rain. My perception of water which is falling at the moment and my present joy are physical events. (Carnap, 1932a, p. 77)

These objections assumed a referential domain which was accessible to only one person and ontologically distinct from the physical. In order to evaluate the objections, Carnap interpreted them as concerning the relation between the physical and the protocol language phrased in the material mode. In this reformulation, the opponent's claim was that the protocol would be essentially private, in the sense of being non-translatable into the physical language. Accordingly, in defending his account, Carnap's objectives coincided with that of a private language argument.

Carnap presented two arguments for holding that the non-physicalist is obliged to assert that intersubjective meaningfulness and the objectivity of science is an illusion. The first considered a singular protocol sentence p_1 concerning the experiential content of a subject S_1 – for example, 'Now Thirst'. How could another subject S_2 express the same fact? It would be insufficient for S_2 to utter p_1, since such an utterance would concern the experiential content of S_2; and more generally, of course, no sentence in the protocol language of S_2 could describe S_1's thirst, since that thirst is not immediately given to S_2.

The only thing actually given, although not immediately, to S_2 is the physical condition of S_1's body, and therefore this is the only thing about S_1 that is testable for S_2. If p_1 is understood as dealing with something beyond this physical condition, such as the thirst sensation of S_1, then S_2 will lack access to this fact. Given that sentences can only refer to testable circumstances, a sentence expressing a non-verifiable fact is meaningless. Hence, S_1's thirst could not be expressed by S_2. More generally, it would appear to be impossible to understand sentences concerning the sensations of other people. As Carnap says: '*Every protocol language could therefore be applied only solipsistically*' (Carnap, 1932a, p. 80, italics original). The argument's established conclusion was that referential privacy would lead to incommunicability, and this was contradicted by the fact that people *could* communicate about sensations.

The second argument would deliver '... even stranger results ...' (Carnap, 1932a, p. 80). Consider two separate domains, one with physical objects and events and the other, the phenomenal, with the contents of experience and sensations. Given that a sentence cannot concern anything that cannot be tested, the physical sentences must stand in some sort of derivational relationship to the protocol language. In other words, from a physical sentence you should be able to derive some protocols. However, this is impossible if we respect our initial assumption, because

> one statement can be deduced from another if, and only if, the fact described by the first is contained in the fact described by the second (Carnap, 1932a, p. 81).

We are bound to arrive, then, at the conclusion that physical descriptions lack empirical testability and are therefore meaningless.

Now this is certainly unacceptable, so instead of referring to two separate domains, a physical and a phenomenal, we must suppose that the physical language concerns complexes of phenomena. Since the phenomena of S_1 are not given to S_2, sentences uttered by S_1, both in protocol and physical language, cannot be tested by S_2; such sentences will consequently be meaningless to S_2. This last step follows once again because the content of a sentence cannot go beyond what is testable. From this it follows that, not only the protocol language, but also the physical language cannot be understood by more than one subject – the one actually experiencing the phenomena. Thus we would in fact be dealing with a private language, and objectivity could not be advocated along these lines: 'There is no solution free from contradictions in this direction' (Carnap, 1932a, p. 82).

It is worth spelling out the close similarities between the two arguments. Both utilize a verification criterion: 'a statement asserts no more than can be verified' (Carnap, 1932a, p. 79). Both assume that the only thing about a subject given to others is his or her physical condition; in the second argument this is highlighted by saying that phenomenal givens of two subjects do not overlap. Given these premises, the assumption best discarded in the first argument is that a subject's sensations are non-physical. In the second argument, by contrast, it is assumed, somewhat paradoxically, that both the protocols and the physical language concern something non-physical. One might also say that, in the second case, it is assumed that neither sensational nor physical domains are shared between subjects. Properly described, then, the first argument is fully anticipated by the second, which generalizes it. For these reasons, I want to examine the second argument in what follows. In effect, I shall treat it as Carnap's private language argument.

Carnap's argument was a demonstration of how much privacy could be accepted within a scientific philosophical framework. Structurally the argument was straightforward: referential privacy leads, via the verification principle, to meaning privacy and the impossibility of communication, which is then contradicted by the actuality of intersubjective discourse. It is important to notice how much Carnap ran against received opinion of the time here. That opinion was that intersubjectivity could be combined with privacy. The classical model involves the so-called 'argument from analogy' to other minds. This argument concedes that no absolute testability can be secured, but claims that there can nonetheless be a high degree of probability.[5] Of course, Carnap could have formulated the verification principle so that it would rule out this possibility, but in fact he directly rebutted the argument from analogy along different lines in the 'Psychology in Physical Language' (Carnap, 1932b), a paper published some months after *The Unity of Science*. Here he pointed out that the original protocol sentences do not contain an ego: 'Now thirst' in the original protocol of S_2 has no entity 'I' which can be replaced by 'S_1'. Accordingly, 'He is thirsty' cannot be understood on analogy with the situation in which I feel thirst.

The first thing to note about this reply is that, although in *The Unity of Science* Carnap took the content of protocols to be determined by scientific means, he argued

---

5   The *locus classicus* of this argument is John Stuart Mill (1867), pp. 237–8.

later that year from the assumption that they did not contain an 'I' or a pronoun. However, this merely emphasizes the peculiar status of the protocol, for given that it concerns what is immediately given in experience to one subject, it has no capacity to transcend its domain; and in particular it is not built into its logic that it can describe the immediately given of another subject. So although Carnap argued against the privacy of the protocol language, he accommodated the idea of the privately given. Indeed he was willing to acknowledge this explicitly. Referring to his preceding article, 'Pseudo-problems in Philosophy' (Carnap, 1929), Carnap accepted that a subject S_1 will associate something different with a protocol sentence p and its physical equivalent P; there will be an additional 'image' ('Vorstellungsgehalt') (Carnap, 1932a, p. 91). Hence it is not meaningless to say that subjects associate something different with identical protocols.

What *was* meaningless was any discussion of the way in which the ontological levels were related – of how the 'image' relates to the physical. Carnap's argument showed that this material-level discussion would imply that intersubjective science was an illusion. He demonstrated that such an ontological discussion was wedded to the view that intersubjective science was impossible. He concluded that it was necessary to move to the formal level.

From this perspective, the distinction between the formal and the material level, and the advocacy of physicalism, amounted to a conservative reply to the criticism, made by Neider and Neurath, of Carnap's methodological solipsism in *The Logical Structure of the World*. Though Carnap appeared to have accepted this criticism, he was not prepared to give up the notion of the immediately given. In *The Unity of Science* he had found a way to keep this 'Cartesian presupposition' (Uebel, 1992, p. 51) and still advocate physicalism and the intersubjective unity of science. For at the formal level we can talk about private episodes publicly and therefore maintain the basic tenet of empiricism. Carnap's stance on the possibility of a private language therefore depends on the level of analysis. At the material level, talking about the content of experiences, a private language becomes possible but paradoxical. At the formal level, where inter-translatability is concerned, a private language is not possible:

> *All statements, whether of the protocol or of the scientific system consisting of a system of hypotheses related to the protocol, can be translated into the physical language.* (Carnap, 1932a, p. 93, italics original)

So Carnap's private language argument was part of an attempt to rescue the basic tenet of empiricism and deploy it in a scientific analysis of the nature of scientific knowledge. It was tied up with Carnap's efforts to explain that we speak about the physical things, but live in a world of immediately given phenomena.

This problem, which Carnap faced in *The Unity of Science*, had already played an important role in the constructional system developed in *The Logical Structure of the World*. The solution Carnap found in the latter work was still very much maintained. This also meant that the formal-level analysis of the protocol language absorbed an important element from the phenomenalism implicit in *The Logical*

Structure of the World, namely: the *unrevisability* of immediate experiences.[6] The immediately given was still seen as the foundation on which objective knowledge was to be constructed. We can use a term of Thomas Uebel's here and say that the protocol language was described as a *quasi-private* language (Uebel, 1992, chap. 10). Methodological solipsism had merely gone undercover, so to speak. As a consequence of this privacy, Carnap could maintain that his protocols were unrevisable and without need of justification. This did not oblige him to treat the immediately given as sense data. The nature of the immediately given was a matter for science to determine. But he thought it necessary to maintain the unrevisability and the self-justificatory status. The peculiarity here was this. Given a tension between a protocol and its established physical correlate, the translation function would have to be revised: given insuperable tension between a protocol and the physical, no appeal could be made to a mistaken protocol in dissolving the dispute. But it also involved maintaining that protocols could not contradict each other (that is to say, 'epistemological atomism'), and how could this be excluded on a priori grounds? To Neurath, all this pointed to one conclusion only: Carnap was not ready to embrace the radical consequences of physicalism for empiricism.

2.4 Neurath's Private Language Argument

We have already seen that the unity of philosophical attitude apparently communicated by the publication of a manifesto was not quite in line with reality; there was substantial disagreement between the members in the Vienna Circle on rather crucial issues. The unity of the Circle was mainly maintained by opposition to the prevailing academic philosophy. Circle members were against unproductive metaphysics conducted by intuition. This opposition united Carnap, Neurath, Schlick and others. It formed a context in which each employed the verification criterion as a reminder that any non-empirical doctrine was devoid of meaning. However, beneath this surface of agreement there was a lot of internal discussion, and this did not pertain merely to minor details. One major disagreement concerned the status of philosophy – whether it was a scientific enterprise (Carnap and Neurath) or delivered elucidations (Schlick). Equally, although neither man ever wearied of stressing the Vienna Circle's unity as a scientific community, Carnap and Neurath had very different conceptions of what scientific philosophy amounted to.

Another issue Carnap and Neurath disagreed over was the nature of protocol sentences. This, of course, was what the *Protocol Sentence Debate* was mainly about. Broadly speaking, Neurath was more radical than Carnap in his departure from the academic philosophy they both denounced. Carnap had advanced a private language argument against the idea that there was an intuitive, untranslatable, but essential content in immediate experience. Now Neurath's private language argument – set

---

6   Carnap said this explicitly, not in *The Unity of Science*, but in the 'Psychology in Physical Language', p. 191. It is clear from Neurath's criticism that the protocols would have this attribute.

out in his article 'Protocol Sentences' published 1932 – was advanced against the remaining element of privacy in Carnap's protocol language.[7]

The protocol sentence debate developed naturally from Neurath's criticism of *The Logical Structure of the World.* We have already seen that Neurath criticized Carnap's methodological solipsism. To him, *The Logical Structure of the World* had not been able to fully transcend the ancient dichotomies of mainstream academic philosophy and appeared altogether to be 'turned more against realism than idealism'.[8] Putting 'methodological' in front of 'solipsism' did not change the matter significantly (Neurath, 1932c, p. 206). In *The Unity of Science* Carnap had conceded that the physical language was the proper language of science, but he had maintained that the protocol language referred to the immediately given. To Neurath, this solution reflected Carnap's unwillingness to take on the full consequences of a scientific philosophy. Carnap's framework possessed a residue of traditional philosophical inhibitions. Neurath's criticism crystallized into two main claims. First, Carnap's system failed to represent actual scientific practice. Secondly, it was not radical enough; there were still a number of idealistic elements in it. In 'Protocol Sentences' Neurath compared the physicalism of *The Unity of Science* and idealism several times.

One problem was that, according to Carnap, the protocols were unrevisable. Unrevisable protocol sentences presupposed atomism. The status of one sentence had to be independent of the status of others.[9] Neurath, on the other hand, could not see any a priori reason for insisting that protocol sentences could not contradict each other, and his criticism extended to Carnap's account of the way in which protocols were linked with the physical. Why suppose that two protocol sentences would never contradict each other? To illustrate, Neurath presented an example in which a subject, Kalon, wrote two contradictory protocols, one with each hand (Neurath, 1932c, pp. 203–4). In such a scenario one of the protocols would have to be discarded, Neurath argued. This argument, however, was directed at the somewhat peculiar constitution of the protocols envisaged by Carnap; it did not really question the framework of Carnap's project presented in *The Unity of Science.*

In his response to Neurath, 'On Protocol Sentences', Carnap was willing to entertain the thought that protocols might be revisable (Carnap, 1932c, p. 462). At least he had, apparently, no principled problem with revisable protocols, as long as they spoke of the immediately given. To Neurath, however, protocols were revisable because they were part of scientific discourse. To Neurath this meant that a protocol, like all scientific sentences, would always have to be evaluated and could not be accepted uncritically. Neurath's private language argument was a systematic way of showing that the need to evaluate a protocol would introduce a refutation of Carnap's conception of the protocol. The protocol could be neither private nor monological in

---

[7]   Neurath's private language argument was first described by Thomas Uebel (1992); my presentation owes a great deal to him.

[8]   Neurath, quoted from Uebel (1992), p. 73, note 4.

[9]   Carnap's underlying thought here was, of course, that the truth of protocols depended on whether they corresponded with the immediately given; but this was a description in the material mode of the just kind Carnap disapproved of.

the sense to which Carnap still subscribed. That is, it could not correspond directly to the immediately given.

Neurath argued against a private protocol language from the perspective of scientific practice. In *The Scientific Conception of the World: The Vienna Circle*, published by leading Circle members in 1929, the scientist was described as having two fundamental roles: to make predictions in sentences which, under certain circumstances, can be tested; and to control these predictions by actually checking their truth (Carnap et al, 1929, pp. 308–9). Consider the situation of an isolated protocolling subject, Robinson Crusoe. In a scientific society consisting of only one subject, the translation of the protocol into the physical would be pointless on Carnap's model. But Neurath's point was that if Crusoe wanted to compare today's protocol with yesterday's he would have to invoke the same procedures as he would to test another person's protocol. Yesterday's protocol, and today's, would have to be translated into the physical if it was to be compared:

> If Crusoe wants to relate what he registered ('protokolliert') yesterday with what he registers today, that is, when he wants to have any sort of recourse to a language, he cannot but have recourse to the intersubjective language. The Crusoe of yesterday and the Crusoe of today stand to one another in precisely the relation in which Crusoe stands to Friday ... *It is therefore meaningless to talk, as Carnap does, of a private language.* ... If, under certain circumstances, the protocol languages of yesterday's Crusoe and of today's are called the same language, then one may also, under the same circumstances, call the protocol language of Crusoe and that of Friday the same language. (Neurath, 1932c, pp. 205–7, italics original)

To maintain scientific practice even Crusoe would have to rely on public testing methods; and if he was to control an earlier prediction made by himself, that prediction would have to be given to him in a suitable medium, presumably a physically instantiated string of symbols. Neurath had adopted this thesis as part of his physicalism (Neurath, 1931, p. 420). In other words, the protocol delivered by Crusoe yesterday would be publicly available. Language needs an instantiation, and it needs to be evaluated by being compared to the set of sentences which is held true. That means that the protocolling subject must give up any privileged access to his protocols. Those protocols, being a physically instantiated string of symbols, are equally intelligible, because equally assessable, to Crusoe and Friday today.

Note that the argument is not sceptical about memory: in so far as memory can be relied on, it is a publicly accessible method; but memory can only be of a protocol, not that to which it refers.

All in all, then, Neurath argued that protocols were not private and could be revised. In his own words: '... *there are neither primitive protocol sentences nor sentences which are not subject to verification*' (Neurath, 1932c, p. 205, italics original).

Neurath's private language argument articulated a disagreement with Carnap about the way in which protocols should be understood, but the disagreement was not confined to this issue. There were also divergences over deeper issues, as it were, underneath. Crucial premises of Neurath's argument emerged from a conception of the nature of scientific language that Carnap did not share. To Neurath, the unified language of science was just part of an 'ordinary natural language' ('historische Trivialsprache') (Neurath, 1932c, p. 200) and therefore contained imprecise, unanalysed terms and vague linguistic conglomerations ('Ballungen'). Neurath believed that this contamination of language was unavoidable. It would be present on every level of scientific discourse, and the clarification of one or some terms would inevitably lead to imprecision in other parts of the body of scientific discourse. This organic conception of language was explained by using his famous Boat simile:

> We are like sailors who must rebuild their ship on the open sea, never able to dismantle it in dry-dock and to reconstruct it there out of the best materials. Only the metaphysical elements can be allowed to vanish without trace. Vague linguistic conglomerations always remain in one way or another as components of the ship. If vagueness is diminished at one point, it may well be increased at another. (Neurath, 1932c, p. 201)

Carnap's account eliminated this historical element from science by focusing on a branch of science that is potentially devoid of imprecision: physics. However, he failed to see, according to Neurath, that this potential perfection was illusory.[10] The 'ballung' criticism was directed at Carnap's overall conception of language, which held that every word in a language could be given rather precise intra-linguistic definition, but Neurath also used it in his more specific attack on Carnap's protocol language. By invoking the historical element Neurath touched upon an issue to which Carnap had given no thought, namely, the problem of how the protocol language was *learned*. Carnap had more or less implicitly assumed the protocol language to be given, although 'In the present state of research it is not possible to characterize this language with greater precision, i.e. to specify its vocabulary, syntactical forms and rules' (Carnap, 1932a, p. 45).

Neurath, on the other hand, thought that the protocol language, like any language, would be a historical product with a relatively stable structure, but one constantly undergoing changes due to the inevitable imprecision scattered throughout the system. If we combine this view of language with the claim that any protocol sentence will have to be tokened, it will follow that nothing about the fact that a protocol was produced yesterday by Crusoe gives him a privileged position with regard to it. Crusoe is in the same position relative to his own protocol as he is relative to Friday's protocol; he must describe them in an analogous manner. 'In this way we can go on to deal with everyone's protocol sentences' (Neurath, 1932c, p. 207). And if any of these protocols are to have any relevance for intersubjective science, they must be part of a language spoken by both Crusoe and Friday. *Pace* Carnap, protocols do not have to be translated into physical language before they can be understood by others.

2.5 Private Language and the Vienna Circle's Agenda

As the presentation in the previous section reveals, Carnap's articulation of protocol language created the immediate context and motivation for Neurath's argument

---

[10]		Neurath did not ascribe a privileged role to physics in his account of physicalism.

in 'Protocol Sentences'. It was this articulation which Neurath disputed. But the premises of his argument also reveal much about Neurath's own views. According to Uebel, Neurath presented his argument for the first time in a private 'Conversation about physicalism' ('Besprechung über Physikalism') in March 1931 at the same time as presenting a 'new conception that there is only physical language' (Uebel, 1992, pp. 129–30). As with Carnap, we witness here a close relationship between the specific conception of physicalism and the private language argument.

The respective conceptions of physicalism adopted by Carnap and Neurath are deeply embedded in the premises of their arguments, but in their work it is not hard to see how the arguments are strategically connected with the relevant versions of physicalism. Carnap conceived of his physicalism in terms of the language of physics. Since the immediately given was not described in this language, the protocols would have to form a different language. He would then have to show how this language could still be connected with the intersubjective; that it was not private. This was done via the formal/material distinction. Following this, his private language argument demonstrated that the material mode of speaking was problematic, implying that the formal level was the correct level of analysis. Neurath, on the other hand, took ordinary language purified of metaphysical elements – the 'physicalistic ordinary language' – to be the language of physicalism (Neurath, 1932c, p. 200). According to his boat simile, this language was a historical product irremediably containing vague terms. Clearly, such a language could not be complemented with an ideal, precise protocol language in the way Carnap envisaged. So Neurath had to show that the situation of the protocols was no different from the rest of language. Protocols could not be used as anchors for the rest of language; they could not be freed of the demand for justification.

Carnap and Neurath's private language arguments are both products of an attempt to accommodate the failure of *The Logical Structure of the World* to meet the demand for intersubjective justification, but they also reflect the differences in the solutions they found: 'In fact the conflict between Carnap and Neurath is usefully conceptualized as one between two kinds of private language argument of different strengths.'[11] What unites Carnap's and Neurath's versions of physicalism is in fact the rejection of a private language.[12] So there is a close connection between Carnap's and Neurath's differing conceptions of physicalism and the private language arguments they presented. But, contrary to the disavowals of both men (Carnap, 1932c, p. 215; Neurath, 1932c, p. 201), their disagreements over the way in which physicalism should be articulated were not minor. Indeed, analysis of their private language arguments reveals important divergences on two very central issues.

One important matter was the status of the basic tenet of empiricism, the claim that all factual knowledge comes from the given. From the way Carnap restricted the application of his private language argument to what is immediately given and not

---

[11]   Uebel, in Cartwright et al. (1996), p.153.

[12]   Incidentally, this is also how physicalism was later characterized in Feigl (1963), p. 227: 'The first thesis of physicalism, or the thesis of the unity of the language of science, is essentially the proposal of a criterion of scientific meaningfulness in terms of intersubjective confirmability.'

to the structure of experience, it is clear that he remained to all intents and purposes within the empiricist tradition. With Neurath, however, the situation is much less clear. Since he chose to speak about protocols, thereby referring to sentences at the justificatory base of knowledge claims, it would appear that he subscribed to the empiricist idea of the given. On the other hand, he defined protocols as ordinary sentences with a specific, slightly peculiar structure:

> Protocol sentences are factual sentences of the same form as the others, except that, in them, a personal noun always occurs several times in a specific association with other terms. A complete protocol sentence might, for instance, read: "Otto's protocol at 3:17 o'clock: [At 3:16 o'clock Otto said to himself: (at 3:15 o'clock there was a table in the room perceived by Otto)]". (Neurath, 1932c, p. 202)

It is far from clear why such sentences should be taken to possess the higher level of inherent justification that makes them particularly suited to form a basis of justificatory support. Our conceptual system is not really attached to the world, or the given, at some particular place in the system in the way Carnap and traditional empiricists envisaged. The tension can be put like this. Neurath remained faithful to the basic tenet of empiricism in the sense that he took reports of individual experience as the justificatory basis of science, but in distancing himself from Carnap's 'idealism', he defined these protocols in a way that makes it hard to see how they could play that role, since protocols are only privileged in virtue of their structure.

The second issue concerns the nature of philosophy. An important aspect of the unity of science thesis concerns philosophy's relationship with science. We can begin by noting what Carnap and Neurath agreed about in 1932. First, philosophy was part of science in the sense that it answered to scientific standards of testability. Secondly, philosophy was a metalinguistic enquiry. Thirdly, both Carnap and Neurath believed that it was important to expose and throw away the metaphysical doctrines that pervaded ordinary discourse. Indeed Neurath kept a list of forbidden metaphysical words and suggested others do the same (Neurath, 1932c, p. 200). In the same vein, Carnap's private language argument exposed the absurdity of a literal interpretation of material level discourse.

We can now turn to the profound differences. Carnap saw the philosopher's job as one of producing abstract constructional systems and clarifications. In *The Logical Structure of the World*, he very explicitly pointed out that he would make no claim about how actual justification proceeds, and conceded that it might very well depend on an intuitive grasp of the claim requiring philosophical justification. In 1932 his project was still one of understanding how objective scientific knowledge could be justified *in principle* – he wished to understand the nature of scientific knowledge. This is why his private language argument discussion attempts to show how a protocol language can be public. Neurath, on the other hand, was considerably more concerned with the mechanisms of *actual* scientific practice, and with the problems the scientist confronts in genuine scientific activity. Therefore his private language argument essentially takes up the problem a scientist will encounter when he considers his own earlier protocols. His concern with actual practice also significantly informed his choice of universal, physicalistic language.

So Carnap's and Neurath's private language arguments mirror their respective revolts against tradition; and deeply embedded in these arguments we find divergences between the two men over the nature of philosophy and the appropriate formulation of physicalism. The disagreement over these deeper issues is reflected nearer the surface in contrasts between their conceptions of protocols; and this explains why Carnap seems to have disregarded much of Neurath's attack on the nature of the protocol language: quite simply, his agenda was very different from Neurath's. However, this should not be allowed to obscure the fact that they struggled with the same problem. This was the problem of explaining how the immediately given, or individual experiences, could be embedded into science in a way that does not jeopardize their crucial justificatory importance. In essence this was the main issue in the protocol sentence debate.

This is suitable point at which to consider whether, and if so to what extent, the arguments of Carnap and Neurath are concerned with private *language*. History has generally answered this question negatively, and the articles considered in this chapter have rarely been taken to contain private language arguments. Even among specialists, this interpretative attitude persists today. Ramon Cirera, for instance, spends a good twenty pages analyzing *The Unity of Science*, but never says that it is an attack on a private language (Cirera, 1994). Cirera's reading is foreshadowed in an earlier commentary:

> These problems [recent problems with private language] differ from the question, debated around 1930, of whether or not it is possible to start with a private language about one's own sensations or 'raw' feelings and arrive at the intersubjective and communicable language of science. (Castañeda, 1967b, p. 458)[13]

The above analysis also shows that, in an important sense, Carnap and Neurath were not primarily concerned with language. Their private language arguments were subordinate to epistemology, and from the beginning their main concern was to understand the scientific enterprise, and the knowledge it generated, correctly. So it was not the nature of language which they sought to understand, but the nature of knowledge and its justification. Apart from its utility value in the anti-metaphysical project, language was discussed largely because it was the medium of scientific knowledge. Underlying this was an implicit conception of the nature of language, and in particular the referential relation between language and reality, which surfaced in the Vienna Circle's acceptance of the verification principle. To bring out this conception we must turn to Wittgenstein's *Tractatus*, for this was the work that provided the impetus towards verificationism. In Chapter 3, then, we shall see how Wittgenstein struggled with the certain (for present purposes, key) elements of the *Tractatus* in 1929. We shall also see how, exactly, the *Tractatus* connects with the Vienna Circle's theoretical assumptions about language.

---

[13]   In correspondence, Uebel has suggested this was probably the first time Carnap's argument was actually called a 'private language argument'. However, the connection appears to have been made earlier at least twice, although with little in the way of elaboration: see Ayer (1954) and Hervey (1957).

As a debate about the justificatory basis of scientific knowledge, the protocol sentence debate did not end in 1932 but continued for some years (Uebel, 1992, p. 26). Remarkably, Neurath, who was the most radical in the period considered here, continued to root the protocols in individual experiences, whereas Carnap, inspired by Popper, came to adopt a more pragmatic approach. However, as a debate about how, and in what form, the immediate given of traditional empiricism, with its inherent privacy, could survive exposure to a verification principle taken at the time to demarcate legitimate scientific philosophy, the protocol sentence debate peaked in 1932. This, then, is what the first private language arguments were really concerned with: how, exactly, traditional empiricism could survive the strictures of consistent scientism and the verification principle. As it happened, neither intuitive content nor unrevisability survived in the end.

Chapter 3

Wittgenstein's Early Concerns About Privacy

In 1932, when the protocol sentence debate was in full swing in Vienna, Wittgenstein was living in Cambridge, England. He had by that time already established a certain distance between himself and the rest of the philosophical community, an isolation which he himself preferred and which would grow over the ensuing years. An exception to this was the correspondence with his friends Moritz Schlick and Friedrich Waismann, who communicated Wittgenstein's ideas to the Vienna Circle.[1] This transmission of his ideas became the focus of attention in May 1932 when Schlick sent a copy of Carnap's *The Unity of Science* to Wittgenstein. The response to Schlick was immediate and was repeated the following August when Wittgenstein claimed authorship of some of the central ideas presented in Carnap's article:

> ... Carnap is conscientious when dealing with the quotations from his own works and has only been silent about his main source.
> 2. that I have not been occupied with the 'Physicalism' question is untrue ...
> 3. I cannot think that Carnap no longer remembers the conversation with Waismann in which he informed him of my conception of ostensive definitions.
> 4. Carnap has his conception of hypotheses from me ... (Nedo/Ranchetti (eds), 1983, pp. 254–5, my translation)

Later that August Carnap received a letter, drafted in a less systematic way, but making essentially the same points. Carnap never responded to this letter. When Schlick had informed him earlier that summer about Wittgenstein's qualms his answer was that to his knowledge Wittgenstein had not been involved in the question of physicalism.[2]

There is little doubt that Carnap was sincere when he expressed his ignorance of Wittgenstein's views to Schlick,[3] since Carnap's physicalism had been developed in discussions with Neurath.[4] The Wittgenstein that Carnap, and Neurath, knew was no

---

[1]   The notes Waismann took of the meetings between Schlick, Waismann and Wittgenstein, and on rare occasions Carnap, were published as Wittgenstein (1967a).

[2]   Wittgenstein's letters to Schlick 8.8.1929 and 8.21.1929, and his letter to Carnap on 8.20.1929, are published in Nedo/Ranchetti (eds) (1983), nos. 358–9. Carnap's and Schlick's responses are presented and discussed in Hintikka (1993).

[3]   See Hintikka (1993), pp. 132–41, for a discussion of the transmission of ideas from Wittgenstein to Carnap.

[4]   The two had even engaged in a priority dispute concerning physicalism; it was only after pressure from Neurath that Carnap added a footnote in *The Unity of Science* crediting his

physicalist. It is also fairly clear that there had been no transmission of ideas in the opposite direction: Wittgenstein had at no point become acquainted with Carnap's and Neurath's arguments for physicalism. It seems that independent pathways had lead to similar conclusions.

Like Carnap and Neurath, Wittgenstein had been struggling to integrate the apparently obvious fact that the world presents itself to us in the immediately given, that what we know about the world comes from the senses. But unlike theirs, Wittgenstein's framework into which this fact was to be integrated was not scientific philosophy, with its emphasis on the intersubjectivity of scientific knowledge. The framework was rather set by some of the 'unassailable and definitive' truths set forth in the *Tractatus* (Wittgenstein, 1921, p. 5). Wittgenstein's physicalism was part of a theory of how obvious ideas would combine coherently.

I will argue that there were other similarities: that Wittgenstein's reasons for changing his mind came from problems he saw with what was essentially a private language. But before doing this I shall demonstrate that Wittgenstein's position, before he adopted physicalism, involved a de facto private language; and that this was an important factor in the period, in 1929, in which Wittgenstein's adoption of physicalism took place. I will then describe what seems to have been the main reason why he felt forced to adopt physicalism: the impossibility of a phenomenological language. These considerations will enable me to evaluate the general situation, and the role of the private language arguments, before 1934. This year, or perhaps the year before, was a watershed. In Rush Rhees's estimate, it was during this period that Wittgenstein started writing down some of the ideas subsequently published as 'Notes for Lectures on "Private Experience" and "Sense Data"'.[5] In these notes he sketched for the first time the thoughts that would evolve later on into §§243–315 of *Philosophical Investigations*.

3.1 The Transition to Physicalism

At the end of World War I, in 1918, Wittgenstein had decided to abandon philosophy and instead become a school teacher. In 1921 the *Tractatus* was published, first in German, and then, in 1922, in an English translation prepared by C. K. Ogden and the young F. P. Ramsey. It soon began to exert an influence and, mainly as a result of encouragement from Schlick, from 1926 Wittgenstein began to attend occasional meetings with Schlick, Waismann, Carnap and other members of the Vienna Circle. During next three years he became increasingly preoccupied with philosophical research, and in early 1929, during a holiday visit to Cambridge, he decided to continue to work on philosophy: 'I have decided to remain here in Cambridge for a few terms and work on visual space and other things ...' (Wittgenstein, 1967a, p. 17). His personal manuscripts are in keeping with this remark and provide more details about the questions he asked himself about 'visual space'. MS 107, which appears to have been written during 1929, although the first 153 pages are undated,

---

physicalist ideas to Neurath. See Uebel (1995), pp. 334–5, for the history of footnote 1 in the German edition of *The Unity of Science*.
   [5]   Wittgenstein (1968), ed. Rush Rhees.

is an important source of evidence and the central text in the present chapter.[6] It begins with a discussion of the following question: How is visual space ('Der Gesichtsraum') to be described, and how will the ordinary, physicalistic language be related to that description?

During 1929 Wittgenstein changed his mind about the correct way to answer this question and as a result adopted physicalism – the thesis that physicalistic language is the primary language. We find the first 'public' pronouncement of his transition in a conversation recorded by Waismann on 22 December 1929, when Wittgenstein was in Vienna for Christmas:

> I used to believe that there was the everyday language that we all usually spoke and a primary language that expressed what we really knew, namely phenomena. I also spoke of a first system and a second system. (Wittgenstein, 1967a, p. 45)

Wittgenstein here distinguishes two systems of language, the first of which is the phenomenological language and the second of which is the 'everyday' language. He often referred to the secondary language as 'the physicalistic language'. The quotation tells us what Wittgenstein used to believe. Immediately after this, his current point of view is presented.

> I think that essentially we have only one language, and that is our everyday language. We need not invent a new language or construct a new symbolism, but our ordinary language already is *the* language, provided we rid it of the obscurities that lie hidden in it. (Wittgenstein, 1967a, p. 45)

This different conception had not come to Wittgenstein without struggle – something his personal manuscripts bear witness to. Were it not for these manuscripts, one might think that Wittgenstein was referring to the *Tractatus* when he described to Waismann what he used to believe. He was, however, speaking about a view he had held earlier *that same year*.[7] At the beginning of MS 107, we find Wittgenstein still clinging to the idea of a phenomenological language, even though problems are emerging:

> If one says: The philosopher must descend down into the kettle and grasp pure reality itself and pull it out into the daylight. Then the answer is that he thereby must leave the language behind and so returns with unfinished business.

> And still there can be a phenomenological language (Where must this language stop?) (Wittgenstein, 1994, p. 3, my translation)

Here he still entertains the idea of a phenomenological language. By contrast, in a later entry, dated 22 October 1929, the idea has been given up:

---

6   References to manuscripts follow von Wright's catalogue in 'The Wittgenstein Papers', reprinted in Wittgenstein (1993), pp. 480–510.

7   Brian McGuinness, the editor of Wittgenstein (1967a), added a footnote to this sequence in which he suggested that Wittgenstein was speaking about a position that he had held fairly recently.

> The assumption that a phenomenological language is possible, and that only it would express what we in philosophy must/want to say, is – I think – absurd. We must learn to live with our everyday language and only understand it correctly. That is, we must not allow it to lead us to speak nonsense. (Wittgenstein, 1994, p. 102, my translation)

So there we are: by 22 October 1929 Wittgenstein had come to regard the physicalistic language ('unserer gewöhnlichen Sprache') as universal. As with Neurath, the physicalistic language is, for Wittgenstein, the language spoken in everyday discourse and not a scientific idealization.[8] This much is clear from Wittgenstein's own remarks. But it is not clear why this transition in his thinking initially brought about a state of despair in Wittgenstein; nor is it clear why he initially thought that there would have to be a phenomenological language in addition to the physicalistic one.

At the root of his despair was the fact that he was still working within a broadly Tractarian framework whose foundation the problem he was tackling threatened to undermine. The general problem he was investigating at this time was the relationship between language and reality; this had also been the dominant theme in the *Tractatus*. The solution which he had presented there, some 15 years earlier, was that all sentences could be analyzed truth-functionally down to elementary sentences, which were then seen as pictures of simple objects. This was the essential lesson of the renowned 'picture theory':

> A proposition is a picture of reality.
> A proposition is a model of reality as we imagine it. (Wittgenstein, 1921, 4.01)

A sentence is a model of what it represents in the sense that, when it is analyzed correctly into its logical form, there will be a correspondence between its parts and parts of the state of affairs of which it is a model or picture; the arrangement of the sentential parts will, moreover, mirror the arrangement of parts in the corresponding state of affairs.

> What any picture, of whatever form, must have in common with reality, in order to be able to depict it – correctly or incorrectly – in any way at all, is logical form, i.e. the form of reality. (Wittgenstein, 1921, 2.18)

He had originally held that all elementary sentences were logically independent of each other, but in 1929 he had changed his mind. He now thought that systems of elementary sentences were held up against reality together (Wittgenstein, 1967a, pp. 73–81). For example, 'This is green' is not logically independent of 'This is red', since a commitment to the truth of the former logically implies a commitment to the falsity of the latter.

All this, however, was theoretical speculation. It had the disadvantage that no examples of elementary sentences or simple objects were given. Norman Malcolm recalls asking Wittgenstein why he did not think it crucial to determine their nature:

---

[8]   The analogy with Neurath goes even further, because where Neurath saw a metaphysical cleansing of the everyday language as necessary, Neurath (1932c), pp. 578–9, Wittgenstein speaks of 'unclarities' ('Unklarheiten') and tendencies to speak 'nonsense' ('Unsinn').

I asked Wittgenstein whether, when he wrote the *Tractatus*, he had ever decided upon anything as an *example* of a "simple object". His reply was that at the time his thought had been that he was a *logician*; and that it was not his business, as a logician, to try to decide whether this thing or that was a simple matter or a complex thing, that being a purely *empirical* matter! (Malcolm, 1984, p. 70)

Apparently, then, he had consciously left their nature undecided when he wrote the *Tractatus*. By 1929, however, when Wittgenstein's attitude to verificationism had changed, the simple objects were no doubt the objects constituting the immediately given: reality here meant the world as it presented itself to us in immediate experience, the immediately given (Gegenwart).[9]

Phenomenological language was defined as the language which speaks directly about the immediately given – more specifically, about items in visual space. Wittgenstein's reason for using a special phenomenological language to speak about the immediately given instead of our ordinary physicalistic language seems to have been that the latter describes visual space by relating it to something outside visual space. When, for instance, I describe my visual field by saying 'I see a vase', I relate it to something external, because vases are not items in visual space; it is not a pure description of what is in the visual field. Furthermore, failure or mistakenness is always a possibility when we use physicalistic language: it can seem to me that there is a vase without there actually being one. If, however, you directly describe the immediately given, there is no sense to a distinction between what *is* the case and what *seems to be* the case; it does not make sense to say that one might be making a mistake.

Two things follow from this analysis. First, since the phenomenological language was intended to be capable of directly describing the immediately given, it was in effect a private language. In fact, compared with Carnap, and the protocol language of 1932, Wittgenstein had taken a further step by explicitly excluding the possibility that his phenomenological language would contain words in the physicalistic language. Secondly, the abandonment of phenomenological language, when it is combined with an acceptance that the physicalistic language is primary and a residual belief that the immediately given is the reality, will compromise the key Tractarian claim that elementary sentences map on to elementary states of affairs. In other words, the picture theory, which was a fundamental doctrine in the *Tractatus*, is intuitively in conflict with Wittgenstein's physicalism. For the time being, however, he was not prepared to give up the picture theory.

---

9   See, for example, his use of 'fliehende gegenwart', and his discussion of colour in Wittgenstein (1994), pp. 1–22; cf. his 'Some Remarks on Logical Form', Wittgenstein (1929), pp. 29–31. In the notebooks, Wittgenstein explicitly took up verificationism. He wrote: 'The verification is not *an* indication of truth, but *the* sense of the proposition.' Wittgenstein (1994), p. 84, my translation.

3.2 The Phenomenological Language Argument

In *The Unity of Science* Carnap had painted with broad brush strokes, leaving it to science to determine the precise articulation of the protocol sentences. Wittgenstein had followed the same strategy with elementary propositions and simple objects in the *Tractatus*. As a logician he had given an argument for their necessary existence, but he had been unwilling to give examples. In 1929 Wittgenstein came to think it was necessary to investigate further, to get a firmer grip on what a description in phenomenological language would look like. I will here present the efforts he made, since it was principally their failure which drove him in the end to give up on the phenomenological language. Although the failure of these attempts did not result in a straightforward argument, I will argue that Wittgenstein saw a recurring pattern, and that this led him to conclude that his determined struggle to develop even a limited grasp of such a phenomenological language could not succeed.

We saw that Wittgenstein's change of mind occurred during the writing of the MS 107 notebook in 1929; somewhere during the writing of these notes he abandoned the idea of an exclusively phenomenological language. Although these are private notes, it is not difficult to see that the phenomenal given, and its potential description, had a dominant role in his thinking. The given was mostly discussed in terms of visual space ('Gesichtsraum'). Consider now the first longer passage (following p. 3) in MS 107 in which he speaks about the objects of visual space. His concern is how such objects can be measured. He compares two distances, *a* and *b*, which are divided into smaller parts, *c* and *d*:

> It is apparently possible that the distances a and b appear to be of equal length to me, that also the pieces c and d appear of equal length, but when they are counted the result is that I have 25 c and 24 d. Here the question is: How can this be possible? Is it here correct to say: This is just how it is and we hereby only see that visual space does not follow the rules – approximately – of Euclidean space. This would mean that the question "how can it be possible?" would be non-sensical and unfounded. Here was nothing paradoxical but only something we would have accepted. (Wittgenstein, 1994, p.18, my translation)

This excerpt opens a passage which contains the crucial elements of Wittgenstein's reasoning about visual space, so it is worthwhile following the line of thought carefully. His topic is a rather trivial empirical fact and the goal of the investigation is to explain how this fact is possible. The first possibility he considers is that the visual space and the objects in it have a non-Euclidean structure. This would dispel the air of paradox, but it is not a solution available to Wittgenstein at this point, because it makes the whole idea of a description absurd, as he notes some pages later:

> But if one cannot say that in a and b there are a determinate number of pieces, how can one then describe visual space? What we see – I think – here, is that visual space is much more complex than it appears to be on a first encounter. What makes it so much more complex is, for instance, the factor that produces the movements of the eye. (Wittgenstein, 1994, p. 19, my translation)

In the earlier passage, his struggle to find the right mode of expression for the phenomenological language continues:

> Or should one now say that also in visual space something can appear to be different from what it *is*? Most certainly not! ... It might, however, be that it is without sense to say about distances in *visual space* that they are of equal length ... so that there exists an *absolute* appearance. (Wittgenstein, 1994, p. 18, my translation)

The gist of his repeated attempts to give a phenomenological description which respects the initially presented empirical fact is evident in these passages. Wittgenstein again and again attempts to develop an account which avoids the distinction between 'seeming to be' ('schein') and 'being' ('sein'). He is obliged, however, either to use relative notions, such as 'unclarity' ('verschwommenheit') or 'indeterminacy' ('unbestimmtheit'), or to introduce contrived delimiters which tell one which objects are identical.

This last solution was actually what he settled for in the end, but setting up the delimiters empirically required the physical language. He presented the following solution to Schlick and Waismann without telling them how he had arrived at it:

> In Euclidean space we thus need a related (but not identical!) relation to render the 'equality' relation of visual space, e.g. the following:

$$a \equiv b, \text{ if } b = a + \varepsilon, |\varepsilon| < \frac{a}{100}$$

> ``$a \equiv b, b \equiv c \rightarrow a \equiv c$`` may be true or not.

> For this reason the geometry of visual space has a different multitude from the geometry of Euclidean space. We must not replace 'equal' with 'equal', 'parallel' with 'parallel', 'straight' with 'straight'. (Wittgenstein, 1967a, pp. 59–60)[10]

In the notebooks we find a much more desperate Wittgenstein attempting, in an exhausting fashion, to achieve this result without appealing to the physical language. In making this attempt he repeatedly encourages himself to give the matter another try,[11] finally concluding, on 22 October 1929, that his efforts have been in vain. At this point he realizes that in order to describe the given, one needs a distinction between *sein* and *schein* – that is, between 'seeming to be' and 'being'. Furthermore, he sees that this distinction is not available in visual space, but only in physical, Euclidean space. The claim that it is necessary to use the physicalistic language to describe visual space is equivalent to this last conclusion.

The upshot of these considerations is a scheme in which the objects in visual space are spoken of as physical objects, but their appearance is absolute. Using the physicalistic language, one can distinguish between 'being' and 'seeming to be' and

---

10   Wittgenstein's frequent references to Euclid and geometry are unfortunate in the sense that the problem which provokes him concerns transitivity, which was also conceived of in the 1920s as an algebraic notion.

11   See, for example, the above quotation from p. 19 of MS 107.

therefore give a logically coherent description of this absolute appearance. This new conception was reluctantly embraced by Wittgenstein once he had seen that his search for a phenomenological language would necessarily fail. Thus the conclusion of his investigations is probably best stated, with Wittgenstein, negatively:

> The phenomenological language, or 'primary language', as I once called it, appears to me no longer to be the target; now I no longer hold it to be possible. (Wittgenstein, 1994, p. 118, my translation)

Only months before this remark, the availability of such a primary language had seemed obvious to him.

The presentation of Wittgenstein's argumentation so far has mainly proceeded by way of consideration of quotations from his personal notebooks. In order to get a more straightforward argumentative structure, I will recapitulate the steps in Wittgenstein's argument. His own reasoning around these steps initially appears, in a scattered form, in notebook MS 107. Much of this reasoning was a result of his reluctance to accept the inevitable conclusion. Nonetheless, one can discern a few fundamental assumptions.

The first premise concerns language in general. It says that a language must be Euclidean. Here 'Euclidean' is probably not meant to refer in a mathematical sense specifically to the standard axioms of Euclid, but rather means that language should obey *some* kind of logic. Secondly, phenomenological words, in particular, are by definition freed of hypothetical content, and phenomenological language therefore cannot support a distinction between 'seeming to be' and 'being'. Hypothetical elements would require the possibility of the subject making mistakes, and this is incompatible with phenomenological languages describing the immediately given. Given these constraints, we are faced with an empirical fact whose possibility will have to be explained. If a,b,c and d are line segments, how can the following four equalities hold in visual space?

$$|a| = |b|, \quad |c| = |d|, \quad |24c| = |a|, \quad |25d| = |b|$$

Wittgenstein considers a solution in which instead of distinguishing 'seeming to be' and 'being', the visual space is made of *absolute* 'being'; but it does not make sense to say that something seems to be unless there is a logical possibility of actually being.

Wittgenstein also attempts to construct similarity classes between appearances, but this presents him with a variant of the Sorites paradox; and, more importantly, 'similar' is a relative notion like 'seeming to be', so similarity must be seen in some kind of relation to identity.

In the end this recurring need to relate a description of the immediately given to something else led Wittgenstein to give up the idea that a phenomenological language could be separately identified and instead hold that phenomenological language was embedded in our ordinary, physical language. He had realized that the commitments you make when you make a claim are not, as he had first hoped, necessarily true when the claim relates directly to visual space. For example, if you claim a rod has a certain length, you also commit yourself to holding that it is not of another length. But in visual space, something can have two lengths or two colours. I will call the argument which led him to this conclusion the 'Phenomenological Language Argument'. This argument does not directly address the issue whether a private language is possible. It relates instead to the question whether certain properties thought to feature in visual space, such as absolute 'seeming to be', can be directly depicted in language. These properties would also feature in Carnap's protocol language, which was not meant to be a private language. As its name suggests, however, the Phenomenological Language Argument exposed a problem with the phenomenological language which Wittgenstein had thought would be the ultimate picture of the phenomenal realm, the privately given.

3.3 Consequences of the Phenomenological Argument

The changes the Phenomenological Language Argument brought about were important to Wittgenstein. One source of evidence for this is MS 107, where his more personal notes around the time of transition bear witness to increasing frustration. This impression is confirmed by the manuscripts, written around 1930, in which he communicated his thoughts to others – that is, by the *Philosophical Remarks* together with the notes which Waismann took of meetings between Wittgenstein, Schlick and himself, which we have already consulted.[12] This is what Wittgenstein tells Waismann and Schlick on 30 December 1929, about two months after his change of mind:

> The essential thing is that we use two languages, a language of visual space and a language of Euclidean space, giving the language of Euclidean space priority. Language indicated this difference by using 'being' and 'appearing' or 'seeming to be'. Thus we say of two stretches in visual space that they *appear* equal but *are* not equal. (Wittgenstein, 1967a, p. 59)

Although he still maintains the idea of two languages, his conception of which is primary has changed. He connects the two languages so that the language for visual space, or phenomenological language, becomes parasitic on the physical language. Despite this, he separates the phenomenal given from the physical. He still finds it necessary to give the phenomena an extraordinary position.

The passage from Waismann's notes given above only states the argument's immediate conclusion – namely, that the description of visual space is parasitic on the description of physical or Euclidean space. We find his reasoning for this in the *Philosophical Remarks*. However, most of it appears in part XX (and to a lesser extent, part VII) of that manuscript, and this makes it practically impossible to guess the connection, between premises and conclusion, which plays a dominant role in one of the book's first passages:

---

[12] Waismann's notes were intended to communicate Wittgenstein's ideas in Vienna; the *Philosophical Remarks* was a typescript delivered to Bertrand Russell to encourage him to recommend an extension of Wittgenstein's research scholarship in Cambridge.

> I do not now have a phenomenological language, or 'primary language' as I used to call it, in mind as my goal. I no longer hold it to be necessary. All that is possible and necessary is to separate what is essential from what is inessential in *our* language.

That is, if we so to speak describe the class of languages which serve their purpose, then in so doing we have shown what is essential to them and given an immediate representation of immediate experience.

Each time I say that, instead of such and such a representation, you could also use this other one, we take a further step towards the goal of grasping the essence of what is represented.

> A recognition of what is essential and what inessential in our language if it is to represent, a recognition of which parts of our language are wheels turning idly, amounts to the construction of a phenomenological language. (Wittgenstein, 1964, p. 51)[13]

Apparently, Wittgenstein now connected the conclusion of the Phenomenological Language Argument with a new conception of the task of philosophy!

The problem was as follows. In a framework incorporating a primary phenomenological language there is a rather obvious way of establishing the basic links between language and world: we are directly acquainted with the referents of this phenomenological language, and from this vantage point more complicated linguistic constructions can be developed with the help of the tools of logic. Given the ineffability of semantics, which Wittgenstein had maintained since writing the *Tractatus*, and which Schlick had adopted,[14] the bridge over which language, so to speak, steps out into the world, cannot be described in language and so must be otherwise characterized. In the *Tractatus* Wittgenstein achieved this by invoking the doctrine that meaning must ultimately be shown. The theoretical solution Wittgenstein had defended in the *Tractatus* was that the meaning of a sentence could be shown by 'completely analyzing' it into a conjunction of elementary sentences containing only primitive signs, or names. Such an exposition of a sentence's logical form would make it transparent to anyone which state of affairs it depicted, because the configuration of objects in the depicted state of affairs would correspond to the configuration of simple names in the elementary sentence (Wittgenstein, 1921, 3.21 and 4.21). But if reality is constituted by what is immediately given in experience, the impossibility of a primary phenomenological language effectively excludes this account of the bridge between ordinary language and reality; there is no final analysis.

It was probably because this analysis bore little resemblance to the way people actually explain the meaning of words or sentences that Wittgenstein later extended the notion of showing to include ostension – the idea that a two-place relation between

---

13   It is peculiar that the passage in MS 107 reads: '... I no longer hold it to be *possible...*' (quoted above), whereas in the *Philosophical Remarks* the word 'possible' is replaced by 'necessary'. Although this certainly makes a difference, I think that it is probably a typographical error; the intended meaning seems to be the one in MS 107; this meaning is also implied by the sentence following it in the *Philosophical Remarks*.

14   See p. 12.

an object and name can be established by pointing to, or concentrating upon, the object while pronouncing the intended name – as a method of giving the meaning of a name or states of affairs.[15] But without an underlying, direct correspondence between names and objects, an ostensive definition like 'This is A' (declared while pointing at something) will not be a transparent elementary proposition. A great deal of understanding is presupposed by ostensive definition; only someone who already knows how the relevant gesture is supposed to work can understand it. Conversely, if someone does not understand what the pointing is supposed to achieve, it will not help to point more. Rather, we will have to explain the meaning of it to him. In this way we see that ostension is really only part of a language and fails to reach beyond it: 'I cannot use language to get outside language' (Wittgenstein, 1964, p. 54). In lectures Wittgenstein described ostensive definitions as connecting two kinds of language:

> One of the implements of our language is ostensive definition. But with ostensive signs we have only a mere calculus.
>
> What we call a connection between language and reality is the connection between spoken language and, for example, the language of gestures. (Lee (ed.), 1980, p. 102)[16]

So, at this time, the bridges between language and world were ultimately down for Wittgenstein: the ineffability of semantics which Wittgenstein had insisted upon since the *Tractatus* (but which in that work had been loosened to allow the act of elucidating) was now fully endorsed. There was no possibility of stepping outside ordinary language. The task for philosophy was still to expose 'which parts of our language are wheels turning idly', or the places where language had gone beyond its purpose of picturing reality; but the method was no longer to provide a complete analysis in transparent form. Instead it consisted in grasping the essence of what an expression represents by substituting for it an expression which you could use instead. The places where language, the medium, had led thought astray would expose themselves through this method via expressions for which no substitution could be given.[17] It would appear, then, that the possibility of the philosopher bridging the gap between ordinary language and reality had after all depended on the viability of a phenomenological language.

The elements of Wittgenstein's philosophy that remained unchanged are more important for our purposes, however. For, in conjunction, these elements ultimately meant that Wittgenstein was still caught up in a picture of the connection between language and reality being a private affair of the subject's own. For one thing, he did not change his idea of what the ultimate constituents of reality were: the phenomenal was still at the centre of his attention. On 1 December 1929, he wrote:

---

[15] See Wittgenstein (1967a), p. 246.

[16] Notice that this strengthens Wittgenstein's case against Carnap over ostensive definitions: at any rate, he had had his ideas on this subject for some time when Carnap published *The Unity of Science*.

[17] See also Wittgenstein (1967a), pp. 182–6.

> The phenomenon is not a symptom for something but is reality.

> The phenomenon is not a symptom for something else that makes the proposition true or false but is itself what verifies it. (Wittgenstein, 1994, p. 128, my translation)

Indeed clarification of an expression was generally thought to proceed by way of provision of the conditions under which it would be verified.

Secondly, Wittgenstein continued to subscribe to the picture theory; it was still the essence of language to represent, or picture, reality.[18] In combination with the claim that the only language available was our ordinary physicalistic language, these theses generated tension. How could a proposition be compared with a reality which is only there in the present? But given his new conception of the task of philosophy, he thought this tension was a result of language gone astray:

> The worst philosophical errors always arise when we try to apply our ordinary – physical – language in the area of the immediately given.

> If, for instance, you ask, 'Does the box still exist when I'm not looking at it?', the only right answer would be 'Of course, unless someone has taken it away or destroyed it'. Naturally, a philosopher would be dissatisfied with this answer, but it would quite rightly reduce his way of formulating the question *ad absurdum.* (Wittgenstein, 1964, p. 88)

The situation after the Phenomenological Language Argument had been pressed into service was therefore as follows. Wittgenstein had maintained the picture theory and the notion that reality was ultimately constituted by the immediately given. Therefore he had, essentially, failed to move beyond a position in which the confrontation between language and reality was a private affair; privacy was still very much a hallmark of his theory. But with his new conception of philosophy, he seems to have thought that this privacy, and hence the problems it would generate for a conception of language as intersubjective, could not be expressed in language, except by misapplying language.

An example of this strategy, and the tensions it generated, is provided by his lengthy treatment, in the *Philosophical Remarks*, of the status of feelings, and in particular the relation between first-person and third-person understandings of feelings. This was a subject on which he had started to reflect directly after abandoning phenomenological language in MS 107.[19] His first impulse was to resolve the problems by looking at translatability:

> We could adopt the following way of representing matters: if I, L.W., have toothache, then this is expressed by means of the proposition 'There is toothache'. But if that is so, what we now express by the proposition 'A has toothache', is put as follows: 'A is behaving as L.W. does when there is toothache'. ... It's evident that this way of speaking is equivalent to ours when it comes to questions of intelligibility and freedom from ambiguity. But it's equally clear that this language could have anyone at all as its centre.

---

[18]   See Wittgenstein (1964), p. 57, and Wittgenstein (1967a), p. 185.

[19]   See, for example, Wittgenstein (1994), pp. 116, 124–5.

> Now, among all the languages with different people as their centres, each of which I can understand, the one with me as its centre has a privileged status. ... The privileged status lies in the application, and if I describe this application, the privileged status again doesn't find application, since the description depends on the language in which it's couched. (Wittgenstein, 1964, pp. 88–9)[20]

Here we see Wittgenstein's new method being applied. Since all the languages describing inner sensations in the first person can be translated into each other, a third person description of inner sensations is intelligible. Furthermore, what makes the first-person description unique cannot be expressed when describing the language: nothing essentially private or privileged is found in the grammar of the language. You cannot doubt your feelings when you have them, but this certainty will not show in the grammar of the language of feelings; it is an empirical discovery, and one that will only appear when the language is applied. In the *Philosophical Remarks*, then, Wittgenstein held the privacy of feelings to be contingent and empirical!

However, this solution would only satisfy him temporarily. In fact it might only have been an idea that was written down to show the direction in which his thoughts on the subject had been moving, because his above comments from *Philosophical Remarks* are followed by a lot of seemingly unanswered questions. It also looks as though he thought that the difference between first- and third-person ascriptions would have to be further explicated. G. E. Moore gave the following account of Wittgenstein's lectures on first- and third-person pain ascriptions, held in or around May 1932 in Cambridge:

> It seems to me that his discussion was rather incoherent ... He said very early in the discussion the whole subject is "extraordinarily difficult" because "the whole field is full of misleading notations"...
>
> ...he said first that it was clear and admitted that what verifies or is a criterion for "I has toothache" is quite different from what verifies or is a criterion for "He has toothache", and soon added that, since this is so, the *meanings* of "I have toothache" and "he has toothache" must be different. (Moore, 1954, pp. 97–8)

Despite his good efforts, in 1932 Wittgenstein was very far from possessing a satisfactory account of the privacy of feelings.

It can be seen, then, that even after his transition Wittgenstein was working within the framework of the *Tractatus*, in the sense that he hung on to the picture theory. He also maintained the notion of the immediately given, and this meant that privacy remained a potential problem for his position: How can I describe my world, my immediately given, to you?

His accommodation of the conclusion, or implications, of the Phenomenological Language Argument consisted in turning other knobs in his philosophical framework which, retrospectively, appear a little like stop-gap solutions. However, Wittgenstein's thought developed rapidly during this period, and his philosophy would soon receive a much more radical revision. This will be the subject of Chapter 4, but before that we

---

[20]   See also Wittgenstein (1994), p. 36.

must settle the matter of how similar the philosophical agendas and private language arguments of Carnap and Neurath were to Wittgenstein's own.

3.4 The Motivation of the Early Private Language Arguments

The Phenomenological Language Argument embodies the considerations that led to a change in Wittgenstein's philosophical convictions in the autumn of 1929 and hence to his adoption of a kind of physicalism. More precisely it involved treating 'our usual physicalistic language' ('unserer gewöhnlichen physikalische Sprache') (Wittgenstein, 1994, p. 3) as the primary language. So, as his letter to Schlick shows, Wittgenstein was preoccupied with physicalism at a time when he was still in contact with the Vienna Circle; and, as passages from the *Philosophical Remarks* show, he was also interested in other issues which Carnap had touched upon in *The Unity of Science*. In view of this, his frustration with Carnap in 1932 was justified. Waismann's notes, which are our main written evidence of the transmission of philosophical ideas from Wittgenstein to Carnap, on the other hand, reveal Wittgenstein's adherence to physicalism only very indirectly and hardly justify Wittgenstein's accusation that Carnap had not mentioned his main source of inspiration or, worse, was a plagiarist.

It would be a mistake to conclude from this 'originality dispute' that in 1932 Wittgenstein and Carnap were dealing with the same problems. Nevertheless, in retrospect it does appear that Wittgenstein, in Cambridge, was personally and introvertedly struggling with issues that were being discussed in the interdisciplinary environment of the Vienna Circle's Thursday evening sessions. The key issue was: What role should be assigned to the immediately given with its essential unrevisability in an otherwise radical departure from the tradition? In essence there was a struggle with the legacy of empiricism.

Despite the superficial similarity and shared historical context of the theses defended by Wittgenstein, Carnap and Neurath, there are salient differences here. This may already be clear from the previous sections, but it is worth elaborating the matter further. To begin with, notice how the role of their respective private language arguments differs. When Wittgenstein began to search for a non-hypothetical, phenomenological language from which our conceptual voyage into the world could start, he was convinced of its possibility; its success was so central for him that he kept on postponing his final verdict and tried, repeatedly, to understand and solve the problems he encountered. So although he ended up rejecting a private language, he was directly concerned, not with problems generated by the privacy involved, but with conceptual issues. His intensive search, and his optimism about what was in essence a private language, stands in stark contrast with Carnap's and Neurath's reservations about private language; to them privacy was, from the beginning, something that had to be avoided. Despite their difference of approach, both Carnap and Neurath were concerned to build a foundation for empirical knowledge that would not be essentially private, and their private language arguments were parts of a discussion about how this should be done. This attitudinal difference was a consequence of differences in agenda.

In 1932, when Carnap and Neurath were disagreeing over the status of protocol sentences, the governing aim underlying discussion was still the one set out in 1929 in *The Scientific Conception of the World: The Vienna Circle*: namely, to understand and explain the intersubjectivity of scientific discourse and the thesis of the unity of science (Carnap et al, 1929, p. 307). From the beginning, then, neither man had any sympathy for a private language, because such a language could not be embedded into scientific discourse. In this context, their disagreement over protocols concerned the way in which scientific knowledge could be generated or, in the material mode, the role to be assigned to the immediately given in the scientific enterprise. So it was an epistemological issue that separated them. In *The Unity of Science*, Carnap's solution was a set of infallible protocol sentences to which all hypotheses, all other sentences, would have to be connected. Neurath did not accept this solution, but he retained the idea of protocols, whose status, pace, Carnap's suggestion, allowed them to be overthrown and required them to be publicly manifestable. It is the verification principle which, in their respective private language arguments, translates this overarching desire to vindicate scientific knowledge to a concern about language. This principle communicates the idea that we can keep asking for justification of a statement until we arrive at a point at which the speaker can say: 'But that is what the statement means!' So in the hands of Carnap and Neurath the verification principle was a bridge from epistemology to semantics; from attainment of information to sentences forming the medium in which scientific information was communicated. Broadly speaking, then, Carnap and Neurath's interest in language was motivated by a desire to understand and justify scientific knowledge. Today, of course, we would treat the latter engagement as an activity belonging to epistemology and philosophy of science.

Wittgenstein, on the other hand, was not, at least, in any way comparable to Carnap and Neurath, guided by a concern to understand the scientific enterprise. The investigations which led to the Phenomenological Language Argument flowed from his wish to understand the connection between the conceptual and the immediately given, the relationship of language to reality. Here it was the conceptual inconsistency of an entity having only relative length which generated the problem of describing length in visual space ('Gesichtsraum'). Wittgenstein discovered that if the meaning of the concept of length is directly tied to the immediately given, logic breaks down. In contrast with Carnap and Neurath, he was not motivated mainly by epistemological concerns. His interest was in the way in which our words have sense and refer – an issue we nowadays think of as belonging to the philosophy of language or semantics. And because he was still treating the picture theory as the general framework within which these questions were to be asked, Wittgenstein did not see privacy as an urgent problem in 1929. This explains why the Phenomenological Language Argument does not directly attack the privacy element of phenomenological language. In this respect, and in so far as Wittgenstein's agenda was not the intersubjectivity of language, the Phenomenological Language Argument is not accurately classified as a private language argument.

From a contemporary perspective, then, Wittgenstein, and Carnap and Neurath were working in different philosophical sub-disciplines. This had important consequences, in particular with regard to the way in which they interpreted the verification principle. One way to characterize this principle is to say that it implies that justifications of knowledge will do double-duty as explanations of meaning. To Carnap and Neurath this suggested that the demarcation between science and non-science would coincide with the demarcation between the meaningful and the meaningless. Accordingly, everything outside the confines of empirical science – like, for example, metaphysical, intuitive insight – was deemed meaningless. The verification principle was an ideal tool in the Vienna Circle's vendetta against certain kinds of traditional, speculative philosophy, since it matched the limits of the meaningful with the limits of science. To Wittgenstein, on the other hand, the principle expressed the notion that the sense of a sentence can be given by a rule that informs you how to apply the sentence – a rule which, at the same time, makes it evident how the sentence is connected to reality. It is, in other words, a semantic principle, and one that does not presuppose any particular method of verification:

> The way a proposition is verified, that is what it says. Compare the universality of real propositions with the universality of arithmetic. They are verified differently and are therefore of different kinds. (Wittgenstein, 1994, p. 84, my translation)

In Tractarian fashion, Wittgenstein sought, not the limits of science, but the limits of language, and thereby the limits of the world.

Chapter 4

Wittgenstein in Transition – The Later Material

Wittgenstein published nothing after 'Some Remarks on Logical Form', which was written in 1929 for the Joint Session of the Aristotelian Society and the Mind Association. It is a measure of how fast his thoughts were developing that he did not deliver the paper at the session and later commented to friends that he thought it quite worthless.[1] Although he tried several times to organize his thoughts and had the intention of publishing something recording his present philosophical position, severe self-criticism brought about repeated postponement. In 1933 he prepared what later became known as 'The Big Typescript', and from November 1936, initially in an attempt to rewrite the *Brown Book*, he worked on what would later become Part I of *Philosophical Investigations*. The latter did not, however, receive a preface of the kind intended for other readers until the second version, which was prepared from some time in the early 1940s (von Savigny (ed.), 1998, pp. 2–3).

The first posthumously published part of Wittgenstein's writing was *Philosophical Investigations* in 1953. This was followed by *Remarks on the Foundations of Mathematics* in 1956; and joint publication of a pair of manuscripts dictated to students, *The Blue and Brown Books*, in 1958. These dictated manuscripts had been in circulation among his followers for a while. Since then there has been a more or less constant flow of publications from Wittgenstein's lecture notes and *Nachlass*, amounting now to over 12,000 manuscript pages (Stern, 1994, p. 436).

The material published to date suggests that Wittgenstein engaged with the privacy issue throughout the period 1932–1945, albeit somewhat infrequently. Here are some milestones. An early trace the privacy topic is a discussion of 'toothache' in the Blue Book, which was dictated in the academic year 1933/1934. That also appears to have been the year in which Wittgenstein started his 'Notes for Lectures on "Private Experience" and "Sense Data"', which was mainly written in 1936.[2] Privacy also makes an appearance in the 'Notes for the "Philosophical Lecture"' (MS 166), which was most probably written in 1941.[3] After that there is a short sequence of passages, §§544–59, in *Zettel*. Although undated, they relate to the

---

[1]   See Wittgenstein (1993), p. 28, for a list of references to comments.

[2]   See Hacker (1990), p. 18. These notes were first published as Wittgenstein (1968), edited by R. Rhees. Rhees' editing was less than ideal. Without indicating the omissions he dropped nearly half of the source material, making it impossible to follow Wittgenstein's train of thought. A full transcription can be found in Wittgenstein (1993), pp. 202–88.

[3]   von Wright initially dated it 'Probably 1935–6', but this seems incorrect. See David Stern's discussion in Wittgenstein (1993), p. 445.

treatment in *Philosophical Investigations*, which in turn received its final revision in 1945/1946.[4]

The sections of *Philosophical Investigations* setting out what is commonly known as *the* private language argument contain some of the most famous passages in twentieth-century philosophy. Although there is no explicit demarcation in the book describing the argument's whereabouts, and although Wittgenstein returns to questions about privacy several times, the relevant passages are usually identified as §§243–315.[5] Other important sections, however, are §202, §580 and p. 542 in Part II. The published edition dates from 1945/1946, but it would be misleading to suggest that these passages provide a snapshot of Wittgenstein's thoughts about the issue. They are in fact rather closely related, in approach, to the 'Notes for Lectures on "Private Experience" and "Sense Data"', and the first drafts of many of the relevant sections in *Philosophical Investigations* were prepared during 1937/1938 (MSS 119–20).[6] Hence the passages are better viewed as the culmination of Wittgenstein's ideas.

I will not scrutinize the development of Wittgenstein's thoughts on privacy between 1933 and 1945 in detail. I will not discuss the difference between the Blue Book, the 'Notes for Lectures on "Private Experience" and "Sense Data"' and *Philosophical Investigations*. There will be no attempt here to trace Wittgenstein's philosophical progress in the period 1933–1945. It is, of course, interesting and relevant, since it could illuminate the way in which Wittgenstein's thought evolved and reached its final form; in so far as he ever reached a settled conclusion, it is probably contained in *Philosophical Investigations*. Moreover, there is little doubt that Wittgenstein's desk was the place where the most significant treatment of the privacy subject occurred during that period. From a chronological point of view, then, the presentation and interpretation of §§243–315 ought to appear here. However, because of the centrality of *Philosophical Investigations* in later discussions about privacy, I believe it is best to postpone discussion of §§243–315 until later. As we shall see, historically, discussion of the possibility of a private language became almost inseparable from debate about the correct interpretation of §§243–315.

One major feature in his development which needs to be brought forward, however, is the much discussed transition in Wittgenstein's approach to philosophy which happened sometime between 1933 and 1936.[7] This transition makes itself felt

---

[4]   The published material on the philosophy of psychology originating after 1945 relates to Part II of *Philosophical Investigations* and does not take up privacy as a distinctive issue. I have here described only published sources. *The Big Typescript*, which has recently been published as Wittgenstein (2005), contains a chapter on 'Idealism etc.', which could be of interest. Stern reports that it discusses '... the dangers of attempting to describe immediate experience, the ascription of pain, solipsism, and memory time', Stern (1995), p. 94.

[5]   See, for example, Strawson (1954), p. 83; Hallett (1977), table of contents; Hintikka/Hintikka (1986), p. 253; von Savigny (1988), table of contents; Hacker (1990), table of contents.

[6]   See Stern's account in Wittgenstein (1993), p. 445. For a list of manuscript sources for the individual paragraphs in the interval §§243–315, see Hacker (1990), p. 13.

[7]   The exact date and character of this transition is a matter of dispute. The Hintikkas locate it in *Brown Book* passages written in 1936, Hintikka/Hintikka (1986), p. 193; Stern (1995) refers to a pamphlet, 'Philosophy', from 1933 discussing philosophical method. The pamphlet is reprinted in Wittgenstein (1993), pp. 160–200, but was first published in 1989.

in Wittgenstein's approach to privacy, in the sense that his discussion in the later period does not flow on naturally from the discussion in MS 107, the manuscript examined above in Chapter 3. This discontinuity is explained, I think, by the fact that where, in 1929, Wittgenstein had a 'privacy-friendly' conception of the nature of language, this subsequently changed into a 'privacy-hostile' conception. I believe that we can only understand what is going on in the discussions from the 1950s and onwards if we have a proper understanding of this change. I have chosen to explore Wittgenstein's transition, and its effects on the privacy issue, through a piece of writing which, remarkably in Wittgenstein's case, is quite self-contained. This is the notes he made for a planned lecture in 1941.

4.1 The 1941 Private Object Argument

Wittgenstein's 'Notes for the "Philosophical Lecture"' (MS 166) was published for the first time in *Philosophical Occasions* in 1993 and has, consequently, played only a minor part in the general philosophical discussion of private language. Nonetheless it has certain features that ought to attract the interest of anyone concerned with Wittgenstein's thoughts on privacy. It was most probably written in 1941, on the occasion of an invitation from the British Academy to deliver the annual public lecture in 1942 on a philosophical topic. Wittgenstein later withdrew, under pressure of other work, but the notes he prepared for the lecture display his efforts to present his thoughts on privacy to a more general audience, an audience unfamiliar with his developing philosophical concerns.

The notes are valuable because they remain relatively focused on the subject in hand, avoiding the usual digressions; they also contain passages somewhat longer than the usual clipped paragraphs, and along the way a number of conclusions are explicitly stated. They are divided into four main parts, together with some smaller paragraphs on the last page that could be preparations for further treatment of closely related topics. Of the four main parts, the first introduces the notion of privacy and the others open with remarks anticipating discussion of referential or denotative theories of meaning: 'Meaning consisting of the word referring to the object', 'As introduction: Word referring to an object' and 'Common idea: a word has meaning by referring to something' (Wittgenstein, 1993, pp. 447, 451, 454). In the present section, I want to describe the line of thought Wittgenstein presents in 'Notes for the "Philosophical Lecture"'. I shall conclude that this line of thought amounts to a coherent argument: it constitutes what I shall call the '1941 Private Object Argument'.

Referential accounts of the way in which meaning is established are Wittgenstein's general target in the 1941 notes, and the three parts complement each other in attacking them. So much is clear, but at the same time Wittgenstein wants to say something about the nature of experiences and feelings. It is also his goal to show that, in the case of feelings and experiences, postulation of a private object becomes unnecessary in the sense that it is irrelevant to the way we speak about them. This conception is controversial in so far as it is a very natural thought that some entity, object, set, structure, or the like, will be the reference of, for example, 'pain'. It also seems natural to allow first-person privileged access to this entity to some degree, because one's feelings can be kept secret from other people. In other words, we have a private technique of use when it comes to feelings: the first-person statement is authoritative when it comes to asserting their presence. So, from the outset, Wittgenstein has two agendas. To further complicate matters, we are still not given straightforward argumentation of the kind that is easy to decipher. Wittgenstein does not start off with the notion to be discarded and derive a contradiction of some sort from it. The overall strategy is better described as closing the gaps through which the notion of a private object is thought to play a role in language.

He begins the notes with some preliminary remarks on privacy: one can distinguish between the privacy of experiences (e.g. experiences of red or green) and the privacy of feelings (e.g. feelings of pain or toothache). Whereas feelings have behavioural correlates, experiences do not, and the privacy we attach to them is, accordingly, a kind of 'superprivacy' (Wittgenstein, 1993, p. 447). So, to begin with, we are warned not to generalize too quickly, since different mental states items have different kinds of privacy attached to them. In the argumentation that follows he concentrates on feelings and generally ignores specific problems that might be raised by, say, visual experiences.

In connection with feelings, privacy can mean:

> '[1] nobody can know them unless I show them, or: [2] I can't really show them. Or: [3] if I don't want to, I needn't give any sign of my feeling but even if I want to I can only show a sign not the feeling' (Wittgenstein, 1993, p.447).

At the outset, then, Wittgenstein expresses reservations about privacy; the concept should be used with caution. The purpose of Wittgenstein's analysis, we might say, is to determine which of these notions is appropriate in the case of feelings.

To determine this we need to examine the nature of feelings. What is the nature of a feeling? Now on a certain conception of language, namely as a picturer of reality, the way we speak about feelings is not obviously relevant here. Grammar is one thing and reality another; the function of words in a language will no doubt be of interest to a linguist, but the problem here is the nature of pain. At most, the way we speak about feelings can *reflect* certain essential properties they have. Wittgenstein expresses the picture conception of language as follows: 'Meaning consisting of the word referring to an object' (Wittgenstein, 1993, p.447). 'Object' is meant to be taken in its broadest possible sense, encompassing structures, dispositions, intentions, and so on. In this model words refer to certain entities and thereby establish a technique of use for describing these objects. The chronological order of things is that, first, we have the reference and then the language; so also in the private case: 'The private object. The naming of the private object. The private language. The game someone plays with himself'. (Wittgenstein, 1993, p. 447)

This model, or picture, of language and the word-world relation is, however, mistaken. It cannot be maintained once we focus on the position the naming process actually occupies in language:

> All ostensive definition explains the use of a word only when it makes one last determination, removes one last indeterminacy ... And we are misled if we think that it

is a peculiar process of christening an object which makes a word stand for an object. (Wittgenstein, 1993, p. 447–8)

He does not argue at length for this point here. He merely hints at the way language is learned and comments that many words have no obvious relation to an object. The general point follows, however, from his discussion of ostensive definition – a discussion summarized above in Chapter 3:[8] ostensive definitions only make sense in a context in which language is already up and running. A word must already have a fairly determinate meaning before you can define it ostensively and this prior determinacy of meaning comes from the word's place in a language.

> And in this very way the technique of use of a word gives us an idea of *very* general truths about the world in which it is used, of truths in fact which are so general that they don't strike people, I'm sorry to say, and philosophers, too. (Wittgenstein, 1993, p. 449)

The grammar of words – the circumstances in which they make sense – explains why we feel the need for a private object in the case of 'pain'; so what role does the assignment of a feeling to a particular object play in our practice of speaking about feelings? What difference does it make?

Wittgenstein now traces the inclination to affirm the privacy of an object in the way we speak about feelings: 'Now why do we say: My feelings are my private property?' (Wittgenstein, 1993, p. 448) This inclination derives from the fact that (a) only I am directly aware of my pain. But we need to be clear about what is meant by this statement; in what way does (a) express something significant about pain?

Wittgenstein briefly considers two possible answers to this question. One is to say that (a) is related to: (b) 'I am directly aware of his pain', a claim that could mean 'I feel the same pain as he does'. In that framework (a) would mean something like: 'Only I feel the same pain as I do.' This would, of course, make (a) a significant statement, but it would not express the inconceivability of someone else feeling the same pain: if this is the right context in which to utter (a), then (a) is not expressing something about the concept of pain, but rather about the world; it is an *empirical* statement that might be falsified in the future.

So we turn to the second possibility, namely, that (a) should express the inconceivability of two subjects being aware of the same kind of pain: (a) should be arranged so that it is a *grammatical* statement pointing to the lack of sense in the statement 'I am directly aware of his pain'. The rule governing the relevant use of words could be this: 'A person is directly aware of his pain only and indirectly aware of the other man's' (Wittgenstein, 1993, p. 448). This would assign a use to the phrase (c) 'He is directly aware of pain' which could not be distinguished from the use of (d) 'He has pain' (or 'He is in pain'). So on this interpretation of (a), the invocation of 'directly aware' *does not* take us any further than ordinary ascriptions of pain; we have not added a new aspect to usage. Speaking about pain as a private object does not add anything to the linguistic practice of ascribing pain to people.

We are nonetheless inclined to say that (c) points to something essential about pain which is not expressed in (d), because it seems to indicate that we are dealing

---

8   See p. 37 .

with a private object to which we think 'pain' refers. Wittgenstein diagnoses the origin of this inclination:

> What gives us the idea that the person who feels pain is aware of an object, as it were, sees it, whereas we are only told that it is there but can't see it? It is the peculiar function of the verbs like feeling, seeing etc. (Wittgenstein, 1993, p. 448)

To recapitulate, we saw above that our linguistic practice does not warrant the assertion of a private object; and Wittgenstein urges us to look at 'the peculiar function of verbs like feeling' in order to diagnose, or explain, why we still feel it imperative to assert the existence of such an object.

So Wittgenstein looks at the way 'feeling pain' or 'having pain' are used and describes how this usage generates the intuition that (c) points to an essence of pain:

> The first point is this: that this verbal expression is, in the first person, used to replace an *expression* of pain. So that if some people say that "having pain" in the end refers to pain behaviour we can answer them that "I have pain" does not refer to pain behaviour but *is* pain behaviour. It corresponds to a cry of pain, not to the statement "I am crying". (Wittgenstein, 1993, p. 449)

The justification here stems from ordinary practice. We learn the handling of the word 'pain' in the first person by being encouraged to utter it instead of screaming or crying. Controversy threatens nonetheless, because even if we grant this picture we are inclined to say that once the correct use of 'pain' is acquired, it not only replaces cries, screams and so on, but refers to something which warrants the ascription of 'pain' to oneself. This something cannot stand in any direct relationship to behaviour, because we can behave as though in pain when we are not and be in pain without letting anyone else know; the use of 'pain' allows these cases. Thus the private object seems to be necessitated by language use. We appeal to it in order to distinguish real pain from fake pain. Its presence therefore seems to underwrite individual usages of the sentence 'I am in pain'. We are here at the origin of the idea that a private object is necessary.

Wittgenstein's strategy for repudiating this picture is to look more closely at usage in order to illuminate the supposedly justificational role of the postulated object.

Let us assume that the model in which a word refers to a private object is correct and consider, first, what role the private mental object would play from a second- or third-person perspective. When would we say that another person is justified in using the word 'pain' – that he has understood the meaning of 'pain'? Well, we imagine some private regularity: the person in question uses the word only when the referential object is present, or maybe his use is guided by a private rule. It might seem explanatory to say that someone knows the meaning of 'pain' when he can use it in accordance with some regularity, but one should dig deeper and elaborate just what is meant by 'private regularity': '...it seems to be something which, if we saw it, we should call a regularity' (Wittgenstein, 1993, p. 451). But what is the criterion by which we compare two applications of the private rule? There is none: we do not wish to use the usual criteria for saying 'I feel what he feels', nor have we given any fresh criteria. None of this is at odds with the picture the model under attack wishes to convey:

> And I course I know perfectly well that we are thinking of criteria similar to the ones of physical objects, only we can't apply any such criteria in our case and *that's* what we mean by talking of the privacy of objects. (Wittgenstein, 1993, pp. 451–2)

But without these criteria the postulated object could be identical to anything whatsoever. Moreover, so far as use of the term 'pain' is concerned, it would be irrelevant which one it was (Wittgenstein, 1993, p. 450); no object would justify an ascription of pain more than any other. So the invocation of a private object cannot explain why we use the term 'private' about feelings. But what can, then?

> Privacy here really means absence of a means of comparison. Only we mix up the states of affairs when we are prevented from comparing the objects with that of not having a fixed method of comparison. (Wittgenstein, 1993, p. 452)[9]

Consider now the situation from the first-person perspective. Could the private object be said to be of any use to the one person supposedly possessing direct access? It would seem that his use of 'pain' will be based on the fact that he recognizes the same object each time he utters the word. Again, however, closer examination reveals problems with this account. One notices to begin with that, in a situation where there is no non-verbal behaviour to go by, his only criterion, or justification, for asserting the presence of the private object is that he utters the word 'pain'. So the use of the word justifies the presence of the private object, which in turn justifies the use. This is not only a full circle; it also makes the object superfluous. To see this, reflect that anything present when the word is used, justifies that use; the speaker has no more reason to think it a particular kind of object than we do.

Granted that the private object cannot play any role in a person's use of 'pain', we seem to be stuck with a problem, because now there is nothing to justify a person's ascription of pain to himself. Wittgenstein does not consider this a problem, however, but a point of view to be occupied:

> What criteria am I using for determining that what I feel is pain, or what I see is red? None. (Wittgenstein, 1993, p. 452)

> "But when I in my own case distinguish between, say, pretending that I have pain and really have pain, surely I must make the distinction on some grounds!" Oddly enough – no! – I do distinguish but not on any grounds. (Wittgenstein, 1993, p. 454)

The attitude taken by the second interlocutor in each of these passages might seem odd. Indeed it would probably take most of us a while to accept, on first encountering the remarks, that the view they express is not necessarily overlooking something. The tension is eased somewhat once we see that Wittgenstein is not denying that

---

9   This is, I think, an example of the kind of remark that makes these lecture notes significant. It is very rare for Wittgenstein's description of his own point of view to be so clear.

there is any justification when someone says to himself 'I am in pain'. But in the case we are considering, where there are no behavioural equivalents, there is no justification: '... I have no justification analogous to the case for calling the sensation identical apart from my use of the word in *other* contexts' (Wittgenstein, 1993, p. 452). In other words, the situation which prompted us to talk of a private object presupposes situations in which we *can* justify the claim that we are in pain, and in these situations the justification alludes to behaviour: 'How would I justify my pain-behaviour in order to show to someone that I wasn't just acting in this way? I would add more expressive behaviour' (Wittgenstein, 1993, p. 454).

Should we now say that Wittgenstein denies the existence of pain? Well, he does not deny that it makes sense to say that someone is in pain. Instead his main concern is the initially proposed model of meaning:

> What I do deny is that we can construe the grammar of "having pain" by hypostatising a private object. Or: The private object functions all right only as long as its grammar is entirely constructed to suit the grammar of the common objects in question. And it becomes an absurdity if its nature is supposed to explain that grammar. (Wittgenstein, 1993, p. 451)

'Grammar' can here be translated by 'use in language'. A private object can figure in a common practice, but cannot explain it; it has no explanatory force vis-à-vis the way we use words like 'pain'. We can speak about a private object, but only in the manner in which people can *show* their pain to others by expressing it; and this way we have a criterion for two 'pains' being identical. Another way of explaining the use of 'pain', the one which Wittgenstein seems to prefer, is to treat the term 'pain' as the name of a common object – and to say that everyone has a private technique of using it (Wittgenstein, 1993, p. 448). Here, in ascriptions of pain, the first-person perspective allows for a use that differs from the third-person perspective. This means that we can return to the possibilities regarding what is meant by idea that feelings enjoy privacy and conclude that they *are* private, but only in the first sense: 'Nobody can know them unless I show them'.

The focal point of Wittgenstein's discussion is clearly the private object – the object which, he argues, can play no essential role in language. But what are we to say about private *language*? Would our possession of a private technique afford us a private language? One can define the terms involved as one sees fit, but a private technique, in the sense Wittgenstein understands it, implies not that others cannot understand the words to which the technique relates, but only that others are not entitled to use them in the same way. To see this, recall how people ascribe pain to themselves. This is what Wittgenstein would call a private technique, but it does not exclude others from understanding the word 'pain'. In fact the opposite is the case. I can only have a private technique for using a word if it resembles a public technique for using that word, and this comparison can only be made if the word is the same. Wittgenstein makes this point in the text with a somewhat obscure analogy between techniques and sewing machines:

> There is a name only when there is a technique of using it and that technique can be private; but this only means that nobody can know about it in the sense in which I can have

a private sewing-machine. But in order to be a private sewing machine, it must be an object which deserves the name "sewing machine," not in virtue of its privacy, but in virtue of its similarity to sewing machines, private or otherwise. (Wittgenstein, 1993, p. 448)

Here, though, the privacy is one which can be abolished; there is no *essential* privacy. So understood (as a language which is spoken by a single person), a private language is possible.

In the last part of the text Wittgenstein deploys the lines of thinking just described to encourage his audience to discard the idea of a mental picture. I will not consider this deployment here. The essential point about privacy has been made, and enough has been said to convey the fact that a lot had changed in Wittgenstein's philosophy since 1929. However, before I turn to broaden the perspective, I would like to recapitulate the main steps of the argument contained, as I have suggested, in Wittgenstein's 'Notes for the "Philosophical Lecture"'.

Consider the proposal that the private object affects first-person ascriptions of pain. The following argument can be given for postulating a private object. (1) If a person knows the meaning of 'I am in pain', he should be able to distinguish cases where it can be warrantedly asserted from those in which it cannot. (2) A claim that is warrantedly assertible has some form of justification. Finally, (3) among the cases mentioned in (1) are some in which there is no relevant public evidence available. From (1)–(3) it is concluded (4) that a private object must be present in the cases where 'I am in pain' is warrantedly assertible. In response to this argument, Wittgenstein looks more closely at the conclusion. He asks: 'How does he who utters "I am in pain" know that the private object is present?' He considers and rejects a number of possible answers. One is that the person experiencing pain asserts 'I am in pain' in cases where the object is present, which creates an explanatory circle. Another is that the experiencing subject does not strictly speaking know, but only thinks he knows, but this only makes sense when one can know (Wittgenstein, 1993, p. 450). This part of the argument proceeds by considering proposed answers to Wittgenstein's question and is probably not exhaustive. However, given that the prospects for finding an unrejectable answer do not look good, we seem to be justified in concluding (5) that the private object has no explanatory value; it could be anything or nothing.

A novel and creative feature of Wittgenstein's reasoning is the solution which allows him to maintain (5): rejection of (2) – or, in other words, a willingness to recognize (6) that it is possible for a claim *without* some form of justification to be warrantedly assertible. This, then, is what I call the '1941 Private Object Argument'.

4.2 The Difference in Approach

The above analysis and that offered in the Chapter 3 highlight the differences between the approach and arguments of the Phenomenological Language Argument from 1929 and the contrasting argumentation of the 1941 Private Object Argument. The extent of Wittgenstein's development here is not at all surprising when one considers his personal preoccupations during the relevant time – the decade or so separating the two arguments was hardly a period of philosophical stagnation for Wittgenstein.

Direct comparison of the two arguments renders the contrasts even more evident. To begin with, observe that there is a potential difficulty in that one argument discusses feelings whereas the other is concerned with the immediately given, or with 'experiences', in Wittgenstein's later terminology. The notes from 1941 begin with the observation that there are differences in the nature of the privacy attaching to these two kinds of mental state. We should keep this in mind, but we can ignore in fact the differences if we compare the arguments at a strategic level, as I shall now explain.

In 1941 the felt need for a private object was motivated by a presumption that ordinary practices are unintelligible without it, and it is this presumption that the argumentation against the object concentrates on. It is not that a private object cannot exist, but rather that it has no use, or can play no explanatory role, in the context in which it is invoked. So the private object the 1941 Private Object Argument concerns is a result of what we think is required to justify ascriptions of feelings. The case with the immediately given, or experiences, is analogous: How can we justify claims about the world by referring to experience if there is no immediately given, if there are no experiences? We can see a similar motivation behind the stage-setting of both arguments, then. In both cases, our justificatory practices generate a story about the way in which public language is created. The story begins with what we ultimately refer to in justification and proceeds to the naming of these private objects, the private language, and finally the public language as a compromise between private languages.[10]

Both arguments attack this story. However, they do so at different levels. The Phenomenological Language Argument attacks the private language, but in it the existence of the ultimate basis of justification, the immediately given, is not called into question. The result is a peculiar, almost paradoxical, theoretical position in which it is held that we speak of the physical but live in the phenomenal. From this perspective, the Phenomenological Language Argument goes only halfway, because it does not attack the root of the picture of the way in which language is generated. The 1941 Private Object Argument, on the other hand, does attack the private objects at the root. It is therefore more radical.

But although there is a pattern here that allows us to say that the arguments are involved in similar projects, it is not their similarities which stand out. To begin with, observe the status, accorded by Wittgenstein, to his targets in 1929 and 1941. In 1929 Wittgenstein had a *positive* attitude to the notion that there is a phenomenological language. He was clinging on to this notion because he was convinced that it had to be correct. When he gave it up, he was in despair and had to take recourse to a solution he still thought was second-best, for a while at any rate:

We must get along with our ordinary language and only understand it correctly. (Wittgenstein, 1994, p. 102)

---

[10]   Compare Wittgenstein (1993), p. 447. Quoted on p. 46 .

What his considerations had demonstrated was the impossibility of a phenomenological language, but they had not undermined its motivation. In 1941, on the other hand, his argumentation not only sought to demonstrate the uselessness of a private object in understanding ordinary practice, but also located and illuminated the misconceived motivation behind its invocation. Here Wittgenstein had a *negative* attitude to the need for a private object. He wanted not only to get rid of it, but to erase the motivation for it. This more thorough-going rejection indicates that Wittgenstein had taken a different view of the essence of language and of what needed to be accounted for.

In a way, one might articulate the difference by saying that in 1929 Wittgenstein took the world for granted and asked how we connect to it, whereas he in 1941 took the connection for granted and asked what this tells us about the world.

In 1929 Wittgenstein was not claiming that ordinary 'Gewöhnliche' language was defective and in need of replacement if the true structure of the phenomenal world was to be captured, but he was holding that such language did not openly exhibit its connection to visual space or phenomenal reality in general:

> [Visual space] can be directly described (but we are far away from knowing the way of expression that describes it) The ordinary physicalistic language relates to it in a v e r y complex and instinctively well-known way. (Wittgenstein, 1994, p. 3, spacing og 'v e r y' original)

Still displaying the grip of the picture theory, this note from his personal manuscripts neatly indicates the general problem he was trying to solve: How could language picture reality? The problem is that it is not open to view how it can do this, and therefore we need a hypothesis to explain how language conforms to its essence. The existence of a phenomenological language was a hypothesis on the road to justification or explanation of ordinary linguistic practice. When the failings of this hypothesis became apparent in 1929 Wittgenstein retained the picture theory and had, therefore, to look for another story about the nature of the picturing relation.

By 1941 Wittgenstein no longer thought that the essence of language is to picture or model reality. Rather, he held what we might call a 'use' conception of language on which the essence of a language lies in how it is being used. From this perspective, ordinary linguistic practice no longer has to be justified, but rather justifies itself: if there is a use or linguistic practice, there is already something to talk about. Use is where the investigation must begin if we want to know the nature of the things we talk about:

> ...the technique of use of a word gives us an idea of *very* general truths about the world in which it is used. (Wittgenstein, 1993, p. 449)

It can be seen, then, that the 1941 Private Object Argument not only demonstrates that the private object offers no justificatory basis for our discourse about feelings, but also attacks the Tractarian picture theory Wittgenstein still subscribed to in 1929. There is, now, no univocal sense in which language has to picture reality in order to be meaningful – that is to say, have a use. Furthermore, the argument shows that a use conception is inherently at odds with privacy of the kind which naturally flows from the twin theses that picturing, or modelling, the world is the essence of language and that the empiricist account of how we confront the world is basically correct. Accordingly, one way to summarize the developments analysed in this chapter and the previous one is to say that Wittgenstein's transition marked his progress from a 'privacy-friendly' conception of the nature of language to a 'privacy-hostile' conception.

The radical change in Wittgenstein's conception of the nature of language that occurred during the 1930s altered his view, not just of privacy, but the nature of philosophy itself. The project of the *Tractatus* had been to show the limits of language by elaborating the way in which language univocally connects to reality; but on a use conception language has no univocal purpose, because the meaning of any given word is tied to the context in which it is used. Accordingly, the limits of language have to be determined for each particular linguistic practice. In the pamphlet from 1933 entitled 'Philosophy', Wittgenstein compared these two conceptions of the nature of philosophy with two different ways of splitting up a strip:

> Unrest in philosophy comes from philosophers looking at, seeing, philosophy all wrong , i.e. cut up into (infinite) vertical strips, as it were, rather than (finite) horizontal strips. This recording of understanding creates the *greatest* difficulty. They want to grasp the infinite strip, as it were, and complain that it //this// is not possible piece by piece. Of course it isn't, if by 'a piece' one understands an endless vertical strip. But it is, if one sees a horizontal strip as a piece //a whole, definite piece//. – But then we'll never get finished with our work! Of course//certainly// not, because it doesn't have an end. (Wittgenstein, 1993, p. 195)

In other words, the transition in Wittgenstein's philosophy was fundamental and changed his approach to problems. This is probably one reason why his views were so hard to grasp, even to his friends. As we shall see in the Section 4.3, some of his close allies continued to believe in the possibility of a private language after he himself had abandoned that belief.

4.3 Wittgenstein's Contemporaries and the Privacy Issue

Neither Wittgenstein's philosophy nor, more specifically, the development of his thoughts on the subject of privacy was taken up in general philosophical debates that took place during the 1930s and the 1940s. In addition to not publishing, he did not engage in any broader philosophical discussions. The only traces of the transition which had occurred in his philosophical thinking, and in his opinion on the subjects he dealt with, were transmitted through irregular correspondence with Schlick in Vienna, and through the influence he had on the rather small circle of students who were allowed to attend his lectures at Cambridge University.

The showdown with privacy was a showdown with the picture theory for Wittgenstein. The picture theory generates privacy because we feel that there must be something we refer to that justifies the way we express ourselves about experiences and feelings. There must be something we talk about whose nature is mirrored in our jargon – hence the postulation of private objects. In 1929 Wittgenstein had concluded from the Phenomenological Language Argument that a simple picture theory could not be true, but he had retained the fundamental outlook of the picture theory. In any case, even if he had wanted to, he could not have abandoned the picture theory at this point, because he saw no alternative. It required exposure to a point of view outside the picture theory for a full confrontation with that theory to occur, and it was this kind of exposure he found in 1941. The radical change in his approach to philosophy which grew from his new conception of the purpose of language placed him outside a historical context. Overwhelmingly, the philosophical community around Wittgenstein was still bewitched – to use a term that Wittgenstein would later use to describe the false attractions of theory-building – by the model of language which the picture theory elaborates.

This is even true of members of the Vienna Circle like Carnap and Neurath who displayed a natural hostility to the possibility of a private language and private objects; they had not taken Wittgenstein's path. As was shown in Chapter 2, they found other ways to deal with privacy – ways that essentially involved declining to face the privacy problem. Equally, the growing threat of Hitler's Nazism to critical thinking (to a large degree) and Jews (to an even greater degree) meant that the Vienna Circle gradually disbanded during the 1930s. Neurath fled to Holland in 1934, and then to England in 1940, where he died five years later without leaving much trace in British philosophy. Influential advocates of its scientific philosophy emigrated to the United States, eventually coming to occupy posts in universities throughout the country. Carnap arrived in 1936 and was first employed at the University of Chicago. He continued to explore and apply scientific philosophy, and substantially influenced the direction of American philosophy.[11]

Among those less persuaded by the physicalist agenda, with its dismissive attitude to traditional philosophical problems, implicit acceptance of mental privacy revealed itself in treatments of our knowledge of other minds. For instance, in 1938 the Oxford epistemologist H. H. Price argued that one proceeds by analogical reasoning when hypothesising the existence of a mind in another body; the basis of the inference is the observation that certain emitted sounds are used in a way in which oneself is inclined to use them. For Price the existence of other minds was a hypothesis which could be imagined to be false. He admitted that the hypothesis was strictly unverifiable, but denied that this would make it nonsense:

> The hypothesis is a perfectly conceivable one ... in the sense that I know very well what the world would have to be like if the hypothesis were true – what sort of entities there must be in it, and what sorts of events must occur in them. I know from introspection what acts of thinking and perceiving are, and I know what it is for such acts to be combined into the unity of a single mind ... (Price, 1938, pp. 446–7)

At Princeton W. T. Stace expressed a similar willingness to accept the privacy of the mind: 'Your colour red, instead of being similar to mine, may possibly resemble what I should call toothache. That we speak familiarly of our sensations proves nothing to the contrary.' (Stace, 1932, p. 31). Again, in 1940 Bertrand Russell, who

---

[11] For an historical survey of the Vienna Circle's emigration to the United States, and their impact on arrival, see Hacker (1996b), pp. 183–8.

had been very close to Wittgenstein when the latter wrote the *Tractatus*, thought it possible 'to invent an artificial language' which was in essence a private language (Russell, 1940, p. 154). Together with A. J. Ayer, who also defended the possibility of a private language, as will be shown in the Chapter 4, Russell was the dominant figure in British philosophy in the 1940s; so to argue against privacy at that time was to set one's face against the philosophical establishment.

Most notably, the possibility of private language was countenanced by Wittgenstein's closest ally from the Vienna days, Moritz Schlick. On at least two occasions Schlick explicitly admitted the possibility of such a language. One was when, still resident in Vienna, Schlick gave three lectures in London in 1932. Dealing with language, and defending a view he described as '... regarding incommunicability as the criterion of inexpressibility' (Schlick, 1932, p. 177), he argued, in a section entitled 'Communication with one's self', that communication was not an essentially intersubjective property. On the contrary, he argued, a universe populated by only a single living being would not exclude the possibility of language. Here memory, or a diary, could be bearers of meaning.[12] This claim was in itself, perhaps, not so very controversial; but pushing the limits of his verificationism, he spoke of *a language where meaning was exclusively constituted in memory*. In this case, the truth of a memory could not be questioned:

> The sentence "I am seeing green" means nothing but "there is a colour which I remember has always been called green". This recollection, this datum of my memory, is the one and only criterion of the truth of my statement. I recall it so, and that is final; in our supposed case I cannot go on asking: do I remember correctly? for I could not possibly explain what I meant by such a question. (Schlick, 1932, p. 179)

Given that others could not verify the truth or falsity of 'I am seeing green', because they could not access the fact that I see the colour I remember as being green (if that is a fact), a language based on such a foundation would be necessarily private – it would be intelligible only to the person in possession of the memory.

The other occasion was in an article entitled 'On the Relation between Psychological and Physical Concepts'. Here Schlick argued for the empirical adequacy of the universality of the physicalistic language. Towards the end of the article, he anticipated the possibility of a world in which the physicalistic language was not universal:

> I can, for example, imagine that my feeling of grief corresponded in no way to any bodily condition. If, for example, I laughed, skipped around, sang and told witty stories, no one would be able to conclude from this that I was gay, rather this behaviour would be as compatible with a sorrowful as with a cheerful mood. ...
> In the described case there would be a world of feeling which could not be talked about in the physical language... it would no longer be universal, for in addition to it there would

---

[12]   Schlick (1932), p. 178. John Cook has conjectured that it is 'very likely' that Wittgenstein was inspired by Schlick to give the diary-example in §258 in *Philosophical Investigations*. See Cook (1972), pp. 44–5.

be a private language in which I could reflect about the world of feeling. (Schlick, 1932, p. 433)

Schlick's persistence with private language is remarkable in so far as he regarded his views on meaning to be largely '... due to conversations with Wittgenstein ... I can hardly exaggerate my indebtedness to this philosopher' (Schlick, 1936, p. 340). Hence, during the 1930s the most explicit statement of the possibility of a private language came from a professed follower of Wittgenstein. From Schlick's description of grief it is obvious that the possible situation he was considering essentially consisted in adopting a privacy thesis about the mind of the kind Price and Stace had defended and adding to it a semantic theory. So, according to Schlick in 1935, physical-psychical dualism would lead to a private language.[13]

Wittgenstein's philosophy now stood in direct opposition to the views of most established philosophers working in related fields. Neither Russell, his teacher before World War I, nor Schlick, his friend from Vienna days and, on the subject of meaning, an enthusiastic student, had followed Wittgenstein in his profound reorientation. The consequence was that confusion prevailed when Wittgenstein's ideas later began to leak into the philosophical community. In Part II I shall look at the way in which this confusion affected the reception Wittgenstein's *Philosophical Investigations*.

---

[13]   Hallett (1977), pp. 311–12, speculates that in 1935 Schlick expressed Wittgenstein's thoughts. The truth of this claim would fortify the picture presented in Chapter 3, but unfortunately it is hard to evaluate. It is, however, certain, as the quotation from 1936 shows, that Schlick regarded himself as building on Wittgenstein's thoughts.

PART II
Post-War Effects of
Philosophical Investigations

Chapter 5

Reviews and Reactions

Wittgenstein died on 29 April 1951. He had been working hard for many years on a major manuscript that would present his philosophical achievements, and although he never managed to bring this project to conclusion, his literary executors did not have to make many editorial decisions before the manuscript in question was ready to be published. *Philosophical Investigations* was published in 1953 in an edition featuring an English translation by G. E. M Anscombe alongside the German original.[1] In the preface, written in January 1945, Wittgenstein characterized the book as the best presentation, though not necessarily a satisfactory one, he could give of the results, or 'precipitate', of his philosophical investigations in the years since his return to philosophy in 1929.

When one reads *Philosophical Investigations* it immediately becomes obvious that, although it employs few technical terms, it requires a substantial degree of active participation from the reader, partly because the material is extremely compressed. Wittgenstein says in the preface to the work that this is intentional: his aim is to encourage those who read him to participate in the enquiries he undertakes. Many of the smaller sections have the character of gnomic insights rather than conclusions derived from argument; and neither the terminology nor the style of the book readily shows how it is to be applied to existing philosophical problems. In short, a lot of decompression and decoding is required – something that leaves considerable scope for interpretation.

Despite these hurdles, early commentators on *Philosophical Investigations* saw clearly that Wittgenstein had identified problems that had to do with the privacy commonly ascribed to sensations, and that these problems were connected with further problems in the philosophy of language.[2] It was also acknowledged that the passages on these issues were extraordinarily difficult. Of these passages, Norman Malcolm wrote: 'This is one of the main inquiries of the book and perhaps the most difficult to understand' (Malcolm, 1954, p. 530). P. F. Strawson went further: 'Studying the sections in which Wittgenstein deals with sensations, one may well feel one's capacity to learn coming to an end' (Strawson, 1954, p. 83).

Many reasons – ranging from attributions of originality to imputations of unnecessary obscurity – have been given for the difficulty involved in understanding these sections. However, the sections certainly received attention and were the subject of intense discussion in the decade or so that followed the publication of

---

[1] The main decision for the executors was whether to include Part II; for editorial details, see von Wright (1979).

[2] An important exception here is the detailed review written by Paul Feyerabend. In this the issue of the privacy of sensations is not addressed directly; see Feyerabend (1955).

Philosophical Investigations. Thus in 1966 George Pitcher noted that 'fully thirty per cent' of the articles discussing Wittgenstein's philosophy in Cambridge dealt with the arguments Wittgenstein had directed against the notion of a private language (Pitcher (ed.), 1966, p. vii).

The agenda, or framework, of this intense discussion was to a large extent set by the first commentators on §§243–315 of *Philosophical Investigations*: by Malcolm, Rush Rhees, Strawson and A. J. Ayer. Malcolm and Rhees had attended Wittgenstein's lectures in Cambridge. The others were leading British philosophers; Strawson and Ayer held chairs at Oxford University and London University. It was in the discussions that took place between these four philosophers that the most important arguments deriving from Wittgenstein's treatment of sensations and privacy came to be disputed and, to some extent, identified.[3]

5.1 The Reductio Argument

As a direct consequence of the style in which Wittgenstein wrote much discussion centred on what was at stake: What notion of privacy did Wittgenstein see as problematic, and how should the problematic language be characterized? It was seen that languages which were private in the sense that their notation was only known to a single person, or involved some kind of code, were not problematic in the required sense. They could be categorized as public languages, and Wittgenstein had allowed them (§243).[4]

Malcolm set out most explicitly the philosophical framework against which Wittgenstein's concerns about privacy should be evaluated. According to him Wittgenstein was concerned with '... the problem of how language is related to inner experiences – to sensations, feelings, and moods' (Malcolm, 1954, pp. 530–31). The problem derived from a conception of inner experiences often called *Cartesianism* after its most famous exponent.[5] On this conception '... there is only a contingent and not *essential* connection between a sensation and its outward expression' (Malcolm, 1954, p. 531). An apparent corollary here is that it can only be a hypothesis that others possess sensations and inner experiences; it is always possible to doubt the presence of a certain sensation.

The view that we possess some kind of private language flows naturally from the Cartesian theory of sensations. Cartesianism implies that I merely know about

---

[3]   The relevant articles are: Malcolm (1954), Rhees (1954), Strawson (1954) and Ayer (1954). All four are included in Pitcher's collection of critical essays on Wittgenstein, Pitcher (ed.) (1966), Jones's collection of articles on the private language argument, Jones (ed.) (1971), and Canfield's collection of influential secondary literature, Canfield (ed.) (1986). Wittgenstein's views had spread from Cambridge through his students, and *Philosophical Investigations* received considerable attention from the beginning. Other early reactions and reviews are Ambrose (1954), Collins (1954), Feyerabend (1955), Findlay (1955), Heath (1956) and Lieb (1954).

[4]   All references to paragraphs will be to *Philosophical Investigations*, Wittgenstein (1953), unless otherwise indicated.

[5]   See, for example, Jones (ed.) (1971), p. 14.

sensations from my own case. If 'pain' or other sensation words are to refer to a particular private experience, it must be possible for me to privately associate the word with the experience. Accordingly, only I can know what these words mean. Others cannot know the meaning of the words; they can only surmise it. If others cannot know the reference of the words, they cannot understand the words. Hence such a language, concerned exclusively with my own inner experiences, would be a private language of necessity, because others could not understand what the words refer to: 'By a "private language" is meant one that not merely is not but *cannot* be understood by anyone other than the speaker' (Malcolm, 1954, p. 530).

Wittgenstein puts the matter this way:

> The individual words of this language are to refer to what can only be known to the person speaking; to his immediate private sensations. So another person cannot understand the language. (§243)

This combination of features leads to a picture of our ordinary sensation language as a compromise between, or construction out of, idiolects in which each individual knows the reference of the words from his own case exclusively: '... certain sentences do serve only to describe the speaker's private experiences and that, this being so they have a different meaning for him from any that they can possibly have for anybody else' (Ayer, 1954, p. 52).

Malcolm, Ayer and Strawson all agreed that Wittgenstein's intention had been to demolish this picture of how sensation discourse arises. They also agreed that Wittgenstein had gone further than Carnap had in rejecting a protocol language expressing 'only what is immediately given'. Carnap had merely argued that it would be impossible to communicate the meaning of terms in this language to others. Wittgenstein had argued that, under these conditions, one would not succeed in saying anything at all, even to oneself.

Malcolm's presentation of the argument was the most elaborate and was to become one of the most influential versions of a private language argument. He argued that Wittgenstein had shown the term 'private language' to be self-contradictory, saying: 'Postulate a "private" language; then deduce that it is not a *language*' (Malcolm, 1954, p. 537). Although it is true that Malcolm, Rhees, Strawson and Ayer all attributed to Wittgenstein (albeit in slightly different terms) a reductio ad absurdum of the notion of a private language, in what follows I shall refer to Malcolm's interpretation as the 'Reductio Argument'.

The Reductio Argument played a major role in subsequent developments in the argumentation against a private language, and for some years, especially outside the circle of Wittgenstein scholars, it was more influential than §§243–315 in this regard. Despite its independent existence, however, it should not be considered apart from the relevant sections of *Philosophical Investigations*, because all the premises originated there. This is why the other reviewers presented similar, if less fully worked out, arguments.

Malcolm begins by pointing out that the construction of the private language presupposes a certain conception of the way in which one might endow a word with meaning: '... I fix my attention on a sensation and establish a connection between a word and the sensation (258)' (Malcolm, 1954, p. 531). I can perform an act that establishes an essential connection between word and object. That such a meaning-producing mechanism is available is the assumption the Reductio Argument is meant to reduce to absurdity. Accordingly, the argument would start with the assumption that I have fixed my attention on a pain as I pronounced the sound 'pain'. It would assume that I can endow the sound we mark with the word 'pain' with meaning by this ritual – that I can make 'pain' into a sign. Because pain has no natural expression, and others cannot infer its presence from my behaviour, others could not know for certain what was being recorded by 'pain', and so they could not understand this sign. Consequently 'pain' would be part of an essentially private language. Furthermore, the privacy involved here is one in which the sensation-word '... not merely is not but *cannot* be understood by anyone other than the speaker' (Malcolm, 1954, p. 530), because, by hypothesis, it is impossible for others to detect its reference; others could not know what was meant by the word; they could not understand it.

To destroy this picture, Malcolm presented an argument which he ascribed to Wittgenstein. The following steps convey the essential elements of his somewhat unstructured argumentation:

1. Suppose '... I fix my attention on a sensation ...' (Malcolm, 1954, p. 531) and thereby define the meaning of a word.
2. 'My private definition was a success only if it led me to use the word correctly in the future. In the present case "correctly" would mean "consistent with my own definition"'
3. 'The concept of a rule requires that there be a difference between "He is following a rule" and "He is under the impression that he is following a rule"'.
4. 'My impression that I follow a rule does not confirm that I follow the rule unless there can be something that will prove my impression correct' (Malcolm, 1954, p. 532); I can determine the above-mentioned difference only if I can appeal to something independent of my impressions capable of showing whether I am following a rule.
5. But there is nothing of this sort in the situation being considered, and therefore there can be no private definition.

The second assumption is that a language can be compared to a system of (linguistic) rules. Using a word correctly should be read to mean 'consistently with my own definition', and this again means following the rule a successful definition lays down. If no sense of correctness characterized subsequent use of the word, it would follow that no definition had taken place and the word had not been given any meaning.

The third assumption is an instance of the Wittgensteinian principle that it is not possible to describe relative notions without invoking the absolute. This principle, which had also figured in Wittgenstein's Phenomenological Language Argument from the late 1920s, is most directly stated in §202: 'Hence it is not possible to obey a rule "privately": otherwise thinking one was obeying a rule would be the same thing as obeying it'. Malcolm pointed out that the principle was also employed explicitly in the sections dealing with a tentative private language. For instance, §258: 'One would like to say: whatever is going to seem right to me is right. And that only means that here we can't talk about "right"'. So the third assumption was clearly derivable from *Philosophical Investigations*, but its role in relation to sensations was not straightforwardly obvious. The assumption seemed to imply that it must be possible to have the impression that pain is present and yet not be in pain. This scenario would allow doubt to arise; and yet, as Strawson had pointed out, Wittgenstein held that doubt had no place in the language game where sensations were concerned (§288). So Wittgenstein's exact employment of the principle was still left open, and with it his views on sensations.

Probably the most problematic assumption was the fourth, because it might be taken as placing the argument in a verificationist tradition, with its emphasis on 'proof'. Since verificationism had for many already become suspect, its dependence on such a framework would render the argument suspect. All of the above premises can be recognized in one of the arguments Strawson presented, and Malcolm was well aware that Strawson's criticism of Wittgenstein's argumentation had in effect been that it employed a variant of the verification principle. Malcolm's comment on this seems to imply that Strawson had misinterpreted Wittgenstein's intentions at this point:

> Strawson attributes Wittgenstein's errors not only to prejudice and, possibly, to 'the old verificationist horror of a claim that cannot be checked' [a reference to (Strawson, 1954, p. 92)], but also to various confusions and muddles ... (Malcolm, 1954, p. 551)

So it would seem that Malcolm had not intended the argument to rely on a verificationist assumption. On the other hand, some of the phrases in his presentation of the argument seemed to point in the opposite direction:

> Now *how is it to be decided* whether I have used the word consistently? ... My impression that I follow a rule does not confirm that I follow the rule, unless there can be something *that will prove my impression correct*. (Malcolm, 1954, p. 532, my emphasis)

This tension was not relieved by the other parts of Malcolm's article, and it soon became a weak point that the critics focused on.

However, after presenting the argument, Malcolm immediately turned to other likely objections to it – objections that had in fact been raised by Strawson and Ayer. Malcolm claimed that Wittgenstein had anticipated them all.

The first objection concerned the status of memory as a tool for determining the difference between merely being under the impression of following a rule and actually following it. A successful attack from this angle would show the falsity of the Reductio Argument's fifth premise. Wittgenstein had considered the appeal to memory and rejected it (§265), but it was not clear on what grounds. According to Strawson's interpretation, Wittgenstein held that one could not justify the use of a word by invoking memory because that would not protect one from slips of memory. To the speaker of the language it would not make any difference if he constantly misremembered the use of one particular word. Strawson had certain reservations about this argument, one of them being that it was too sceptical: 'It is also *just* worth asking, in connexion with some of Wittgenstein's arguments here: Do we ever in fact find ourselves misremembering the use of very *simple* words of our common language, and having to correct ourselves by attention to other' – use?' (Strawson, 1954, p. 85).

Another reservation focused on the apparently excessive demand for justification where memory claims are concerned. Strawson and Ayer both argued that one might raise the doubt that Wittgenstein seemed to be raising in relation to memory about any public justification. Justification had to stop somewhere, and Wittgenstein did not give any special reason for supposing that memory could not be at the bottom of a 'pyramid of justifications'. Ayer, alluding to §265, wrote:

> I check my memory of the time at which a train is due to leave by visualizing a page of the time-table; and I am required to check this in its turn by looking up the page. But unless I can trust my eye-sight at this point, unless I can recognise the figures written down, I am still no better off. It is true that if I distrust my eyesight I have the resource of consulting other people; but then I have to understand their testimony, I have correctly to identify the signs they make. (Ayer, 1954, p. 54)

Even if one held that the possibility of consulting other people provided a foundation for epistemic justification, the Reductio Argument would make no essential reference to the privacy that Malcolm had described as the argument's target, but it could easily be extended to languages which are only contingently private; all that would be required is that the initial definition be lost in time. One might suspect some kind of verificationism lurking here. Against this, Malcolm's claim was that there was nothing to remember, since no initial definition had been secured:

> 'My memory' will not even mean – my memory *impression*. For by a memory impression we understand something that is either accurate or inaccurate; whereas there would not be, in the private language, any conception of what would establish a memory impression as correct, any conception of what 'correct' would mean here. (Malcolm, 1954, p. 534)

So it seemed that the argument was not dependent on memory-scepticism. The central point of the argument was not that in the private scenario one could not distinguish between following and seeming to follow the rule initially laid down. It was rather that no rule had been laid down in the first place, and that there was therefore nothing to remember correctly.

Let us suppose that this was Wittgenstein's point. It remains hard to see the reasons he might have had for believing it to be correct. How could this be the consequence? Is Wittgenstein not bluntly rejecting an obviously available solution? Ayer and Strawson both noticed that Wittgenstein had spend considerable time on the question of how one might endow a word with meaning, or define the meaning of a word, but they could not figure out why he had done this. Strawson thought Wittgenstein had forgotten a straightforward solution:

> He might simply be struck by the recurrence of a certain sensation and get into the habit of making a certain mark in a different place every time it occurred. (Strawson, 1954, p. 85)

Ayer took Wittgenstein to be making the point that all available methods for attaching meaning to a sign would make the sign's meaning available to others (Ayer, 1954, p. 55).

Malcolm again pointed out, in response to this objection, that Strawson and Ayer had not understood Wittgenstein correctly. He insisted that Wittgenstein had weighty reasons for refraining from the position on which Strawson openly relied and elaborated Strawson's and Ayer's attitude as follows: 'One wants to say, "surely there can't be a difficulty in knowing whether a feeling of mine is or isn't the *same* as the feeling I now have. I will call this feeling "pain" whenever it occurs. What could be easier than to follow that rule?"' (Malcolm, 1954, p. 534).

To undermine this attitude, Malcolm, following Wittgenstein, utilized the analogy of a language with a system of rules.[6] Consider a pupil who has been taught to write down the natural numbers (§185). He is now taught how to write down other series of cardinal numbers and gets to a point where he writes down series of the form $n,2n,3n,4n,...$ upon hearing the order '+n'. The teacher takes some samples to check whether he has really mastered the technique, but the samples have never been taken above the figure 1000. Suppose that we let the pupil extend the series '+2' beyond 1000, and that to our bewilderment he writes down '1000, 1004, 1008, 1012...' What could support the claim that he has not continued the series in the *same* way after 1000, other than the explanations we have already given him? The answer is: nothing. He might very well reply that he did continue in the *same* way. For in our previous explanations there was nothing that made it impossible for him to regard his written responses as the continuation of the series.

This argument does not depend on the teacher and pupil being two separate individuals. It also applies to the case of a private language – that is, to a case in which the teacher and pupil are identical:

> The point to be made here is that when one has given oneself the private rule 'I will call this same thing "pain" whenever it occurs', one is free to do anything or nothing. That 'rule' does not point in any direction. On the private-language hypothesis, no-one can teach me what the correct use of 'same' is. ... What I choose to call the 'same' will *be* the same. (Malcolm, 1954, p. 536)

What Ayer and Strawson had envisaged as an obvious, commonly adopted and easy method of laying down a rule, Malcolm showed to be an act that would not impose restrictions on future use.

Despite their criticisms of it, Strawson and Ayer took Wittgenstein'sargument to have a similar structure to that described by Malcolm. So the structure of the argument was more or less agreed on. There was also agreement over the conclusion of the argument: its immediate conclusion was that it is not possible to associate a word with a private experience.

One can now work backwards towards the rejection of Cartesianism. If it is not possible to associate a word with a private experience, and if the word 'pain' refers to some kind of sensation, then it follows that I do not know from my own case what that sensation is. But then I must know what a particular kind of sensation is partly by having been acquainted with the sensations of others. Since I only have access to the behaviour of others, it follows that I know about others' sensations by observing their behaviour. Hence, there must be a *non-contingent*, or essential, connection between a sensation and its outward expression.

---

[6] The following presentation is Malcolm's; see Malcolm (1954), pp. 534–6.

5.2 The Solitary Language Argument

Neither Strawson nor Ayer was convinced by the Reductio Argument. They both saw two main problems with it. First of all, Wittgenstein had imposed too strong a justificatory requirement by constantly asking for an independent test to determine whether a sign had been used correctly. Ayer and Strawson thought that justification must stop somewhere: 'But unless there is something that one is allowed to recognize, no test can ever be completed.'[7] And it seemed that the only thing Wittgenstein would accept as an answer was some kind of external check which others could corroborate.

This trail led naturally to the second objection: the kind of ultimate test Wittgenstein demanded seemed to exclude the possibility of contingently private languages. Malcolm had presented the argument as one applying only to necessarily private language – i.e. to language 'that not merely is not, but *cannot* be understood by anyone other than the speaker' (Malcolm, 1954, p. 530). However, everything he said seemed to apply to contingently private languages – to private languages spoken by only one person because no other happened to speak the language – as well. Ayer and Strawson both argued that the speaker of a contingently private language had available no other tests of word meaning than the ones available in the necessarily private case. Accordingly, Wittgenstein's conclusion would have no special relevance to sensations (Strawson, 1954, pp. 84–5; Ayer, 1954, pp. 55–9). Ayer claimed, and Strawson insinuated, that this effectively refuted the argument.[8]

The claim that the Reductio Argument applied to both necessarily and contingently private languages was most elaborately argued for by Ayer. In order to show that this distinction had no decisive significance, he constructed the fiction of an infant called Crusoe (Ayer, 1954, pp. 55–7). The thought experiment imagined Crusoe alone on his island while still an infant, having not yet learned to speak. Crusoe survives through childhood and adapts to the island's conditions. Ayer starts out by observing that it is at least conceivable that he can develop a language:

> The development of language, it might be argued, is a social phenomenon. But surely it is not self-contradictory to suppose that someone, uninstructed in the use of any existing language, makes up a language for himself. After all, some human being must have been the first to use a symbol. (Ayer, 1954, p. 55)

So it is conceivable that Crusoe should develop his own notation for keeping track of, and speaking to himself about, the wildlife and food resources on the island; and Crusoe's use of this notation would constitute a contingently private language.

Granted this possibility, why should we not allow that Crusoe could invent words to describe his sensations? His use of words for describing physical objects and sensations would in both cases only be justified by reference to his memory of the

---

[7]   Ayer (1954), p. 54. Compare Strawson (1954), p. 85.

[8]   Because one could construct a secret language that would be contingently private, and because Wittgenstein had claimed that secret languages were possible (§243), the applicability of the argument to contingently private languages would definitely mean that Wittgenstein had not been fully aware of the argument's consequences.

way in which he has used the words previously. Given that the justification is the same in both cases, Ayer pointed out that it is unlikely, as long as Crusoe remains alone on the island, that he will even draw the distinction, made in society, between 'outer' and 'inner' objects (Ayer, 1954, p. 57). His sensations happen to be private in the sense that other people have no access to them, but this property is not visible to an individual in isolation.

If, on the arrival of a Man Friday, it turns out that Crusoe can only teach Friday his use of words referring to physical objects, it would by no means follow, says Ayer, that the sensation language is now useless, or meaningless, to Crusoe: 'The ability to teach, or rather the ability of someone else to learn, cannot therefore be a prerequisite for understanding' (Ayer, 1954, p. 57). If Crusoe is allowed to invent a language, that language could incorporate descriptions of sensations which might turn out to be unintelligible to other people. Thus Ayer concluded that a contingently private language was possible, and that the possibility of a contingently private language implied the possibility of a necessarily private language. Wittgenstein was mistaken.

The challenge Ayer raised was one Malcolm had to take seriously. What exactly is the difference between a language about objects and one about sensations if both are spoken by a solitary speaker? At this point Malcolm was a little unclear about his position, but he definitely regarded it a consequence of the discussion of sameness that there was a crucial difference between a contingently private language and a necessarily private one. His response essentially amounted to a paraphrase of Wittgenstein: whether someone understands 'same' in the public case is determined by his mastery of various techniques exhibited in practice, but this does not apply to the private case, because a practice presupposes a distinction '... between believing that you have that practice and having it' (Malcolm, 1954, p. 537). In a second attempt to explain the crucial difference, Malcolm insisted that in the public case if I recognize two things as same '... I can express my recognition in some other way', whereas the '... notion of a private language doesn't admit of there being "some other way"' (Malcolm, 1954, p. 537). At bottom, then, if one is puzzled about the basis of Wittgenstein's remarks on the notion of practice, Malcolm's remarks do not help.

The crucial premise in Ayer's argument was that the distinction between inner and outer would only be visible in actual intersubjective discourse; it was a distinction that we would discover empirically. In other words, the claim was that it was no part of the definition of a sensation that it was private; it was not essential to pains that they be private.[9] Ayer might have anticipated that discussion of his argument would revolve around this assumption; the discussion would become a debate about the distinctive nature of sensations.

Ayer had probably not foreseen, however, the immediate reply his article received from Rush Rhees.[10] Rhees claimed that Ayer's Crusoe did not have the necessary means to invent a language at all; and that the public aspects of language, and the

---

[9] As was argued in Section 3.3, Wittgenstein had entertained a similar view in *Philosophical Remarks*.

[10] Rhees (1954). Ayer's and Rhees's articles were actually presented together in a symposium: see *Aristotelian Society Proceedings*, supplementary vol. XXVIII, pp. 63–94.

distinction between outer and inner, were not the main targets of Wittgenstein's attack. Rhees had been Wittgenstein's pupil. He had also been appointed by Wittgenstein as one of his literary executors and had edited *Philosophical Investigations* together with G. E. M. Anscombe.[11] He could therefore claim to be one of those most familiar with Wittgenstein's views.

According to Rhees, Wittgenstein would not have regarded the sounds made by Ayer's Crusoe as words:

> Defoe's Crusoe could have kept a diary, but Ayer's could not. ... Ayer's Crusoe may use marks for particular purposes – to show where he has hidden something, perhaps – and with as great regularity as we care to think. This is not what we mean by the regular use of an expression in a language ... But so long as he never has learned a language, in the sense of taking part in a language, it is as meaningless to say of him that he follows words as it would be of an electronic computer. (Rhees, 1954, pp. 70 and 72)

So Wittgenstein, according to Rhees, would disagree with Ayer over the assumption that Ayer's Crusoe could develop a language. This much was clear, but the reasons Wittgenstein might be supposed to have given in support of this view – the details, that is, of what we might call the 'Solitary Language Argument' – were notoriously hard to decipher in Rhees's article. The following is an attempt to extract some premises from the key passages (Rhees, 1954, pp. 73–4):

1. A solitary speaker cannot learn his language, so he must invent it himself.
2. If a language is invented by a single speaker, the meaning of words is not independent of the solitary speaker's use of the words.
3. Were there no independence of meaning, a word could not be misunderstood.
4. If words could not be misunderstood, there would be no possibility of distinguishing between their correct and their merely apparently correct applications; and the meaning of a word would then be the meaning it seemed to have. (This is the negation of the consequent in the third premise in the Reductio Argument.)

From Rhees's perspective, then, Wittgenstein had not been especially concerned with the nature of sensations and other inner items. Instead he had intended to point toward the essential social dimension of language. Apart from straightening out the conclusion of the line of thought, however, Rhees's account did not contribute to a better understanding of Wittgenstein's treatment. The style in which the article is written reveals very clearly that Rhees had been a student of Wittgenstein, and Benjamin F. Armstrong expressed what many people probably thought, saying that some interpreters, '... produce accounts, or explications, that are no easier to follow than Wittgenstein's own account (Rhees)' (Armstrong, 1984, p. 48, parenthesis original). Apparently, the argument had been that if meaning was to be manifested in the actual use of the words, at least two users were necessary to generate a divergence between correct and incorrect use. But unless something is added such an argument seems to imply the impossibility of a secret language which is translatable into a common language. This would be a rather intolerable consequence, and it was

---

[11]   R. Rhees, G. E. M. Anscombe and G. H. von Wright were appointed by Wittgenstein as his literary executors. Later Anthony Kenny and Peter Winch became involved.

explicitly denied by Rhees: '... I can decide to use expressions of a secret language or the signs of a code in a particular way' (Rhees, 1954, p. 66). Rhees must have had something to add to the above argumentation, then, but what it was remained obscure.

At this point the position was therefore roughly this. It was generally recognized that Wittgenstein had presented an argument against the possibility, in principle, of private language, and that such an argument would have wide-ranging consequences in the philosophy of mind since it would initiate the dismantling Cartesianism. But it was also clear to a neutral observer that even the most comprehensive interpretation of the argument available, Malcolm's Reductio Argument, needed to be elaborated to become convincing. Somewhere, hidden in *Philosophical Investigations*, an extra argument would have to be found. In this respect the disagreement among Malcolm and Rhees was strategically problematic in the promotion of their teacher's thoughts. For if not even Wittgenstein's followers could understand his intentions, how could others?

5.3 The External Argument

In addition to the Reductio Argument, Malcolm thought that Wittgenstein had presented another argument against a private language. This 'external' attack, unlike the 'internal' attack of the Reductio Argument, was directed against the idea that commonplace sensation language is a compromise between, or construction out of, idiolects – a language grounded in a collection of private languages:

> What is attacked is the assumption that once I know from my *own* case what pain, tickling, or consciousness is, then I can transfer the ideas of these things to objects outside myself (283). (Malcolm, 1954, pp. 537–8)

Suppose I learn from my own case what pain is. I then notice a correlation between my experiencing this sensation and my bodily conditions. Suppose that I now observe other human figures with a body condition similar to the one I have when I am in pain. Observing these other human figures, I might start to use my word 'pain' in second- and third-person contexts. If I observe that the other human figures make a sound similar to the one I make when I say 'pain' in most of the situations I am inclined to apply 'pain', then I have inductive evidence for believing that others can feel pain, and that they use 'pain' to refer to what I call pain. This picture was a central part of the Cartesian picture adumbrated earlier; it formed part of the story of how our ordinary sensation language arises.

Ayer, among others, had also argued this way in seeking to substantiate the conclusion that it is probable that another person uses the word 'pain' with the same meaning as I, or that it is probable that that human figure, by 'pain', is referring to the same thing as I (Ayer, 1954, p. 58). This, then, was the essential structure of the 'Argument from Analogy', an argument that can be seen as a natural corollary of Cartesianism: I inductively discover a correlation between my pain and my bodily condition and then observe that other organisms have similar bodily conditions; I am then warranted in inferring, inductively, that they have the same sensation as I have.

In his review of *Philosophical Investigations*, Malcolm's construal of Wittgenstein's argument against this approach was quite short and taciturn: if I have learned the concept of pain exclusively by perceiving my own pain, the concept will include the property that pain can only exist when *I* feel it; and obviously this concept cannot accommodate the possibility that others have pain. However, four years later, in 1958, both Strawson and Malcolm had worked out more elaborate arguments against the Argument from Analogy. These seem to have involved the same idea.[12]

Strawson's argumentation came closest to the case adumbrated by Malcolm in 1954. Faced with the challenge that reference to another subject's feeling is meaningless, I might, if I were advocating the Argument from Analogy, reply that the sentence 'That human figure has thoughts and feelings' means that the human figure in question sometimes has the same intellectual and affective mental states as I have. Such an answer would commit me to being able to identify another subject of experience, the 'he' in the sentence. So I might then say: I am 'the subject of those experiences which stand in the same unique causal relation to body N as *my* experiences stand to body M' (Strawson, 1958, p. 339). But in order to say this, I will need to have noted a relation between *my* experiences and the body M, and in order for 'my' to have any significance here, I will need to have the concept of an experience that is not mine; otherwise it will be the case that 'my experience' can be replaced by 'experience' in the above sentence. But this is impossible on the assumption that I have learned the concept of pain exclusively by perceiving my own pain. It follows that in order to arrive at the foundation upon which I conduct my analogical reasoning I must already have an idea of experience of the kind that connects to bodies other than my own. But this makes the analogical reasoning superfluous.

Malcolm's rebuttal relied on the semantic significance of the notion of *criteria*. Underlying the Argument from Analogy is the Cartesian assumption that there is a contingent relationship between sensations and behaviour; otherwise the argument would not be needed. The conclusion it is meant to establish is that it is probable that that human figure (pointing to a figure distinct from one's own) has thoughts and feelings. The aim of Malcolm's argumentation was to show that these claims could not be held in conjunction – that they generated a dilemma. He puts the case in this way:

- **Motivation:** It can never be established with certainty by anyone that the sentence 'that human figure has thoughts and feelings' is correctly asserted ('that human figure', of course, refers to someone other than the speaker).
- **Problem:** Does he have a criterion for a determining whether a human figure has thoughts or feelings?
- **First horn:** 'If he had a criterion he could apply it, establishing with certainty that this or that human figure does or does not have feelings (for the only plausible criterion

---

[12]   The relevant articles are Malcolm (1958) and Strawson (1958), both published for the first time in 1958. Strawson's argument was repeated in Strawson (1959).

would lie in behaviour and circumstances that are open to view) and there would be no call to resort to tenuous analogical reasoning' (Malcolm, 1958, p. 970).

- **Second horn:** 'If ... [he] has no criterion for the existence of feelings other than his own then in that sense he does not understand the sentence "that human figure has feelings" and therefore does not understand the sentence "It is *probable* that that human figure has thoughts and feelings"' (Malcolm, 1958, p. 970).
- **Dilemma:** Therefore *either* one does not need the argument from analogy *or* one cannot make sense of another human figure having thoughts and feelings.

Furthermore, it would not help to repair the Argument from Analogy to claim, say, that 'He is in pain' means that he has the *same* thing I have when I have a pain. This would simply require us, in the above argument, to substitute the demand for a criterion governing 'he has a pain' with the demand for a criterion governing the notion that he has 'the same as I have': 'If I do not know how to establish that someone has a pain then I do not know how to establish that he has the *same* as I have when I have a pain.'[13] This, then, was Wittgenstein's *external* private language argument, or, as I shall call it, the 'External Argument'.

The direct target of both Strawson's argument and the External Argument was the Argument from Analogy, but their conclusions also undermine Cartesianism. For if there is a problem of knowledge of other minds to which the Argument from Analogy is an appropriate response, we will be led to a position in which that problem rapidly becomes unintelligible. Accordingly, the diagnosis here is that the problem with the Argument from Analogy lies with acceptance of the problem of knowledge of other minds to which it is a natural response. But this problem is an integral part of the Cartesian position, so this position is now compromised. This does not show the absurdity of Cartesianism, but only that the model on which the Cartesian construes ordinary discourse about sensations – a discourse generally agreed to be meaningful to more than one person – as highly suspect. Ordinary discourse about sensations is not a compromise between, or construction out of, private languages in which each word is ultimately defined by reference to the speaker's sensations.

5.4 Pain-Expressions as Criteria

Obviously the External Argument relied heavily on the adequacy of explaining the meaning of sensation words in terms of criteria. The criterial account of sensation language was not elaborated in the 1958 article, but Malcolm had given an account of it in 1954. In his review of *Philosophical Investigations* Strawson had also focused on criteria. According to him the notion of criteria had wrongly led Wittgenstein to advance the Reductio Argument.

The difference between the strengths of the Reductio Argument and the External Argument was paralleled by a difference in strength between two theses which Strawson, in his review, had taken Wittgenstein to oscillate between. The External Argument yielded the weaker thesis: 'The weaker thesis says that certain conditions

---

[13] Malcolm (1958), p. 970. A similar point about 'sameness' had been argued for in Malcolm (1954), p. 534. See p. 67.

must be satisfied for the existence of a common language in which sensations are ascribed to those who have them' (Strawson, 1954, p. 84). Strawson had agreed with this, conceding that we require criteria for the third-person ascription of pain. Part of the use of the public word 'pain' is that it can be ascribed to others on the basis of criteria which might be overruled.

However, Strawson also believed that Wittgenstein had further assumed that meaning was exhaustively accounted for in terms of criteria:

> What he has committed himself to is the view that one cannot recognise or identify anything, unless one uses *criteria*; and, as a consequence of this, that one cannot recognise or identify sensations. But of course this is untrue. (Strawson, 1954, p. 86)

It was this extra assumption which had motivated Wittgenstein's persistent demand for criteria or proof of correct use in the Reductio Argument and which, ultimately, led him to misunderstand self-ascriptions of pain. Since we do not use criteria for this, Wittgenstein had thought that we do not recognize our own pain.

That Wittgenstein had made this extra assumption was evidenced in another argument Strawson found in *Philosophical Investigations*. That is, the assumption was part of an argument of Wittgenstein's which took as its point of departure two facts about self-ascription demonstrated by the language game in which we use 'I am in pain':

1. 'the expression of doubt has no place in the language game ...' (288)
2. 'what I do (when I say "I am in pain") is not to identify my sensation by criteria' (290).[14]

For suppose that 'pain' is the name of a sensation. Then, so Strawson conjectured, we would require criteria for the identity of the sensation – criteria that we do not use according to the second fact described above and do not even have according to the Reductio Argument. Moreover, these criteria would introduce the possibility of error, which has no place according to the first fact described. Consequently 'I am in pain' does not refer to a sensation, but is instead '... an *expression* or manifestation of pain, alongside such natural expressions as crying or groaning, but of course, one which, unlike these, is the result of training (*Inv.* 244, 288, etc.)' (Strawson, 1954, p. 86).

Thus two distinct arguments with a common underlying assumption had led Wittgenstein from the weaker thesis to the stronger thesis '... that no word whatever stands for or names a special experience' (Strawson, 1954, p. 83). This was more than Strawson could accept. He believed that to think of meaning as exhaustively characterized in terms of criteria would saddle one with verificationism, and as a consequence he was persuaded by neither the Reductio Argument nor the argument elaborated above. He did not claim that Wittgenstein would have subscribed to verificationism. He said merely that because Wittgenstein had stressed the common language, and the features it necessitated, too much, he was committed to a

---

[14]   Strawson (1954), pp. 85–6. The numbers in parenthesis refer to paragraphs in *Philosophical Investigations*; Strawson is paraphrasing Wittgenstein's text to an extent.

verificationist approach (Strawson, 1954, p. 88). Wittgenstein's semantic theory had confused him about the nature of sensations: 'Wittgenstein here seems to me to be in a muddle: The weaker thesis is being muddled with the stronger thesis' (Strawson, 1954, p. 86). Strawson's diagnosis of the problem with the Reductio Argument was that it relied too heavily on the notion of criteria – a mistake avoided by the External Argument.

Against this Malcolm pointed out that the stronger thesis, that no words name sensations, which Strawson had ascribed to Wittgenstein had been explicitly denied by Wittgenstein himself. Malcolm presented substantial evidence that Wittgenstein had not held such a view (Malcolm, 1954, p. 551). But the explanation Malcolm gave here was not one that would convince Strawson. For what had led Strawson to believe that Wittgenstein held the stronger thesis was that he had apparently defended an asymmetry between first- and third-person sensation ascriptions, holding that 'pain' would mean different things in the two cases. Malcolm seemed to acknowledge the accuracy of this description of Wittgenstein's view: it was the wording of Strawson's stronger thesis that Malcolm essentially objected to. He alluded to an observation made much earlier in *Philosophical Investigations*:

> We call very different things 'names'; the word 'name' is used to characterize many different kinds of use of a word, related to one another in many different ways (§38).

So the reason we can say that words name sensations is that the naming relation is used in many different ways.

This, however, did not address the essence of Strawson's criticism, and indeed Malcolm seemed rather to agree with that. That is, Malcolm agreed with Strawson that according to Wittgenstein 'I am in pain' should be taken as an expression of pain. One way to realize that 'I am in pain' is an expression of pain is by looking at the way in which the use of this sentence is learned. Immediately after providing the definition of a private language in §243, Wittgenstein had described one such process in which the primitive, natural pain-expressions are connected to the words. The process is one in which a child hears parents use the word 'pain' every time he or she cries. This leads one to see, that '...: the verbal expression of pain replaces crying and does not describe it' (§244). By this Wittgenstein had not meant that the verbal utterance could not have a use distinct from its being a cry of pain. He had intended to illuminate the important similarity that both are 'incorrigible' – there is no possibility that 'I am in pain' may be claimed by mistake. So, according to Malcolm, the intention had been one of

> ... bringing to light the arresting fact that my sentences about present sensations have the same logical status as my outcries and facial expressions. (Malcolm, 1954, p. 542)

The fact that first-person pain ascriptions and outcries are incorrigible indicators of pain makes it possible for them to be criteria for pain. First-person pain ascriptions have the logical status of a criterion for pain; by contrast third-person pain ascriptions are ascribed on the basis of criteria.

Malcolm noted that this concession to Strawson presented the Wittgensteinian with the problem of presenting an alternative. The External Argument's rebuttal of

Cartesianism had been a step in the right direction, but now there was no ready-made replacement for Cartesianism to hand:

> When his thinking is freed of the illusion of the priority of his own case, then he is able to look at the familiar facts and to acknowledge that the circumstances, behaviour, and utterances of others actually are his *criteria* (not merely his evidence) for the existence of their mental states. Previously this had seemed impossible.
> But now he is in danger of flying to the opposite extreme of behaviourism, which errs by believing that through observation of one's own circumstances, behaviour and utterances one can find out that one is thinking or angry. (Malcolm, 1958, p. 976)

If the criteria for 'He is in pain' are to be found in behaviour, and if 'He is in pain' uttered by one person can express the same as 'I am in pain' uttered by another, then it seems to follow that the criteria for 'I am in pain' are to be found in behaviour. This conclusion was viewed by Malcolm as tantamount to the acceptance of behaviourism, and behaviourism was regarded as a rather unattractive position by most philosophers at the time, including Malcolm.

Avoiding behaviourism was one problem for the advocate of criteria. But there was also a more general problem with the notion. For what, it was asked, was the relation between a criterion and that of which it was a criterion? The way Malcolm explained the role of criteria, that relation involved two elements whose compatibility was not obvious. Malcolm, of course, held that they were compatible.[15] On one hand, the relation between criterion and that of which it is a criterion was one of *conclusive evidence*, and understanding a concept would involve grasping its criteria: 'The satisfaction of the criterion of *y* establishes the existence of *y* beyond question; it repeats the kind of case in which we were taught to say *y*' (Malcolm, 1954, p. 544). Strawson saw this as disguised verificationism. On the other hand, and in tension with the first claim, it was insisted that satisfying the criterion for being in pain did *not logically imply* that one was in pain. This was so because it was only against certain background conditions that expressions of pain were criteria of pain; only in conjunction with other facts would a certain expression count as a criterion of pain. For example, a scream would not normally be a criterion of (genuine) pain when uttered on the theatre stage. Furthermore, the set of conjunctions in which an expression would count as criterion was open-ended and indefinite, so a verdict that someone was in pain might always be overruled by the appearance of new evidence (Malcolm, 1954, p. 545). The case with pain and criteria might be compared with that of a chair and criteria: it does not follow from my sense impression of a chair that there is a chair before me, but part of the concept of a chair is that it can be perceived.

The problem that arises when we combine these two claims is this. If a given kind of behaviour and circumstance do not entail that another is in pain, what kind of logical connection do they have to pain, and how is this connection such that it can be certain that another person is in pain? Malcolm admitted that the answer to this

---

[15]   What follows here is the view of criteria presented in Malcolm (1954). Although, as we have seen, Malcolm made substantial use of the notion in Malcolm (1958), he did not address the question of how this notion should be characterized.

question was not easy to spell out. It seems that he saw Wittgenstein as appealing to *actual* practice and its contextual character: '... what we sometimes do is draw a boundary around *this* behaviour in *these* circumstances and say, "Any additional circumstances that might come to light will be irrelevant to whether this man is in pain"' (Malcolm, 1954, p. 547). Obviously, the semantic connection between an entity and the criteria for its presence was a subject for further investigation.

Clearly, then, the reliance on criteria in the anti-Cartesian External Argument made urgent an explanation of this seemingly fantastic notion. Here two problems presented themselves. One was to say how it was possible to avoid identifying criteria with bullet-proof, contingent evidence. The other was to account for the apparent asymmetry in the role of criteria in first-person and third-person ascriptions of sensations. Although this is somewhat implicit in his review article, Malcolm essentially thought these problems would dissolve within the distinctive approach to philosophy that Wittgenstein had developed.

5.5 Malcolm on Use and Ordinary Language

Wittgenstein's use of the term 'criterion' was problematic, but it was reasonably clear from Malcolm's review what role it was supposed to perform in the argument against private language – namely, to isolate the reference of a word. Only by being associated with criteria could a word mean something. Wittgenstein's understanding of the term 'practice', and of the allegedly connected terms 'use', 'language game' and 'form of life', was more obscure in Malcolm's review.

According to Malcolm, the concept of a form of life was very important: 'One could hardly place too much stress on the importance of this latter notion in Wittgenstein's thought' (Malcolm, 1954, p. 549). As we saw in the Section 5.4, Malcolm appealed to practice in his explanation of criteria, saying that what was to count as a criterion was revealed in practice. Somehow all of these notions were meant to draw attention to the importance of use. To understand a concept, one should examine the human behaviour in which it is used. Furthermore, actual use was meant to provide the rock-bottom of justification: 'As philosophers we must not attempt to justify the forms of life, to give reasons for *them* ...' (Malcolm, 1954, p. 550). Rhees had also stressed the importance of these notions in his article (Rhees, 1954, p. 69). However, in the commentary of neither man was it at all obvious how to explain the fact that an isolated infant Crusoe could (Malcolm) or could not (Rhees) develop a language for describing his surroundings. Despite its importance, Malcolm dealt with this problem only briefly. What he did say did little to defuse the worries identified in the previous sections.

What Malcolm had in fact done, by merely mentioning these notions in passing, was to avoid going into details about the distinctive methodological break in philosophy that he associated with Wittgenstein. This neglect can be explained in part by the formal restrictions which apply to book reviews. Malcolm did not have the space to treat all of these general issues properly and had to restrict himself to a single topic (Malcolm, 1954, p. 530). Intentionally or not, however, he had made Wittgenstein's treatment of private language appear less idiomatic. Certain indications of the relevant methodological assumptions were detectable in Malcolm's review, to be sure. One of these was quoted in part above:

> As philosophers we must not attempt to justify the forms of life, to give reasons for *them* – to argue for example that we pity the injured man, because we believe, assume, presuppose, or know that in addition to the groans and writhing, there is pain. (Malcolm, 1954, p. 550)

Unfortunately, however, these indications were, as was remarked above, somewhat opaque, because no deeper account of their import was provided for those not already initiated into Malcolm's Wittgensteinian approach.

One way to repair Malcolm's picture of Wittgenstein is by attending to the connections he saw between Wittgenstein's philosophy and the work of another leading Cambridge philosopher, G. E. Moore. Malcolm had first-hand knowledge of Moore's common-sense philosophy,[16] and in fact it is in an early article on Moore's philosophy that Malcolm's methodological convictions are revealed most explicitly. Consider the following passages, for instance:

> I hold that what Moore says in reply to the philosophical statements in our list[17] is in each case perfectly true. .. The essence of Moore's technique of refuting philosophical statements consists in pointing out that these statements *go against ordinary language*. (Malcolm, 1942, p. 8)
>
> Moore's great historical role consists in the fact that he has been perhaps the first philosopher to sense that any philosophical statement which violates ordinary language is false, and consistently to defend ordinary language against its philosophical violators. (Malcolm, 1942, p. 23)

In Malcolm's conception, Moore's defence of ordinary language was also an attack on traditional philosophical hypothesising: Philosophical claims which conflict with ordinary usage in one way or another can be ignored because '... ordinary language *is* correct language' (Malcolm, 1942, p. 15). For instance, the Berkeleyan claim that there are no material things could be refuted by pointing to the fact that in ordinary usage we do not accept such a statement; a refutation would simply consist of saying: 'You are certainly wrong, for here's one hand and here's another; and so there are at least two material things' (Malcolm, 1942, p. 6).

Moore's influence on Malcolm was, however, secondary to Wittgenstein's, and the latter might be making itself felt in the above account.[18] At any rate, Malcolm still regarded his 1942 article as an accurate description of Moore's procedure[19] when, twenty years later, he proclaimed

---

[16] Moore had agreed to supervise Malcolm's Ph.D. in 1938.

[17] Malcolm had arranged a list of twelve philosophical statements (including the following: 1. there are no material things, 2. time is unreal, and so on).

[18] Moore himself rejected Malcolm's account of his philosophical procedure. See Chappell (ed.) (1964), p. 2.

[19] In a short postscript to his article in Chappell's book. See Chappell (ed.) (1964), p. 23.

that in order to grasp Wittgenstein's idea that a philosophical problem is essentially a confusion in our thinking, and that philosophical work cannot interfere with the actual use of ordinary language ..., one must understand what is right in Moore's defence of ordinary language. The latter was an advance in philosophy because it brought us nearer to a true understanding of philosophy itself. (Malcolm, 1963, p. 183)

Malcolm was not alone in viewing Wittgenstein as a promulgator of Moore's methods. In 1956, another of Wittgenstein's students, G. A. Paul, wrote about Wittgenstein, 'He follows Moore in the defence of Common Sense and in a regard for our common language' (Paul, 1956, p. 88); and even earlier Gilbert Ryle had described Wittgenstein as extending Moore's methods (Ryle, 1951, p. 257).

Underlying these statements alleging a kinship between Moore's and Wittgenstein's methods was a conception of Wittgenstein as an exponent of ordinary language philosophy. The term 'ordinary language philosophy' began to be applied in the 1940s to the philosophy emanating from Wittgenstein in Cambridge and Gilbert Ryle and John Austin in Oxford. I shall comment on its appropriateness as a generic term later, but for now it is sufficient to notice that it is Malcolm's view of Wittgenstein as an ordinary language philosopher that explains the methodological assumptions that occasionally surface in Malcolm's review of *Philosophical Investigations*. Immediately after the passage quoted at the beginning of this section, he wrote, quoting from *Philosophical Investigations*:

'What has to accepted, the given, is – one could say – *forms of life*' (p. 226). What we should say is: '*this language-game is played*' (654). (Malcolm, 1954, p. 550)

Connected with this idea of ordinary language as a fundamental source of justification was the conviction that philosophy should remain purely descriptive. It should only describe the structure and mechanisms of language. Thus earlier in his article Malcolm had stressed that Wittgenstein did not advance any kind of theory (Malcolm, 1954, pp. 538–9). The aim should not be to replace one philosophical theory with another, but to clear up the confusions that create philosophical problems: '... we may not complain at the absence from the *Philosophical Investigations* of elaborate theories and classifications' (Malcolm, 1954, p. 539). It was from this methodological perspective that the Reductio Argument and the External Argument had been launched. The perspective also explains why no alternative position had been set out in Malcolm's review.

Alas, clarification of the underlying methodology did not in itself make the arguments easier to follow. It seemed to imply that the premises would be either those held by 'opponents' – in this case, Cartesians – or those acceptable by the standards of ordinary language. Neither alternative seemed to apply to the fourth premise. It would probably not be accepted by a Cartesian; and it seemed to be connected more closely with a verificationist principle of meaning than with what, to adopt the jargon of the time, 'we would ordinarily say' about the meaning of words. And what about memory? Was it not an ordinary practice to appeal to memory when asked about the meaning of words? More generally, then, it would seem that before one could even begin to answer such questions, a general description of what exactly constituted 'ordinary language' and 'common sense' was needed; the only thing that was clear was that it was not the common sense of a philosopher like Descartes to which an appeal was being made. The 'no-thesis' part of Malcolm's ordinary language philosophy was set aside, in practice, when he used the term 'criteria' in his review and his 1958 article. For clearly, in the use Malcolm made of it, 'criteria' was more of a technical term than an element of ordinary speech.

All in all, the publication of *Philosophical Investigations* brought new vigour to the debate at a time when the Cartesian was generally felt to have the upper hand. Wittgenstein's contribution was made at several levels. To Malcolm and many other observers, Wittgenstein had introduced a new approach to classical problems; he had introduced a new terminology, and he explored new territory by presenting fresh arguments against privacy which would have extensive implications. It should be made clear that the discussion contained more than one argument, more than one theme. Several arguments were in play from the beginning.[20] Even a follower of Wittgenstein could not expect all these novelties and their internal connections to be absorbed and accepted immediately.

More than any other source of commentary, the reviews of *Philosophical Investigations* defined the context in which these novel themes would subsequently be discussed. Thus Malcolm's account of the arguments, and Ayer's and Strawson's criticism, were constant points of reference throughout the philosophical debate about privacy conducted over the ensuing decade and a half.

Rhees's Solitary Language Argument was less influential in these circles. However, when, in *The Idea of a Social Science*, Peter Winch attacked the idea that social science '... must follow the methods of natural science rather than those of philosophy if we are to make any significant progress' (Winch, 1958, p. 1), he relied heavily on Rhees's argumentation, whose conclusion he accepted. Accordingly, the private language argument came to be involved in an interdisciplinary discussion about the proper methodology of the social sciences.[21] This latter discussion did not, however, focus on the proper formulation of a private language argument; it concerned the consequences of that argument for the social sciences. We can therefore ignore it here, especially since, elsewhere and at the same time, the viability of private language and its consequences for Cartesianism were being assiduously examined.

---

[20]   The origin of the term 'the private language argument' is unclear. The earliest use of the term I have come across is in the proceedings of a symposium with that title held in 1962 with the participation of H. N. Castañeda, J. F. Thomson and V. C. Chappell. My best guess is that it evolved as a common term in the early 1960s, becoming so common that it was discussed separately in the *Encyclopedia of Philosophy* edited by Edwards from 1967, Castañeda (1967b).

[21]   See, for example, Gilbert (1983), p. 313, and Bloor (1983), p. 4.

Chapter 6

The Availability of an Argument

The reviews we have been looking at were at least as important for the way in which the debate about privacy evolved during the late 1950s and 1960s as the enigmatic book they dealt with. Although the details of the arguments and their scope were mainly discussed with reference to *Philosophical Investigations*,[1] it was the reviews that defined the direction of discussions about privacy.

It soon became generally recognized that Cartesianism was the target of Wittgenstein's remarks on private language in *Philosophical Investigations*. This meant that the External Argument was the more straightforward argument, because it directly concerned the relationship between sensations and behaviour and the Cartesianism conception of this relationship. By contrast, the Reductio Argument specifically attacked the notion that the Cartesian could construct a language in which he could refer to sensations.

In both cases, however, Malcolm had taken the arguments to involve a claim about the justification of meanings: the claim, that is, that the Cartesian could not account for the meaning of certain terms in the way he imagined. This subject now became the focus of the debate. What kind of justification was required for meaning? Was memory not enough? Was justification needed at all? The demand for justification indicated to many observers that a verificationist link between justification and meaning was presupposed by both the Reductio Argument and the External Argument, and there was a general consensus that the verification principle was problematic.

It can be seen, then, that the availability of a sound argument came to depend on the provision of a non-verificationist position on two topics: first, the link between justification and meaning presupposed in the argument; and, second, the essential connection between sensations and behaviour. In each case, Wittgenstein's notion of a criterion was central. In connection with the second topic, a criterial approach would undermine the Cartesian picture. This possibility was taken up by so-called ordinary language philosophers. Accordingly, it will be useful to begin by briefly considering how deeply grounded Cartesianism is in the way we talk about sensations.

The following seems to be a trivial but substantial feature of our conception of sensations, and one which points towards privacy: in the epistemology of sensations there is radical first- and third-person asymmetry. That is, third-person access to sensations is mediated by prior access to behaviour, and this means there is a possibility of overruling a third-person sensation judgement in a way that has no parallel in the case of first-person judgement. Consider, for instance, the allegedly

---

[1] The Blue Book and the Brown Book, which were published in 1958, were also very influential in shaping the discussion of criteria.

pre-philosophical opening remarks made by Pitcher in a chapter on sensations and sensation language:

> You cannot feel my toothache, nor I yours. But your toothache is doubtless qualitatively similar to mine, since the structures of our bodies are very similar. And so, although many words in our language denote physical things and events which are publicly observable by all, other words denote items in each of our separate consciousnesses, things directly observable only by the one person in whose consciousness they occur. All this seems undeniable. (Pitcher, 1964, p. 281)[2]

The philosophical relevance of intuitive observations such as these has lent credibility to Cartesianism – that is, to the idea that there is a contingent relationship between an experience and its outward expression.[3]

However, for Cartesianism to be the theory characterized in §243 and criticized by Wittgenstein, a model of language needs to be added to the above. Hence, when Malcolm, in his review of *Philosophical Investigations*, took the attack on a private language to be directed against Cartesianism, he was implicitly extending the Cartesian position to incorporate a theory of language explaining how sensation words refer to sensations. Malcolm assumed that, to respect the essence of Cartesianism, it was necessary to think of sensation words as referring directly to sensations without detour through bodily behaviour. This assumption eventuates in a picture of 'Cartesian' sensation language which fits the characterization in §243: 'The individual words of his language are to refer to what can only be known to the person speaking; to his immediate private sensations.'

Whether it was natural or not, the semantic view Malcolm attached to the Cartesian position was by no means arbitrary. It contained the essence of the semantics that Descartes' heirs developed when they embarked on semantic theorising. In view of this, Peter Hacker has a point when he says that John Locke is Wittgenstein's opponent, because Locke's *Essay Concerning Human Understanding* contains a recognizably Cartesian theory of meaning.[4] Memory plays an important role in Locke's semantics: the meaning of words is fixed by a private exemplar of each experience type within our minds. This account is applied to sensations. The place in our minds where these exemplars are stored is memory, and its function is to produce a correct exemplar for each word that is used when we are thinking or speaking (Hacker, 1972, p. 226). In this way memory is, for Locke, essential for language. It ensures that words are not misunderstood by the mixing up of exemplars, or devoid

---

[2]   Compare Hacker (1990), p. 96: 'What could be more plausible than to hold that I know what 'pain', 'fear', or 'cheerful' mean simply by experiencing such feelings and naming them, ...?'

[3]   I am not seeking to describe a position Descartes actually occupied. To see why this caveat must be entered see, for instance, Cottingham (1992). During the 1950s and 1960s, however, Descartes was regularly associated with this position; see, for instance, Kenny (1966).

[4]   Hacker (1972), p. 217. Hacker noted that the only reference to other philosophers in these passages is an implicit one to Frege in §273, but he agreed that the roots of the position Wittgenstein attacks are best located in the work of Descartes.

of meaning by being associated with no exemplar. Thus scepticism about memory, here, would leave language without a vital foundation.[5]

So Cartesianism is in keeping with Pitcher's plausible-looking picture of the nature of sensations. It gives a natural explanation of the obvious fact that a person might be undetectably shamming pain. It leaves the person experiencing the pain in a privileged epistemic position: 'Well, only I can know whether I am really in pain; another person can only surmise it' (§246). Cartesianism respects the essence of this kind of claim by allowing other people only indirect access to a person's pain through his bodily behaviour and verbal exclamations. Again, claims such as 'Another person can't have my pains' (§253) express the feature that each individual possesses his own exemplar of sensations. They respect the uniqueness that we feel attaches to an experience.

How intuitive was this picture? So far as the history of philosophy is concerned, section 4.3 shows that the pictured kind of privacy was still conspicuously present in philosophical thinking in the late 1930s. It made itself apparent not merely as an intuitive starting point of philosophical reflection, but as a datum which, along with dualism, lay at the core of philosophy of mind. There can hardly be any doubt that the position was not a curiosity in the history of philosophy in middle of the twentieth century and so Wittgenstein's contemporaries possessed what according to Malcolm was prerequisite to understand Wittgenstein's thoughts: 'In order to appreciate the depth and power of Wittgenstein's assault upon it you must partly be its captive. You must feel the strong grip of it' (Malcolm, 1954, p. 531).

So a showdown with Cartesianism was believed to be a showdown with 300 years of deeply felt background. It would not be overruled by pointing out that the common concept of sensations was a public one. Even Descartes might have conceded that, but he was believed to have told a story of the foundation upon which that common concept should be reconstructed.

6.1 Post-War Doubts about Cartesianism

The sharp separation of the mental and the behavioural – that is, the insistence that they are contingently related – which the Cartesian uses to explain the privacy of the mind received sustained critical attention during the 1950s from several corners.

In 1956 Wilfrid Sellars gave a series of important lectures under the title 'The Myth of the Given: Three Lectures on Empiricism and the Philosophy of Mind' at the University of London. In these lectures Sellars questioned an assumption that appeared to be threatened by Wittgenstein's Reductio Argument – namely, the assumption, so important for phenomenalism, that sense data are simple. En route, as it were, Sellars devoted several sections to problems pertaining to the privacy usually ascribed to sense data. Here he expressed agreement with B. F. Skinner, Carnap and Wittgenstein, that '... the fact that language is essentially an *intersubjective* achievement, and is learned in inter-subjective contexts ... is compatible with the "privacy" of "inner episodes"' (Sellars, 1956, p. 189). Although

---

[5] Compare Schlick's account of a private language in section 4.3.

Sellars did not elaborate the views he attributed to Wittgenstein, it was clear that he saw Wittgenstein and himself as philosophers opposing the Cartesian picture of the mind. Sellars, however, compared the relationship between the mental and the behavioural with that between theoretical entities, like electrons, and our inductive evidence for them. This view would soon gain a number of powerful advocates,[6] but few philosophers believed it to be one Wittgenstein accepted. For one thing, it implied that we might propose a better mental 'theory' with subsequent revision of our discourse as a consequence, whereas Wittgenstein had held that 'ordinary language is all right'[7]. Secondly, Wittgenstein's use of criterion seemed to imply a stronger relation between, for instance, pain and pain behaviour than one of mere inductive evidence.

Wittgenstein's approach was understood by his followers as more closely related to Gilbert Ryle's employment of categories in his attack on the Cartesian 'Ghost in the Machine' in *The Concept of Mind*, published in 1949. Ryle, whose concern with categories had developed in discussions with Wittgenstein (Ryle, 1970, p. 5), had also touched upon privacy as a part of his attack on the Cartesian mind-body dichotomy. Apart from spelling out the apparently insurmountable barriers faced by anyone respecting the dichotomy while trying to understand the relationship between the mental and the physical, Ryle argued that it was founded on 'category mistakes'. In essence these consisted in taking superficially similar linguistic patterns to reveal an identity of category. Thus from the syntactical similarity of statements about the mental and physical, the mental is described within a framework applicable to physical entities; at the same time, mental items are agreed to differ from bodies or things: 'Minds are things, but different sorts of things from bodies; mental processes are causes and effects, but different sorts of causes and effects from bodily movements' (Ryle, 1949, p. 19). The mistake here is reminiscent of the reason Strawson had given for attributing to Wittgenstein the view that 'No words name sensations'.[8]

In the assault on private language and Cartesianism, then, Wittgenstein had an important contemporary associate in Ryle. It is clear, however, that the Reductio Argument and the External Argument presented by Malcolm on Wittgenstein's behalf were more ambitious than anything put forward by Ryle and Sellars, because they purported to demonstrate that the Cartesian position was inherently unstable.[9]

Around 1960, therefore, various currents of thought were undermining the Cartesian theory of mind. Some of these showed the influence of Wittgenstein. But if the arguments Wittgenstein had allegedly advanced against privacy were to gain currency, they would have to be presented in a way that avoided the verification principle and other problematic premises more obviously than they did in Malcolm's initial elaboration.

---

[6]   See Chihara/Fodor (1965), Castanĕda (1967a), Rorty (1965), Feyerabend (1965), Putnam (1965), and Quine (1966).

[7]   Wittgenstein never uses this phrase; the slogan derives from *Philosophical Investigations* §98.

[8]   See Section 5.4.

[9]   Although Sellars did hold the phenomenalist position to be paradoxical; see Sellars (1956), p. 176.

The general consensus at this time was that the verification principle was inadequate for a number of reasons. Herbert Feigl had criticized the status of the principle: it was, he pointed out, neither analytical nor empirical. W. V. O. Quine had argued that verification is holistic and always a matter of decision. But most importantly, the application of the principle simply failed to produce adequate accounts of the meaning of key terms. Accordingly, when philosophers like Ayer continued to speak about verification even in the 1950s, they acknowledged that verification would have a much weaker grip on meaningfulness than had at first been implied by proponents of the verification principle (Ayer, 1954, pp. 60–61).

Arguments against private language with the verification principle as a premise would have to be rejected, and this was in fact the reason why many of Wittgenstein's opponents concluded that they should reject the private language argument. This conclusion was not unfounded, as we will see in the next section.

6.2 The Reductio Argument and Verificationism

I want now to turn from the problematic nature of the premises required by Malcolm's argument and look at the evolution of the discussion of the private language argument that took place in the wake of Malcolm's review of *Philosophical Investigations*. This discussion – which had its heyday in the 1960s – focused on various presuppositions of the arguments Malcolm had given against the possibility of a private language.

Section 5.5 demonstrated that, in Malcolm's understanding of Wittgenstein's methodology, the notion of a practice deployed in the Reductio Argument was closely tied to the slogan 'ordinary language is all right'. Malcolm had been very indirect, to say the least, in his allusions to the slogan when he presented the Reductio Argument; and this gave the impression that the assumption, or methodological attitude, signalled by the slogan was not essential. Discussions now followed this lead. They centred on the question, what premises would render the idea of a private language paradoxical? Answers here often involved mention of the verification principle, especially when they were being evaluated by Wittgenstein's opponents. As early as 1954 Strawson remarked that Wittgenstein had displayed a '... hostility to the idea of what is not observed (seen, heard, smelt, touched, tasted) ...' (Strawson, 1954, p. 90); he had claimed that Wittgenstein's views on 'private' or 'inner' items might have been guided by verificationist ideas: 'Perhaps what is really operating here is the old verificationist horror of a claim that cannot be checked' (Strawson, 1954, p. 92). And indeed several critical examinations of *Philosophical Investigations* in the 1950s had noticed its close affinities with Carnap's views of the early 1930s. Despite these indications, however, the general attitude concerning these matters was somewhat timid, especially when it came to attributing to Wittgenstein a principle which, as all acknowledged, was criticized elsewhere in *Philosophical Investigations*.

In 1962 J. F. Thomson, for example, was reluctant to attribute the verification principle to Wittgenstein. He concluded instead that Wittgenstein had not been clear on the privacy issue: 'He does not, I think, ever make it clear what is the way of thinking that he wants to expose and discredit' (Jones (ed.), 1971, p. 172). A more radical defence of Wittgenstein, provided by Judith Jarvis Thomson in 1964, distinguished sharply between Wittgenstein and the 'Wittgensteinians' and sought to expose the verificationism in Malcolm's Reductio Argument. This defence was presented in Thomson's influential article, 'Private Languages', to which I wish to turn now.

Thomson claimed that Malcolm's Reductio Argument was actually no more than an elaborate way of stating the verification principle. She wrote that the argument '... is, properly understood, something very familiar and rather trite' (Thomson, 1964, p. 183), adding that '... it seems to me clear that Wittgenstein himself would never for one moment have subscribed to it' (Thomson, 1964, p. 203). Thomson's strategy in supporting the above claim was to assemble the verification principle from acceptable formulations of premises that she had identified in Malcolm's presentation of the argument. Deflating the dramatic effect somewhat, I will reverse the process and dissect the verification principle in order to trace its connections with Malcolm's argument.

The principle with which Thomson was concerned had the following formulation:

> what purports to be a kind-name 'K' has meaning if and only if it is possible to find out whether or not a thing is a K. (Thomson, 1964, p. 200)[10]

This principle, Thomson showed, could be derived from the premises of the Reductio Argument without much trouble. To begin with, observe that nothing essential is lost by the following rephrasing: what purports to be a kind-name 'K' is a kind-name in a man's language only if it is possible to find out whether or not a thing is a K.[11] This principle can be derived, with insignificant changes in wording, by removing the middle terms from the following three steps:

> [1] If a sign 'K' which a man uses is to be a name of a kind of thing in a language, his use of it must be governed by a rule of the form, Xs and only Xs are to be called 'K's. (Thomson, 1964, p. 189)
> [2] If a sign 'K' which a man uses is to be a kind-name in a language, it must be possible that he should call a thing 'K' thinking it is an X when it is not an X, when it is Xs and only the Xs which (in his use) are to be called 'K's. (Thomson, 1964, p. 192)[12]

---

[10]   It will be observed that Jarvis Thomson took the verification principle to concern kind-terms, whereas Schlick's formulation concerned sentences. However, the only difference is that whereas sentences are associated with specific methods of verification, kind-terms need to be used in such sentences.

[11]   Thomson (1964), p. 200. The substitutions are from 'has meaning' to 'is a kind-name in a man's language' and from 'if and only if' to 'only if'. Leaving out the right-to-left implication by no means weakens the substantiality of the claim.

[12]   In order to render the implication involved in this step more transparent, the sentence might be construed like as follows. Suppose a sign 'K' which a man uses is to be a kind-name in a language. If it is X's and only X's which (in his use) are to be called 'K's', then it must be possible that he should call a thing 'K' thinking it is an X when it is not an X.

[3] There is no such thing as a man's thinking a thing is of a kind to be called 'K' and it not being so unless it is logically possible that it be *found out* that it is not so. (Thomson, 1964, pp. 195–6, emphasis original)

Thomson claims that these three steps are the bones of Malcolm's Reductio Argument. Not only can Malcolm be interpreted in this way, but in some of his formulations of the argument – formulations we examined in Chapter 5 – he seems almost to explicitly endorse equivalents. To recapitulate:

[1] My private definition was a success only if it led me to use the word correctly in the future. In the present case 'correctly' would mean 'consistent with my own definition' ...
[2] The concept of a rule requires that there be a difference between 'He is following a rule' and 'He is under the impression that he is following a rule' ...
[3] My impression that I follow a rule does not confirm that I follow the rule unless there can be something that will prove my impression correct. (Malcolm, 1954, p. 532)[13]

Thomson sought to justify her claim that she had correctly interpreted these passages by pointing out that other interpretations either had not been given or were counterintuitive; and Malcolm himself never argued for an alternative interpretation in which verificationism was avoided.

The association of the Reductio Argument with the verification principle, together with the fact that an alternative interpretation had failed to materialize since the publication of Malcolm's review, was probably adequate reason for most philosophers in the mid-1960s to discard the argument as flawed. But Thomson had not merely found the argument to rely on the verification principle as others had argued. She had demonstrated that the Reductio Argument was a disguised formulation of that very principle, and that the premises of the argument constituted a *derivation* of that very principle. The Reductio Argument was not only a private language argument, but an argument for the verification principle. So if the premises were reasonable, the verification principle would have to be taken seriously; it would have to be revived. Accordingly, the main part of Thomson's article was an analysis of Malcolm's Reductio Argument as she had construed it. It contained a subtle diagnosis of the structure of the argument, and therefore the structure of the verification principle, which, as it turned out, anticipated events.

The first two steps concerned rules and, in particular, the appropriateness of modelling language as a system of rules. Inspired by Wittgenstein, Malcolm had adopted this model in his presentation of the Reductio Argument when he construed the meaning of a word as a rule whose extension was determined by a definition. This was the first step in the above. Thomson noted that Malcolm had given an example of such a linguistic rule: 'I will call this feeling "pain" and will thereafter call the *same* thing "pain" whenever it occurs' (Malcolm, 1954, p. 534). Although Malcolm's claim had been that such a linguistic rule would not in itself determine a difference between 'correct' and 'seems correct', he seems to have accepted the view that meanings were rules in the above sense. What he had denied was that a rule

---

[13] Jarvis Thomson's interpretation is also very reasonable given the interpretation in Section 5.1.

such as the one above would in itself allow a speaker to decide between correct and seemingly correct use in the private case:

> ... when one has given oneself the private rule 'I will call this "pain" whenever it occurs' one is free to do anything or nothing. (Malcolm, 1954, p. 536)

Malcolm had, however, equivocated over the factors that would limit such freedom.[14] Thomson pointed out that an explanation of the way in which a rule, be it private or public, would determine the use of a given word had not been provided: if the meanings of words were described as rules, how could those meanings guide use? In other words, how must a rule be stated if it is to guide use? Malcolm's example of a linguistic rule (quoted above) was clearly inadequate here; it sounded more like a statement of policy. Should 'pain' be uttered every time a pain occurred? (Thomson, 1964, p. 188)

Thomson's treatment remained tentative, but she indicated a demand for further explanation here which did not concern private languages specifically and which left Malcolm fumbling. A certain general model of language, not just private language, needed an explication and the fact that it had not been carried out affected the argumentation: '... the notion of a linguistic rule is at least as much in need of an explanation as any of the things philosophers make use of it *to* explain' (Thomson, 1964, p. 188–9). Eighteen years later, Saul Kripke put this issue at top of the agenda and argued that Wittgenstein's private language argument was merely an application of the solution Wittgenstein had offered to this problem.

Thomson thought that anything that could be invoked to show that a private language did not comply with the requirements laid down in the first and the second steps above would also exclude public language (Thomson, 1964, p. 195). The critical step in the argument was the third: '... *without* this claim, the argument simply stops dead in its tracks, since nothing which has so far been said rules out the possibility of a private language' (Thomson, 1964, p. 196). Without the third step the private language speaker might reply in the following way:

> 'Indeed there must *be* a difference between my sensations' being of the kind I had decided to call "E" and its seeming so to me if "E" is to be a kind-name of a sensation; but why should it follow from the fact that my sensations are strongly private that there is no such difference?' It might be said. 'Well how is it to be established that the sensation is or is not of the required kind?' and now if the argument is to proceed, there must be something which rules it out that L.W. [the private language speaker] should quite acceptably reply: Perhaps it can't be found out that my sensation is or is not of the required kind, but all the same it may be that it is. (Thomson, 1964, p. 196)

Against this, the third step essentially claims that only those rules laying down justification conditions can be meaning-giving. Suppose that I, the private language speaker, '... did fix my attention on a pain as I pronounced the word "pain" to myself' (Malcolm, 1954, p. 532), and that by this initial ostension I singled out a particular sensation – or, in Thomson's terminology, designated a rule that determines which

---

[14]   Malcolm (1954), pp. 534–7. See Section 5.1.

of all my future sensations will be like the one present initially and which will not. This is not enough to secure meaning for the word 'pain', or 'E', according to the third premise: only if, by this stipulation, I define a procedure that enables me to find out whether a certain sensation is or is not pain, or E, will I have endowed the word with a meaning.

In this way the argument against a private language made the semantic question of how a word acquires meaning depend decisively on the epistemic question of how one can check, with justification, that one has used the word correctly. Accordingly, a condition excluding the possibility of correcting one's own judgement in the case of a private rule-giving act would have to be added:

> Now add to the strong privacy of the sensations whatever it is that you need to make out in addition that L.W.'s later impressions that he was or wasn't mistaken can't count as L.W.'s finding out that he was, and you now have it that no one can find out whether or not he is now mistaken. (Thomson, 1964, p. 199)

However, to offer an argument that would rule out private languages specifically, a further condition would be needed, namely, that whatever was added should preserve the public language: 'ace' should not be ruled out as an English kind-name on the ground that someone could destroy a playing card without looking at it, making it technically impossible to find out whether it was an ace (Thomson, 1964, p. 197). So allowance had to be made for public, 'technical' methods of checking.

It now seemed that the argument was relying either on memory scepticism or a claim that memory would always need justificatory back-up: it is necessary to claim either that you cannot check any claim by consulting memory or that you have only remembered something when you have a memory-independent method of justifying your memory impressions. The latter route would bring you back to the problem of saying why memory impressions of public items can always, in principle, be independently checked when private ones cannot. Only in that way would the public case be left intact. And since Malcolm had not addressed this problem satisfactorily, a sound argument would apparently have to appeal to memory scepticism.

Summing up, we might give the following general formulation of Thomson's argument:

1. that which purports to be a kind-name 'K' has meaning if and only if it is possible to find out whether or not a thing is a K. (Thomson, 1964, p. 200)
2. In the case of a private language, nothing, and in particular not later memory impressions, can count as finding out whether or not a thing is a K.

Thomson's claim that the Reductio Argument was an application of the verification principle must have been a nuisance to Malcolm. For he had claimed that Wittgenstein was opposed to the idea that philosophers should advance any theses, and that Wittgenstein's method had been one of illuminating the confusions which tempt philosophers to formulate such theses. In particular Malcolm ascribed to Wittgenstein the view that it '… is philosophically pointless to formulate a general theory of language or to pile up descriptions for their own sake' (Malcolm, 1954, p. 539). What Thomson had concluded was that the Reductio Argument could not be understood unless it was taken to rely on the verification principle. Stating this conclusion in a wider perspective, so to speak, she had construed the argument against the possibility of a private language as one depending on a certain general, and ultimately problematic, idea of how the meaning of a word should be characterized. Indeed, the Reductio Argument was an application of the verification principle to a particular area of discourse (Thomson, 1964, p. 201). Stripped of all the promises that it had failed to fulfil after ten years, Malcolm's Reductio Argument was essentially a combination of verificationism and memory scepticism.

With Thomson's contribution, the debate about the possibility of a private language more or less reached an impasse, for her interpretation of the Reductio Argument proved hard to counter. During the second half of the 1950s, and the 1960s, several presentations of the private language argument appeared in print, all of which claimed Wittgensteinian origin and sought to establish essentially the same conclusion as Malcolm's Reductio Argument.[15] None of these arguments was written in ignorance of the case Malcolm had made in 1954, so they might have been expected to improve or repair his reasoning, or to state more clearly how the alleged *reductio ad absurdum* proceeded. However, although the later contributions either contained superficially different premises or presented their moves in a different way (or both), Malcolm's Reductio Argument remained the focal point of the debate.

One reason for this is probably that Thomson's complaints could be applied to these other arguments against the possibility of a private language. Certainly, N. Garver's and J. D. Carney's version of the Wittgensteinian argument were actually given such treatment by W. B. Smerud in 1969.[16] Leonard Linsky also seemed to invoke an equivalent of Thomson's third step to block any attempt to construct a private language when he asked, rhetorically:

> If it seems to me that I am using 'E' in accordance with my remembered intention that is as far as I can go toward settling the matter. But if there is no difference between seeming and being correct use, doesn't the notion of correctness itself, and with it the idea of a language, become inapplicable? (Linsky, 1957, p. 287)

The newer versions of the private language argument could all be regarded, then, as minor variants of Malcolm's Reductio Argument. As such they were vulnerable to similar lines of criticism. This, at least, was their fate from the 1970s onwards.

6.3 Malcolm's Account of Criteria

The External Argument shared with the Reductio Argument the problem of distancing itself from verificationism. Failure to do this would not only reduce its impact, but also ensure that it was reminiscent of Carnap's private language argument.

When it is separated from Carnap's formal-material distinction and applied specifically to sensations, the conclusion of Carnap's private language argument

---

[15]   The more influential include Carney (1960), Garver (1959), Pitcher (1964), and Linsky (1957). See also Buck (1962) and Perkins (1965).

[16]   See Smerud (1970), Chs 2 and 5.

can be characterized as follows: if the meaning of sensation words such as 'pain' goes beyond behavioural facts, and if therefore private content partly constitutes its meaning, then the fact that I feel pain cannot be expressed by other people. Carnap had argued that since all I have access to in another person is physical appearance, this is all that can go into the meaning of mental terms. The External Argument reversed this strategy. The problem it confronted is the Argument from Analogy's solution to the problem of other minds – namely, that although I cannot know with certainty that someone is in pain, I can collect inductive evidence by observing his behaviour. Against this solution it is argued that since we can meaningfully ascribe mental states to others, it must be possible to know from someone's behaviour what mental state he is in.

Essentially, then, these two arguments employed opposing strategies. Carnap applied epistemic considerations to a semantic problem, whereas the External Argument applied semantic considerations to an epistemic problem. Actually, however, this difference can be removed merely by switching a premise and the conclusion in either argument: Carnap's conclusion figures as a premise in the other argument and vice versa. Apart from this, both arguments employ very similar starting points. Both begin with a statement that discourse about sensations is *actual* and a principle bridging epistemology and semantics. It is differences in the formulation of the statement that explain why, in the 1960s, Carnap's argument was generally neglected, while the External Argument (in Malcolm's version) was still very much at the centre of the debate about private language.

For one thing, Malcolm identified behavioural facts as features to which sensations were conceptually connected (Malcolm, 1958, p. 970), without, admittedly, specifying what the term 'behaviour' covered. Carnap's physicalism, on the other hand, was much more specific and comprehensive. According to him, sensation discourse, like all other discourse, could be translated into the language of physics. His avoidance of any particular philosophical view on behaviour, especially physicalism, meant Malcolm was able to interest a wider audience with his argument.

Significant as this might have been, a second difference is more likely to be the main reason why Malcolm's argument overshadowed Carnap's. Carnap's argument had employed a version of verificationism: 'a statement asserts no more than can be verified' (Carnap, 1932a, p. 79). From this principle, he inferred that the relation between sensation discourse and behavioural discourse was a reductive one – i.e. that any utterance about sensations could be translated without loss of content into one about behaviour.[17] Consequently, the assertion 'I'm in pain' meant, according to Carnap, that certain behavioural facts had been obtained, and of course these could be publicly scrutinized. Avoiding this principle of reduction to testable facts, Malcolm had appealed to the notion of criteria – a notion which had been used repeatedly by Wittgenstein and to which Malcolm had devoted space in his review of *Philosophical Investigations*. Accordingly, the conclusion of the External Argument

---

[17]   This holds only on a very wide interpretation of 'behaviour', because Carnap seems to have held that at least part of the meaning of a sensation concept would be constituted by neurophysiological states. In general Carnap held that such details in his physicalism would be decided by science.

was that sensations were conceptually tied to criteria with behavioural conditions of satisfaction. On the surface, at least, this was a much more plausible claim. Strawson, for example, had accepted it in 1954.

The nature of criteria was inadequately clarified, however, in Malcolm's writings. It was clear that Malcolm intended a criterion to stand in neither a merely evidential (Malcolm, 1958, p. 976) nor defining relation (Malcolm, 1954, p. 544) to what it was a criterion for. Consequently, he implicitly intended his account of sensations to differ from that given in Carnap's in *The Unity of Science*. But these were Malcolm's intentions; it was another question whether he had succeeded in fulfilling them. In an article published in 1962 called 'Non-other Minds' Roger Buck argued convincingly that in his 1958 paper Malcolm's criterialism was essentially a form of the old verificationist dogma from the Vienna Circle (Buck, 1962, pp. 195–9). Buck even explicitly referred to the question of the relationship between the satisfaction of criteria and verification as the 'criteria problem' (Buck, 1962, p. 196). Malcolm, he argued, had presented no ready solution to this problem, because his use of the term 'criteria' had been equivocal. On one hand, he had used the term to stand for 'that by means of which, or through the noticing of which, we verify our statements' (Buck, 1962, p. 196). Several passages in Malcolm's article indicated such use according to Buck:

> In contrasting the 'one's own case' philosophy with 'behaviourism' he [Malcolm] writes '... according to behaviourism the self-observation would be by means of outward criteria, available to all' [footnote referring to [87], p. 976]. The important point here lies in the idea of 'observation *by means of* criteria'. The context is one in which the verification of what we say is constantly invoked. (Buck, 1962, p. 196)

On the other hand, Buck pointed out that Malcolm tied criteria intimately to the idea of meaning. For instance, he quoted Malcolm's claim that

> ... it is of the essence of his [the analogist's] viewpoint to reject circumstances and behaviour as a criterion of mental phenomena in others. And what else could serve as a criterion? He ought therefore to draw the conclusion that the notion of thinking, fear, or pain, in others is in an important sense meaningless.[18]

Consequently, Malcolm had not managed, in any obvious manner at any rate, to distance his position from verificationism; he had failed to present a fundamentally new semantic foundation:

> To run together one use of 'criterion' which is oriented towards verification with another whose orientation is towards meaning is to make the notion of 'criteria' carry essentially the burden of a verificationist theory of meaning. (Buck, 1962, p. 197)

In effect, Buck's conclusion was that on Malcolm's construal, *criterialism* (i.e. the thesis that the notion of a criterion is a fundamental semantic category) was old-fashioned verificationism in disguise. The consequence for the External Argument,

---

[18]   Malcolm (1958), p. 975, quoted in Buck (1962), p. 197.

in Malcolm's version of that argument, was that it collapsed into Carnap's private language argument.

Malcolm's statement that he (and in his presentation, Wittgenstein) had not resorted to the old verificationist beliefs when arguing against a private language had not survived detailed scrutiny. But others had been more cautious in their characterization of the criterial relation. In so far there was a private language argument in play in the 1960s which had the potential to avoid recourse to the verification principle, it involved these characterizations. Again, the claim that a genuine non-verificationist account of criteria could be given was considered by many to be Wittgenstein's position. The term was loosely employed in *Philosophical Investigations*, but in *The Blue and Brown Books*, which was published in 1958, the term was discussed and employed repeatedly.[19] It was noted early on that Wittgenstein's use of the term in these books had not been quite consistent (Albritton, 1959). As a consequence, in part, of this, the potential of the term was the subject of intense discussion during the 1960s.

An example of the criterial relation Wittgenstein had mentioned was that between someone's engaging in pain behaviour and his being in pain. Rolling on the ground and screaming was described as a criterion for being in pain. Wittgenstein had distinguished criteria from two other notions. Since it was conceivable that a criterion might obtain in the absence of that for which it was criterial – for example, in cases of acting on stage, the criterion was not a defining characteristic. On the other, a criterial relation is not purely contingent on and discovered by induction. Accordingly, the notions of 'non-inductive evidence' and 'necessarily true evidence' characterize the criterial relation:

> If so and so's being the case is a criterion for the truth of a judgment ... the assertion that it is evidence in favor of the truth of the judgment is necessarily (logically) true rather than contingently (empirically) true. (Shoemaker, 1963, p. 31)
>
> X is a criterion of Y ... if the very meaning or definition of 'Y' ... justify the claim that one can recognize, see, detect, or determine the applicability of 'Y' on the basis of X in *normal* situations. (Chihara/Fodor, 1965, p. 397, emphasis original)

The existence of such a relation was generally supported by arguing that it played a central role in the process by which concepts are formed and words learned, or by arguing that inductively known evidence could not be collected if there were no criteria. Both of these arguments can be found in Wittgenstein's discussions. Elaborating them is beyond the scope of the present book,[20] but if something like the criterial relation existed between sensation and behaviour, this would certainly have an impact on the private language debate.

A criterial relation, in the sense of a special sort of evidential relation, would provide an argument against the claim that we do not have knowledge about other minds. This epistemic claim would spill over into semantics, for if there is such an

---

[19]   It was not generally recognized during this period that the views Wittgenstein presented in the Blue Book and the Brown Book, on the one hand, and *Philosophical Investigations*, on the other, were quite different.

[20]   See Lycan (1970) for an overview.

epistemic relation between sensation and behaviour, it will follow that we do not learn sensation language by generalizing from our own case. So growing recognition that we do not have merely contingent, inductive evidence for the states of others' minds led to the general view that the Cartesian or Lockean model of sensation discourse was incorrect. The problem, of course, was to clarify the semantic significance of criteria and, in so doing, formulate a bridging principle that would not reduce to verificationism.

6.4 Sensations and Sensation Language

The External Argument had failed to cast off its verificationist shadow. It was not clear that Malcolm had a general non-verificationist account of criteria. So the semantic relation the argument had relied on was regarded as problematic. However, the conclusion here – the view that the relation between sensations and behaviour was non-contingent, and that there was some kind of necessary connection between sensations and their bodily expression – attracted considerable attention; there was growing sympathy for it.

Accordingly, even if no general account of criteria could be given, the argument might still be sustained vis-à-vis second- and third-person sensation ascriptions. The question was: How had Wittgenstein envisaged the relation between sensations and behaviour? A coherent description of this relation incorporating necessity would revive the argument. Indeed the prospects were promising, because Wittgenstein had rejected behaviourism as well as Cartesianism.

Cartesianism was widely regarded as the target of §§243–315. In so far as the traditional framework for discussing the status of sensations was the dichotomy between Cartesianism and behaviourism, this would saddle Wittgenstein with behaviourism. Behaviourism had been defined, by Malcolm in 1958, as the view that a first-person sensation ascription is justified by attending to one's own behaviour (Malcolm, 1958, p. 976). Wittgenstein had, however, explicitly denied in §244 that this was a correct description of what we do.

Malcolm's definition was somewhat idiosyncratic. Behaviourism was commonly regarded as an ontological view, but it could easily be extended in an epistemological direction, since it involved a denial that sensations occur in a domain to which the subject has privileged access. So his definition fits neatly with *crude behaviourism* of the sort excluding the occurrence of private experiences (Mundle, 1966, p. 103). Against this it was noted that several passages in *Philosophical Investigations* discouraged such an interpretation. In §308, for example, behaviourism was explicitly characterized as a mistaken view of sensations.

Refining the picture, Alan Donagan showed that some passages in *Philosophical Investigations* even rejected *dispositional behaviourism*, i.e. the view that sensations are to be identified with dispositions to pain behaviour that may, or may not, be held in check (Donagan, 1966, p. 335). It appeared, then, that Wittgenstein had rejected all the ways in which the meaning of 'pain' would reduce to the criteria by which we establish its presence. Somehow he had positioned himself *between* behaviourism and Cartesianism.

It was commonly held in the 1960s that Wittgenstein had distinguished sharply between ontology and semantics.[21] Many felt that Wittgenstein was concerned only to reject the idea that sensations themselves can play any role in language: the reference of 'pain' cannot be the particular experience which presents itself to consciousness.[22] The phrase often invoked to describe such a view was 'linguistic behaviourism'.[23] Mundle's explication of this phrase is a useful preliminary guide to its content:

> If Wittgenstein had formulated this view explicitly, it would presumably have run something like this: that words which are ostensibly used to name or refer to private experiences can have meaning only by referring to overt behaviour (as in 'he is in pain') or by deputising for other, and 'natural', forms of behaviour (as in 'I am in pain'). (Mundle, 1966, p. 103)

There is a concession to Cartesianism of sorts here, because it is not denied that sensations exist; it is insisted merely that the role of sensations in language is nothing like that of a publicly observable object (Pitcher, 1964, p. 298).

The essential questions, for those who held that linguistic behaviourism contained the bones of Wittgenstein's position, were now these: What semantic rules governed the language game where sensations were concerned? What meaning did pain ascriptions possess? Notably, Wittgenstein was regarded as holding that first- and third-person pain ascriptions had a radically different status and were not cases of the same general ascription-type 'x is in pain'. I have already remarked several times that Wittgenstein saw the role in language of 'I am in pain' as one of more or less replacing natural pain behaviour (e.g. groans) and of making more sophisticated pain behaviour possible. §244 was usually invoked as evidence here. But it was also noted that Wittgenstein regarded the transition from a brute utterance of pain to a deliberate description of the state of one's feelings to be one of degree.[24] Thus a description of one's pain to a doctor could more appropriately be construed on the model of third-personal ascription. The illumination of Wittgenstein's view of these third-person pain ascriptions was no easy matter, because reductionism had somehow to be avoided.[25]

Donagan argued that Wittgenstein had elaborated 'quasi-technical terminology' to explain the difference between referring to publicly observable objects and to pains or sensations in general (Donagan, 1966, pp. 329–32). Accordingly Wittgenstein held that the content of sentences about physical objects could forcefully be compared to pictures, but that representing its content in this manner required a distinction to be drawn. A *picture* ('Bild') would contain nothing it did not directly represent whereas

---

[21]   See, for example, Pitcher (1964), Donagan (1966), Mundle (1966), and Chihara/Fodor (1965).

[22]   Pitcher (1964), p. 299. Compare Carnap's view in *The Unity of Science*.

[23]   Essentially the same view also went under the name 'Logical Behaviourism'; see Chihara/Fodor (1965), p. 387.

[24]   See, for example, Wittgenstein (1953), pp. 187–8.

[25]   Reductionism had also been a problem in Malcolm's explanation of criteria, Malcolm (1954), pp. 545–6.

as an *imaginative representation* ('Vorstellung') would be capable of representing indirectly.[26] As an example one might consider the drawing of a balloon above a tight vertical string tied to it. It would not be a picture of a balloon filled with helium, but it could be an imaginative representation of one. It was this distinction that Wittgenstein had alluded to in the otherwise enigmatic §301: 'An image ['Vorstellung'] is not a picture ['Bild'], but a picture can correspond to it.'

Donagan's point was that in §300 Wittgenstein had regarded this distinction as useful in explaining how pain enters into the language game with 'pain'. There cannot be a picture of pain in the way that there can be one of pain behaviour, but a picture of pain behaviour might correspond to an imaginative representation of pain. The distinction had also been present in Wittgenstein's thought when he wrote:

> Of course, if water boils in a pot, steam comes out of the pot and also pictured steam comes out of the pictured pot. But what if one insisted on saying that there must also be something boiling in the picture of the pot? (§297)

Some years earlier Pitcher had thought that §297 was an analogy invoked to illuminate the contention that private sensations do not enter into pain-related language games (Pitcher, 1964, p. 299). He tried to explain the circumstances under which pain could and would be predicated of a person or animal. In response to the equivalent enquiry, about when a picture of pain behaviour would contain an imaginative representation of pain, Donagan was remarkably silent. In his account, Pitcher remarked that certain modes of pain behaviour were essential to the concept of pain, and in a footnote he referred to Malcolm's account of criteria. The criterial relation seems to have been regarded by Pitcher as holding between the meaning of a word and the circumstances in which a word is learned or taught; but his account was most rewarding when regarded as extending and explicating the concept of pain-criteria that Malcolm had introduced somewhat vaguely in 1954.[27] Although he avoided a theoretical exegesis of Wittgenstein's ideas, and therefore made no progress with the problems Malcolm had faced, Pitcher devoted considerable space to explaining when 'He is in pain' could be uttered; and he connected his claims to sections in *Philosophical Investigations*. First, only of what behaves like a human being can one predicate pain. This is a consequence of the necessary connection with behaviour.[28] Secondly, third-person pain ascription is context-dependent: it is only by referring to circumstances, and in particular by pointing to various sorts of surrounding condition, that one can explain why a pain ascription is made (Pitcher, 1964, p. 307). Here no reference to sections of *Philosophical Investigations* was made. Thirdly, believing someone to be in pain is a matter of attitude (Pitcher, 1964, pp. 310–12). Saying 'He is in pain' does not stand alone, but involves pitying the sufferer, for example. Here Pitcher referred to §§287, 299 and 310. This last point

---

[26]   Donagan (1966), p. 330. For background information about translating 'Vorstellung' as 'imaginative representation', see Donagan (1966), p. 330, note 6.

[27]   Pitcher (1964), p. 305. The footnote reference to Malcolm explained that Pitcher's account of the discussion of sensations and private language owed much to Malcolm (1954).

[28]   Pitcher (1964), p. 306; here he referred to §§281–3.

revealed and emphasized the many purposes one might have in uttering the sentence 'He's in pain' (§304).

The identification of Wittgenstein's as linguistic behaviourism was supported by the seemingly plausible approach to *Philosophical Investigations* Pitcher apparently took.[29] The division of the book into sections, and the fact that, very often, no obvious connection between neighbouring sections can be found, invites us to see *Philosophical Investigations* as a collection of loosely connected thoughts, where issues are condensed in certain areas of the book, but are nonetheless commented on throughout the book. This encourages a certain eclecticism of interpretation: the job is to rearrange the 'salient' sections and paragraphs. Approached in this way, Wittgenstein seems to start by stating a theory and then develop his criticism of it by examining associated issues as he proceeds, so that he is constantly referring to the initial, stage-setting theory.

Since the book starts with a criticism of the Augustinian picture of language, it is natural to interpret §§243ff as sections still essentially concerned with this picture. If that is not the case, at any rate, it is hard to see where any transition takes place.[30] Apart from providing stylistic evidence for linguistic behaviourism, §293 played an important part in supporting the notion that, for Wittgenstein, the sensation itself had no role in language.[31] Pitcher took that section to hammer home the final nail in the coffin of the idea that sensations play a vital role in language. According to him, Wittgenstein had shown that sensations had no part in language before §293, but was now considering the objection that this would fail to reflect the obvious purpose of sensation reports:

> ... when a person is in pain, the really important thing for him is the sensation which he is feeling, for that is what is unpleasant and even horrible; hence it seems necessary and desirable to have a name for this sensation, so that one can tell other people that one has it (Pitcher, 1964, p. 297).

The beetle analogy in §293 told another story. In this analogy we are asked to imagine the case in which everyone has a box whose content is referred to as 'beetle'. If no one can look into anyone else's box, the reference of the word might be different for everyone, depending as it does on what is in the box; the box might even be empty. To Pitcher, this analogy clearly stated that, contrary to appearances, nothing was gained by hypothesizing the same sensation behind the appearances; and so that hypothesis should be omitted from any account of language. Nothing would be lost even if we were to imagine that *nothing* goes on 'behind the curtain' (Pitcher, 1964, p. 298). Pitcher even quoted §304, where Wittgenstein apparently summed up his results:

---

[29] Several writers probably took this approach, perhaps including Hacker (1972), to whom I will return. But Pitcher's book is a very clear example.

[30] Compare Baker (1981), p. 44.

[31] Hacker even gave it a name: the famous beetle-in-the-box example. Hacker (1972), p. 237.

'And yet you again and again reach the conclusion that the sensation itself is a *nothing*.'
– Not at all. It is not a *something*, but not a *nothing* either! The conclusion was only that
a nothing would serve just as well as a something about which nothing could be said.
(§304)

What Pitcher did not mention was that he had had to leave out the first part of the
section in order to invoke it in support of his interpretation of Wittgenstein:

'But you will surely admit that there is a difference between pain-behaviour accompanied
by pain and pain-behaviour without any pain?' Admit it? What greater difference could
there be? (§304)

Donagan improved Pitcher's interpretation of this passage, but at the cost of allowing
§293 to be intelligible:

The existence of the 'object', of what accompanies natural pain-behaviour, is not only
not irrelevant to the meaning of pain words, it is cardinal. What is irrelevant is not the
existence of the object, *but what it happens to be*. (Donagan, 1966, p. 347, my emphasis)

Leaving aside the philosophical problems raised by the views ascribed to Wittgenstein
by Pitcher and Donagan, it is obvious that the textual evidence they called on was
equivocal; to take either view seriously, one has to assume that Wittgenstein had
been quite slipshod in his formulations.

The interpretation of Wittgenstein's analysis as one concerned with the way we
speak about sensations, not their nature, was an attempt to respect Wittgenstein's
dictum that philosophy should remain purely descriptive. In several sections in
Philosophical Investigations, Wittgenstein explicitly denied that he was advancing
philosophical theses and stressed that philosophy must remain descriptive.[32] In the
discussion of private language Wittgenstein had, accordingly, somehow managed
to free himself of the dichotomy between Cartesianism and behaviourism – a
dichotomy that shaped the debate and in which any denial of Cartesianism would
have to struggle with the discomforts of behaviourism and vice versa. Concentrating
on language, and on how it is used, Wittgenstein had resisted the temptation to fall
into philosophical theorizing.

However, many commentators who were impressed with other aspects of
Philosophical Investigations found it hard to accept this apparently dismissive
attitude to the role of philosophy. They also felt that Wittgenstein had not been
consistent on these matters. Consider, for example, Michael Dummett's comment on
Wittgenstein's 'philosophy without theses':

This is probably the weakest part of his work, and doubtless affected his manner of
presentation; but there is nothing in what he says on any other topic the arguments for
which presuppose acceptance of these views, and indeed it seems to me that his actual
practice belies them – it is, e.g., quite easy to formulate philosophical theses which
Wittgenstein advanced. (Dummett, 1960, p. 434)

---

[32]   §§109,124, 126 and 309 are some well-known examples.

Likewise, linguistic behaviourism could very well be formulated as a thesis, in the way Mundle demonstrates.[33] In this perspective, it can seem that many of those who saw Wittgenstein as mainly concerned with the description of language either ignored the sections indicated above or followed the approach Dummett finds in Wittgenstein's work, i.e. advanced theses and then denied having done so.[34] However, when it is formulated as a thesis, linguistic behaviourism essentially amounts to a defence of Cartesianism. It denies neither the Cartesian motivation nor the conclusion drawn from it. It insists only that language cannot pass beyond behaviour. In other words, it introduces a sharp separation of philosophy of language and philosophy of mind.

This is why we must distinguish linguistic behaviourism from ordinary language philosophy as it is described in the Chapter 7. The common element was that both approaches were intended to remain purely descriptive; but whereas ordinary language philosophy generally sought to undermine the Cartesian picture by showing that it is motivated by the way in which we ordinarily conceive of sensations and their relation to behaviour, linguistic behaviourism sought to accommodate it. Philosophers of ordinary language tried to harmonize Cartesianism with the contention that the Reductio Argument and the External Argument were sound.

This also meant that linguistic behaviourism tended to take the private language arguments for granted. The account of Wittgenstein's positive views on the structure of ordinary sensation language that was offered was hardly suitable to support the External Argument.

---

[33] See p. 95.

[34] See, for example, Donagan (1966) who sees Wittgenstein as advancing theories. He also gives Pitcher's account, Pitcher (1964), the name 'Linguistic Behaviourism', Donagan (1966), p. 329.

Chapter 7

Ordinary Sensation Language

The previous chapter showed that, during the 1950s and 1960s, several expositions of the Wittgensteinian private language argument failed to dissociate the argument from reliance on a verification principle. At this time, then, the viability of the argument stood and fell with a principle which had fallen into discredit.

There was, however, another line of argument against Cartesianism with Wittgensteinian origin. Rather than aiming to show that the Cartesian position was absurd, this line proceeded by arguing that the Cartesian picture gained plausibility by misrepresenting ordinary sensation discourse. This approach (and indeed Malcolm's rather loose presentations of the Reductio Argument and the External Argument) was closely associated with a distinctive philosophical method often called 'ordinary language philosophy' — a method widely acknowledged to have been developed and employed by Wittgenstein in the period following his return to philosophy in 1929.

This method is detectable in Malcolm's approach to Wittgenstein, although it was somewhat muted in his review of *Philosophical Investigations* in 1954. At any rate, his interpretation of Wittgenstein fits well with the characterization V. C. Chappell gave of ordinary language philosophy in 1962:

> Here the conviction is that 'ordinary language is all right' and that philosophical difficulties, which are indeed linguistic in origin, arise not because our language is faulty but because philosophers misdescribe and misconstrue it. It follows that the way to achieve success in philosophy – and this again means understanding and the solving of problems – is to determine how our language is in fact used, and thence show where and how philosophers have gone astray. (Chappell (ed.), 1964, p. 2)[1]

In this summary the philosophical methodology has two goals: to describe correctly, and gain an understanding of, the ways in which language is actually used; and to use this understanding to show where traditional philosophy has gone wrong. A corollary of this method, and one that can be traced in Malcolm's review of *Philosophical Investigations*, is that philosophy should not go beyond descriptions to advance theoretical constructions.

The context in which Chappell made the above remarks was one in which he was describing a dominant, post-war philosophical orientation originating in Britain; but the description in fact serves a dual function. First, it presents a common view of the

---

[1] Note that the slogan 'ordinary language is all right', which was never used by Wittgenstein, was derived from *Philosophical Investigations*, §98: 'On the one hand it is clear that every sentence in our language 'is in order as it is'. That is to say, we are not *striving after* an ideal ...'

philosophy advocated by the 'later Wittgenstein' — a term referring to the philosophy Wittgenstein had developed during the 1930s in Cambridge. Accordingly, the later Wittgenstein's work is represented at one and the same time as a break with, and a continuation of, the philosophy Wittgenstein had practised earlier when he wrote the *Tractatus*. Both the early and later Wittgenstein held 'the view that philosophy is essentially linguistic' and that a study of language would yield results relevant to traditional philosophical problems in other areas (Chappell, 1964, p. 1). But whereas Wittgenstein had, in the *Tractatus*, believed that a view of language should be achieved by constructing 'a logically perfect language', because '... ordinary language is somehow deficient or faulty, at least for philosophical purposes, ...' (Chappell, 1964, p. 2), the latter had believed that philosophical advance could only be achieved by attending to ordinary use.

Secondly, as a characterization of ordinary language philosophy, the above quotation was meant to concern not only the philosophy conducted by Wittgenstein and his students, like Malcolm and Rhees, but also the philosophy emanating from Oxford under the influence mainly of Gilbert Ryle and John L. Austin. The generic term sometimes applied to this school was 'Oxford philosophy'.[2] Talking about Oxford philosophy would, however, only make the reference to Wittgenstein slightly more indirect. Even before his death in 1951, Wittgenstein's ideas were the dominant influence in post-war Oxford. The influence exerted itself through Gilbert Ryle, who knew Wittgenstein personally and had attended some of his lectures in Cambridge, through Wittgenstein's students G. E. M. Anscombe and Friedrich Waismann, and through typescripts of what came to be known as the Blue Book and the Brown Book around 1950. I shall not concern myself much with the appropriateness of using 'ordinary language philosphy' as a generic term, with the unity it signals. G. J. Warnock was right in pointing out that there were significant differences between its Oxford practitioners in the 1950s:

> It can only have been from a *very* great distance, or through glasses of highly imperfect focus, that everyone at the time looked much alike, like devotees of 'school'. (Warnock, 1976, p. 51)[3]

He was definitely right in so far that no 'school' or general orientation of the kind exemplified by the Vienna Circle's 'scientific world conception' was ever defined. In Chapter 6 we saw disagreements among philosophers usually classified as ordinary language philosophers in the debate between Malcolm and Strawson. Besides disagreement on specific issues, the distance between Strawson's descriptive metaphysics (Strawson, 1959), and Malcolm's anti-theoretical practice was

---

[2]   See, for example, Dummett (1960). The origin of the term 'ordinary language philosophy' is unknown, but Hacker (1996b), pp. 309–10, notes that by the mid-1950s the term had become common.

[3]   Recently the term has been exposed to detailed criticism by Hacker (1996b) and Cook (2000). Hacker and Cook accept that shared features were collected under the term, but both writers would probably find a more fully determined account such as Chappell's misleading. See also Shanker (1986).

considerable. There was also disagreement over the way in which Wittgenstein had implemented the method.

It is, however, crucial to understanding the logic of the private language debate during this period to acknowledge that it was deeply tied up with a discussion about proper philosophical method. Increased attention to the mechanisms of the way we speak led to a growing recognition that we are not inevitably led from our ordinary discourse about sensations to the Cartesian position. Our sensation concepts do not possess Cartesian features such as privacy and a contingent relation to behaviour. The connection here with what was said at the end of Chapter 6 is that this criticism of Cartesianism refused to rely on a general unifying principle bridging the epistemology of sensations and the meaning of sensation terms; it refused to link the criteria for sensations and the reference of 'sensation'.

7.1 Cook on Privacy and Ordinary Language

One of the most energetic attempts to demonstrate that the philosophical idea of a private language is motivated by a mistaken or confused view of the privacy of sensations was provided by John Cook in 1965. Cook had been introduced to Wittgenstein's later work through Malcolm and O. K. Bouwsma. He also took *Philosophical Investigations* as vantage point in his discussion. Providing an interpretation of §§244–55, he defended Wittgenstein against Hector-Neri Castañeda, who, in 1962 at a symposium on the private language argument, had complained amongst other things '...that the ordinary language of pain is still a mixed private language in several senses and remains, therefore a counterexample against some interpretations of Wittgenstein's thesis' (Castañeda, 1962, p. 142). Castañeda urged that '... the idea of a private language is so obscure that there are many senses of "privacy" ...' (Castañeda, 1962, p. 179). Cook took this to be an utterly mistaken interpretation of Wittgenstein and undertook to defend him by examining in detail the roots of the idea of privacy in ordinary language. He concluded that the philosophical idea of a private language is a consequence of the following argument:

> No one can know whether another person is in pain or is dizzy or has any other sensation, for sensations are private in the sense that no one can feel (experience, be acquainted with) another person's sensations. (Cook, 1965, pp. 281–2)

Cook showed that Wittgenstein had criticized the two elements involved in this kind of argumentation separately in §§244–55 of *Philosophical Investigations*. The first claim in the argument is that knowledge of another's sensations is impossible. The truth of the sentence 'Well, only I can know whether I am really in pain; another person can only surmise it' (§246) (call it A_1) seems to justify a private language in so far as only one person could know when this sentence can be asserted. Wittgenstein showed that A_1 does not point in that direction on any sensible interpretation; a syntactically well-formed sentence is not automatically endowed with sense. The notion that A_1 has sense presupposes that it make sense to say 'I know that I am in pain' and that in turn requires us to find a genuine use for this latter sentence (Cook, 1965, p. 285). Several such uses suggest themselves. The sentence might, for example, be uttered in exasperation by a man to his wife, who is urging him to attend a doctor: 'I know I am in pain, but we can't afford a doctor!' This, however, does not sufficiently support the idea of a private language, because as an expression of exasperation it does not indicate any special certainty that only one person might have; the knowledge referred to by the husband might also be shared by his wife.

So, Cook argued, one needs to find a genuine use for the sentence 'I know I am in pain' in which it functions as an expression of certainty, and this was what cannot be done (Cook, 1965, p. 287). The thought that it can be done rests on a mistaken idea of the homogeneity of language. Compare 'I know it is raining'. The addition of 'I know ...' functions here as an expression of certainty, because the term can be added to 'It is raining' in order to indicate that one is in as good a position as one could be to assert that it is raining. The misleading thing here is that one cannot automatically generalize such a use to sensations, because it does not make sense to ask whether a person is in an optimal position to make the claim 'I know I am in pain'. Cook stated this conclusion quite explicitly:

> More generally, for 'I know that ...' to be an expression of certainty, it is at least necessary that the sense of the sentence filling the blank allow the speaker to be ignorant in some circumstances of the truth value of statements made by means of the sentence (or equivalents thereof). But now, it is just this, as Wittgenstein points out (*Inv.* 246 and pp. 221–2), that does *not* hold for 'I am in pain'. (Cook, 1965, p. 286)

So there is no use for 'I know I am in pain' as an expression of certainty; the addition of 'I know ...' has no function, and therefore A_1 says nothing significant about pains. Cook pointed out that this claim rests on Wittgenstein's idea that first-person present-tense sensation statements are incorrigible. He was less certain about this, but he conjectured that it might be argued for by appeal to the way in which sensation language is *actually* taught (Cook, 1965, p. 288). Here he seemed to have something like §244 in mind: 'words are connected with the primitive, the natural, expressions of the sensation and used in their place. A child has hurt himself and he cries; and then adults talk to him and teach him exclamations and, later sentences'. Since the initial natural expression was not subject to correction, its replacement, the sentence, would also fail to be.

Wittgenstein's point, according to Cook, might be summed up by saying that the incorrigibility of first-person sensation reports makes it impossible to meaningfully interpret A_1 as a sentence expressing anything about the nature of sensations. In particular, A_1 cannot be assumed to point towards a private language as the Cartesian takes it to do. Cook had also diagnosed the origin of the idea that such a claim might make sense in certain superficially similar cases. What had been ignored was that despite this similarity they were nonetheless quite distinct: 'Or as I would like to put it... the moves that are part of the one language game are not part of the other' (Cook, 1965, p. 288). As an expression of certainty 'know' is not a part of the language game with first-person sensation ascriptions, and so A_1 does not express anything about the nature of sensation. Consequently the sentence (C) 'No one can know what sensations another person's having' could not have any sense in which 'know' refers to something possessed by the person having the sensation (Cook, 1965, pp. 283–4).

Wittgenstein discusses the statement that 'Another person can't have my pains' a few paragraphs later in §253. Essentially this statement is the second claim in the argument motivating Cartesianism. In 1964 George Pitcher had argued that Wittgenstein had accepted this statement (call it A_2) as part of a demonstration of the absurdity of the view that 'pain' is the name of a private sensation: if 'pain' were such a word, I could not determine whether another person feels the same sensation as I do, because that would require me to feel his pain, and that, following §253, is impossible; hence 'pain' is not the name of a private sensation (Pitcher, 1964, p. 288).

Cook provided the foundation of a better understanding here by showing that the correctness of A_2 must be evaluated by considering which criterion of identity ranges over ordinary sensation discourse. Again, the apparent homogeneity of language misleads us into holding A_2 to be true. We assume that there is only one such criterion available and have an inclination to think of sensations as objects of perception (Cook, 1965, pp. 305, 309). Such a mistake leads us to consider the pain case as one that is analogous to the case of physical objects.

As an example of a philosopher making such a mistake, Cook mentioned Ayer. Ayer, in a passage reminiscent of the argumentation he had given against a private language in his 1954 paper, had claimed:

> The question of whether an object is public or private is fundamentally a question of … the conventions we follow in making judgements of identity. Thus physical objects are public because it makes sense to say of different people that they are perceiving the same physical object; mental images are private because it does not make sense to say of different people that they are having the same mental image; they can be imagining the same thing, but it is impossible that their respective images should be literally the same. (Ayer, 1956, p. 200)

Here we find the physical criterion of identity applied to sensations, but this creates confusion. Instead, Cook insisted: ' "Same" must always be understood together with some general term, such as "build" or "coat", and the criterion of identity in any particular case is determined by the general term involved.'[4]

Cook pointed out that, on the usual criterion of identity ranging over the domain of sensations, pains are identical when they are described in the same way. If we have two people in pain, who behave in similar ways and describe their pain in the same words, then 'qualitatively similar' has the meaning of 'same'. We even say, sometimes: 'We always get the same pain whenever it rains: an intense aching in the joints' (Cook, 1965, p. 306). Such ideas are granted by Ayer, among others; but the claim was that we have here one of the practical short-cuts of ordinary language; 'same' is a convenient way to express oneself here, but it should not be taken literally.

---

[4]   Cook (1965), p. 305. Cook's concern with 'same' here can be compared with Malcolm's discussion in 1954. Cook argued that no consistent usage of 'same' would span the entire language automatically. In other words, we cannot simply assume that we know what 'same' means.

Against this Cook held, referring to §253, that where it is correct to say 'His pain is the same as mine', it is also possible for people to feel the same pain (Cook, 1965, p. 306).

Even if our opponent concedes that much he is unlikely to admit defeat, because his main concern is numerical identity. There is something about pain, and sensations in general, which makes it impossible for two people to have the same one. The pains of two people cannot be numerically identical: there is '... a familiar use of sensation words with a criterion of identity that is reflected in "But surely another person can't have *this* pain!" ...'[5] Cook admitted that there is a use of such words on which certain sensations are counted and identified according to place and time: 'Toothaches are episodes of pain, just as dizzy spells are episodes of dizziness so that answering the question "How many toothaches have you had?" requires a reference to particular occasions' (Cook, 1965, p. 308). This, however, would not support A_2, because on this understanding it would not even make sense to suppose, of a single person, that he could experience the same toothache twice, because the senselessness of the alleged sameness of two spatially or temporally distinct episodes of sensations would be a defining criterion on this use. Such a criterion of identity would make it impossible for two people to have the same pain, but it would still not lend support to a statement like A_2. The impossibility would not rest on these pains being ascribed to different people, but on the senselessness of spatiotemporal locations recurring. Here, the statement that two toothaches are 'exactly alike' would mean that the toothaches are 'rather alike'; it would not entail 'sameness':

That is, it would not be asked: "Do you suppose they may have had the same one or just two exactly alike?"

> ... the identification question "Did they have the same one?" has no place and so neither do its answers. That is it would not make sense to say, as if in answer to that question, *either* "They had the same toothache" or "They did not have the same toothache" (Cook, 1965, p. 308).

To conclude, Cook had found two identity criteria applying to sensations, one referring to qualitative similarity and another referring to spatiotemporal location. Because neither of these would yield any special category of my sensations, neither could support the Cartesian picture. Since we do not identify sensations by reference to the person having them, I might very well have the same feeling you are having. I can know very well how you are feeling because I can have the same feeling.

So because the identity criteria in the Cartesian conception of the mind differ from those deployed in actual discourse, that conception cannot be motivated by appeal to actual discourse; worse still, it cannot explain actual discourse: 'the idea of the private object is not one that turns up in our common thought and practice ...' (Cook, 1965, pp. 313–14). The analysis which led to this conclusion accomplished at least two things: it refuted Castañeda's claim that ordinary sensation language was private, and it provided a convincing interpretation of *Philosophical Investigations*

---

[5]   Cook (1965), p. 307. The sentence alludes to §253, where Wittgenstein imagines a person saying it while hitting himself on the chest.

§§244–55. Whether it presented a problem for the Cartesian was a matter for serious discussion.

7.2 The Ordinary Language Methodology

In an influential, critical examination of recent discussions of Wittgenstein's views on the privacy of sensations, Richard Rorty had argued that Cook's analysis involves a problematic methodological premise which leads him to conflate senselessness with uselessness or obviousness. Just because the answer to 'Did they have the same toothache?' is obvious and therefore not very informative, it does not necessarily follow that it is senseless (Rorty, 1970, p. 291). Rorty advances a similar criticism of §246. When someone proclaims that he is in pain, the remark 'I am sure you have something, but are you certain that it is pain that you're having?' is senseless, according to Cook, because neither the answer 'I doubt that I am in pain' nor the answer 'I know that I am in pain' would make sense (Rorty, 1970, p. 296). It would seem that Cook had conflated obviousness and senselessness by embracing the following principle:

> (I) If a yes-or-no question does not normally occur in extra-philosophical discourse (although all the words used in it do), then the question, and all direct answers to it, are senseless. (Rorty, 1970, p. 291)

In his paper, Rorty makes a devastating criticism of such a principle, and given that Cook did not offer any illuminating remarks on why he would hold the relevant question and its possible answers senseless, this criticism would appear to be warranted.

Rorty's criticism undermines much of the work done within the ordinary language philosophy circles; it also reflects an internal discussion within these circles: Gilbert Ryle had explicitly warned against a similar use of ordinary language in 1953 (Ryle, 1953, p. 30). But against Cook, the criticism is misplaced. Rorty's distinction between statements that make sense and those that do not fails to coincide with the distinction between statements that 'normally occur in extra-philosophical discourse' and those that do not. It is true that Cook had appealed to ordinary language, but he had not relied on an idea of what would normally occur in the sense that he could have conducted an empirical survey of common uses to warrant his claims. Instead he had investigated whether a connection *could be found* between sensations and privacy which would support the Cartesian notion of the privacy of sensation. The situation with toothache certainly involves a connection with privacy, but not one peculiar to sensations; on that construal tantrums would be private too. In line with the Wittgenstein whose views he claimed to clarify (Cook, 1965, p. 288), Cook's distinction was rather between empirical statements and meaning-explaining statements; between 'empirical propositions' and 'grammatical propositions' (§251).

Nonetheless, Cook's use of the term 'senselessness' was broader than Wittgenstein's category of 'grammatical propositions'. First, Cook had insisted that, in the case of toothaches as episodes of pain, the question 'Did they have the same pain?' was senseless because the person asking the question would not have understood the meaning of the words it involves. That is, the questioner would not have understood how 'toothache' was used in this context. So the question was senseless because the fact that it was being raised would show that the questioner did not know what he was talking about. This was one kind of senselessness.

The second use of 'senselessness' did correspond to Wittgenstein's category of 'grammatical propositions'. In fact Cook's choice of terminology had probably been inspired by §§248, 251 and, especially, §252: '"This body has extension." To this we might reply: "Nonsense!" – but are inclined to reply "Of course!" – Why is this?' What Wittgenstein had pointed out here was that 'This body has an extension' was not an empirical statement expressing a fact about the world, but a *grammatical* statement explaining something about the use of words. Accordingly, the answer 'They did not have the same toothache' was senseless in the sense that it explained something about the language game being played. It was a statement about the rules of the discourse, and so it did not say anything about the nature or essence of toothache. Clearly it could not express anything essential about sensations, because one might speak about toothaches in a manner that would make the answer false.[6] To call these statements senseless was not to imply that someone expressing them would demonstrate a lack of understanding. It was just to say that the speaker would not be talking about pains but about the rules of the discourse.

So empirical statements made claims about the domain of the relevant discourse; grammatical statements set out the rules for the discourse, the rules of the game. Cook's analysis shows how the road to Cartesianism is paved by failures to respect this distinction.

The crucial element in Cook's analysis is that only by observing actual use could one distinguish grammatical from empirical propositions; the difference between these propositions is hidden, so to speak. The Cartesian, assuming too readily that the structure of language reflects the structure of the world, is misled into thinking that sensations and physical objects are individuated the same way: '... the idea that sensations are private results from construing the grammar of sensation words on analogy with the grammar of words for physical objects' (Cook, 1965, p. 313). Two mistakes are in fact made here: to assume, first, that the distinction between empirical statements and statements about language is reflected in form; and second, that this distinction is uniform, irrespective of the domain of discourse. To use Wittgenstein's term, it is assumed that there is only one language game. The second mistake derives from the former, because the formal structure of language is indeed fairly uniform. By contrast, an analysis of the empirical-grammatical distinction requires us to attend to actual use and to ignore superficial formal similarities.

The Cartesian's ignorance of the distinction was most straightforward in the analysis of 'knowing about pain' (§246). Since the sentences 'I know I am in pain' and 'I know that there is a table in the kitchen' have a similar syntactical structure, we conclude that the knowledge relation is the same. In this way we fail to notice that

---

[6]   One might, for instance, classify them by referring, not to time and place, but what had caused it – fist fights, bad teeth-brushing habits, and the like.

the latter is an empirical statement, whereas the former is a grammatical statement expressing the rule that when I say I am in pain you are not allowed to doubt it.

Cook reckoned the line of reasoning that leads to the mistake of thinking that two people cannot have the same pain to be a little more subtle. In thinking of '... sensations as being objects of perception', and in construing '... first person statements on analogy with eyewitness reports' (Cook, 1965, p. 309), we are lead to apply to sensations '... a criterion of identity of the same kind as in the case of the crocuses ...' (Cook, 1965, p. 290). Confronted with the question 'Can two people feel the same toothache?', and influenced by the physical criterion of identity, as Ayer had been, one is bound to exclude one alternative a priori, because 'It cannot be the *same* toothache if there are *two* people in pain'.

> But with one of the pair of 'answers' thus excluded a priori, it will seem that the one *must* be true, and thus 'No two people can feel the same toothache' comes to be called 'a necessary truth.'

> This, then, is the complicated story behind the idea that in 'sensations are private' we have a 'necessary truth' or that 'No one can feel another's pain' expresses a 'logical impossibility'. (Cook, 1965, p. 309)

In other words, since the reasoning had been a priori, the proposition that 'No one can feel another's pain' appeared to describe an essential property of pain. However, from Cook's analysis of the identity criteria that are available in talk about sensation, it followed that the statement was either an incorrect grammatical statement or, at best, a grammatical statement partly describing the rule that sensations are individuated spatio-temporally. Once we see this we appreciate that the idea that sensations are private objects '... turns up only in those odd moments when we are under the influence of a false grammatical analogy' (Cook, 1965, p. 314).

The obstacle to using this argument against the Cartesian position directly was that, in order to draw the distinction between the grammatical and the empirical, an existing practice was required. For it is only relative to a practice that one is able to decide whether a statement is grammatical or empirical. This was one way in which Wittgenstein's methodological adage that 'Meaning is use' would apply: only by looking at the way in which statements in some range are actually used can we isolate the meaning-giving statements. But equally, only by doing something more than merely stating this slogan, only by saying something substantial about the conditions for setting up a practice, could the possibility of a private language be shown to be incompatible with the idea that meaning is use. In particular, why could one not set up a practice of speaking about sensations by ostensively defining the terms? Or, why would this presuppose an already existing practice? Answering such questions proved to be very difficult within the general strictures of ordinary language philosophy. Since these demanded that one should not engage in theory but stick to describing the structure and implications of natural language, the argument against the idea of a private language was that it would not describe anything we know from our already established discourses; that is, since a private language would not connect to our ordinary sensation discourse, it could not be speaking about sensations. This would essentially amount to claiming that philosophical analysis is exhausted by attending to actual use. Those who made this claim said almost nothing about what was essential for use.

But without a claim about what is essential for language it would not be possible to demonstrate the impossibility *in principle* of a private language. Clearly, merely to point out that ordinary language was not private, would not rule out the latter's possibility.

Without further explanation of the authority of ordinary language, however, the Cartesian would not feel (nor would he be) refuted, because his project was not to describe ordinary language, but to unravel the essence of sensations. Descartes did not take himself to be analysing the structure of ordinary discourse when he characterized cogitatio. Rather, his project was to clarify, and thereby deepen our understanding of, the nature of the mind. Descartes reached his result through careful investigation of the possibility-conditions of knowledge. Nothing in his method required all the conventions of ordinary language to be respected as literally true.

In contrast with this, the typical ordinary language philosopher would not have seen his investigations as continuous with science, or as extending our knowledge of the world.[7] Arguing against the possibility of a private language, he would have had the negative purpose of showing where traditional philosophy, through the legacy of Descartes, had gone wrong in its construal of the nature of sensations. The correct philosophical task consisted in illuminating, and removing the motivation behind, any metaphysical extrapolations through an analysis of the ordinary use of key expressions; in examining what was actually accomplished by using the terms. The project was not one of improving ordinary use, or replacing it with a scientific language, but attaining a correct understanding of an existing linguistic practice. Accordingly, an analysis of sensation language would show what characterized pain and what characterized 'pain' – and show which statements were concerned with the objects of sensation discourse and which were concerned with its rules.

Although the relationship between these two approaches, and hence the nature of philosophy, was the subject of intense debate,[8] the most that could be accomplished by attending to ordinary language was a demolition of the motivation for the Cartesian position.

7.3 Reinterpreting Wittgenstein

The fact that private language could not be shown to be impossible in principle by attending to actual use, leads to a further difficulty. This difficulty concerns the sections in *Philosophical Investigations* in which Malcolm had claimed to find a reductio ad absurdum of the idea of a private language. In his review, Malcolm seemed to make an indirect appeal to practice in the substructure of the Reductio Argument, but no properly explained connection between the argument and the

---

[7]   Hacker (1996b), p. 229, notes that this was generally (and perhaps uniquely) agreed by philosophers generally regarded as conducting ordinary language philosophy.

[8]   See, for instance, Chappell (ed.) (1964) and Rorty (ed.) (1967); see also Strawson (1959), pp. 9–12.

doctrine evolved.[9] How, if he had applauded the dictum that 'ordinary language is all right', could Wittgenstein have argued for the impossibility in principle of a private language? Apparently, the argument could be advanced only if the premises were either ascribed to Cartesianism or regarded as justified by appeal to ordinary use.[10]

The latter solution might actually have been the one intended by Malcolm. In one of the first general expositions of Wittgenstein's later philosophy, Pitcher painted a picture not altogether different from Malcolm's;[11] and in the two chapters Pitcher devoted to Wittgenstein's methodology, some remarks had a familiar ring. For example:

> ... the philosopher's job is to give a certain sort of description of the uses of words; his task is a purely descriptive.

> The philosopher puts before us familiar data about our language-games and arranges them in such a way that we achieve a clear overall view of the uses of certain expressions. In this way he attempts to dispel the puzzlement which has plagued us. (Pitcher, 1964, pp. 319–20)

Unlike Malcolm, however, Pitcher did not present Wittgenstein's argument against the possibility of a private language as a step-by-step reductio ad absurdum. Instead, he described the argumentation over the course of several pages, apparently trying to justify the stages of the argument by appealing to the way in which we ordinarily conceive of language. Despite this, certain premises are quite easy to make out, but the origin of these is not explained:

> The alleged diarist – call him Paul – has no way whatever of *knowing* whether he always applies the sign 'E' to a different one each time, or whether he sometimes applies it to the same sensation, sometimes to a different one. ..
> under these conditions the question of correctness or incorrectness (rightness or wrongness) of Paul's use of the sign 'E' cannot arise, and that hence the very concept of correctness and incorrectness fails to apply ...
> [and so ...] Paul's mark 'E' is not the name of one of his private sensations – it is not a sign or a word of any sort. (Pitcher, 1964, pp. 295–7, my emphasis)

Here, one is bound to ask: Where does the demand that the private diarist should *know* (in a sense he cannot) whether his application was consistent come from, if 'There are no philosophical doctrines or theories' (Pitcher, 1964, p. 321)?

Cook's account of §258 in 1972 made a much more direct appeal to ordinary usage. Distancing himself immediately from the Reductio Argument Malcolm had claimed to unearth, Cook suggests that Wittgenstein is not presenting any argument at all:

---

[9]   See Chapter 5.

[10]   See Chapter 5.

[11]   Pitcher (1964). The front inside-flap of Pitcher's book promoted it as the first joint treatment of the *Tractatus* and *Philosophical Investigations*, thereby overlooking a Danish book by Hartnack (1960), which was also published in a German version (1962).

The imagined diary case is not, then, as some have supposed, the first step in an argument of the *reductio ad absurdum* form but merely an (admittedly devious) heuristic device. There is, in fact, no argument here at all. Rather we are being invited to consider a certain deliberately restricted description and being asked whether we could recognize from this description alone that a sensation has been named. (Cook, 1972, p. 46)[12]

Cook took Wittgenstein to be imagining a case in which all the human activities and bodily functions that are normally necessary in order to teach children the use of language have been removed. This brings us to a Cartesian disembodied mind to whom (or to which) we are to ascribe the wish to keep a diary of a certain sensation by writing down 'E' on its occurrence. How, then, can we describe what this disembodied authors does? 'What he does, we are told, is to associate the sign "E" with a certain sensation' (Cook, 1972, p. 64). Following Locke, we seem committed to claiming that the association must become fixed in memory if its use is to have any justification.[13] The appeal to memory, however, presents a problem: '... given the supposition that this is a disembodied being who neither does nor seems to participate in any form of life, there could *per hypothesis* be nothing whatsoever that differs between a supposed case in which he remembers and a supposed case in which he is mistaken' (Cook, 1972, pp. 65–6). Is this the general principle that a difference should be provable that Cook is appealing to? He seems to hold that in the normal, everyday case one could meet this demand merely by saying that the difference is preserved by the fact that one may, or may not, be using 'E' in conformity with an actual memory. But in the diary case, the disembodied author could not make this response, because in that case 'memory' is a product of human conduct from which he has, by hypothesis, been separated. In fact, the private speaker who is permitted to use notions like 'sensation' and 'association' is already granted too much:

> The problem, rather, is one of trying to describe a faculty of memory or association in complete independence of any human – or human-like – activities. And what we soon discover is that we do not know what we are doing when we try to do this. (Cook, 1972, p. 66)

This is a condensed version of Cook's argumentation, but it suffices to show the way in which Cook presupposed that memory and association cannot be described apart from their use in ordinary human (or human-like) activities. The ideas drawn upon here were used to argue that private language was, not just impossible, but unintelligible. For instance, Cook ascribes to Wittgenstein the view that a description even of the diary case would presuppose '... *inevitably* that which only the stage-setting, i.e. a human childhood etc. could provide, namely, the mastery of the words of the dialogue itself ...' (Cook, 1965, p. 65). Marking the confinements of human language, Wittgenstein had captured the frustration of those seeking to exploit the private diary example by saying in §261: 'So in the end when one is doing

---

[12]   This perspective was not unique to Cook; others taking it included Wisdom (1972), p. 26, and Thomson (1964), p. 183.

[13]   Probably deliberately, Cook eschewed the term 'meaning' here and employed the less worn term 'use'.

philosophy one gets to the point where one would like just to emit an inarticulate sound'.[14] The diary case had taken Wittgenstein beyond the confines of intelligible discourse (Cook, 1972, p. 40). From Cook's point of view, then, Cartesianism had lost its motivation, because it had been relocated to a powerless position far removed from the phenomenon it was supposed to explain.

7.4 Lessons from Ordinary Language Philosophy

Although Cook had been concerned, in both of his articles, to analyse the use of sensation language, his analysis focused on *sensations* and not merely sensation language. His point had not been the linguistic behaviourist's – i.e. that we do not *talk* about sensation as if they were private objects. Rather it was that sensations *themselves* are not private objects in the Cartesian sense.

In relation to the wider discussion of private language, Cook's analyses, along with other ordinary language analyses, had made a strong case against the Cartesian picture of the mind by removing much of the motivation for that picture. First, it was now clear that we are not led directly from our ordinary sensation discourse to the idea of sensations as private objects; a great deal of (perhaps uncritically) presupposed privacy, and with it the motivation for a dualism of mind and body, would evaporate in any attempt to locate that privacy in our 'pre-philosophical' handling of psychological concepts. We do not speak about our sensations as though they are objects beyond the reach of other persons. Secondly, it would be a huge challenge to construct ordinary sensation discourse from a collection of Cartesian private languages. The two types of language have very different characteristics. Thirdly, Cook had offered a diagnosis of the mistakes which lead to Cartesianism: that position was motivated by a conflation of empirical and grammatical propositions, by a failure to separate statements concerned with the objects of discourse and statements concerned with the rules of the discourse. This mistake was in turn the result of taking syntactical categories to have semantic significance – the result of a category mistake, to use Gilbert Ryle's terminology (Ryle, 1949).

Underlying these conclusions were analyses of ordinary discourse that were much more sensitive than had previously been seen in analytic philosophy. For instance, Cook's strategy in his 1972 article consisted in analysing the way in which the concept of memory is learned, and in asking what we usually, perhaps without being unaware, take for granted when such a concept is acquired. From that platform, he asked whether the relevant process could inspire and motivate a theoretical position that would secure the possibility of a private language; whether, detached from its natural habitat, the concept could still be characterized as memory. Cook here showed a much more sensitive awareness of actual practice than Russell had in 1940, when, under the influence of a theoretical framework, he tried to explain how he had learned the concept of something's being hot:

Let us begin with 'meaning', and let us take the word 'hot' for the purposes of illustration. I shall suppose a schematic simplicity in the experiences by means of which I learnt the

---

[14] Quoted in Cook (1972), p. 65.

meaning of the word in childhood: there was an open fire in my nursery, and every time I went near it someone said 'hot'; that they used the same word when I perspired on a summer's day, and when, accidentally, I spilled scalding tea over myself. The result was that I uttered the word 'hot' whenever I noticed sensations of a certain kind. (Russell, 1940, p. 157)

Likewise, Cook's 1965 article presented an assiduously thought-through picture of the way in which we discourse about pain. Through an analysis of germane paragraphs in *Philosophical Investigations* this picture explicated the role of privacy and privileged first-person access here; and here, too, the phenomenology of sensation discourse was the material which turned the tables with regard to the burden of proof: the Cartesian was no longer permitted to wait for an opponent to present a more appealing account of sensations, but had to demonstrate that in *his* account he had captured the essentials.[15]

All in all, then, the case made by way of close analysis of ordinary discourse against the Cartesian position and its corollary the argument from analogy was a strong one – one capable of standing independently of the specific ideology of ordinary language philosophy; and that case was made, to a considerable extent, by analysing sections in *Philosophical Investigations* which dealt with the possibility of a private language.

However, these analyses characteristically appealed to actual discourse, or to what we mean when we speak about sensations. Several other expositions appeared in the late 1960s and early 1970s that tried to harmonize Wittgenstein's argumentation with the methodology of ordinary language philosophy. In some cases, where the External Argument was considered, this amounted to requiring a merely possible private language to answer to the working demands of ordinary usage. For instance, Chihara's and Fodor's widely read account of Wittgenstein takes his argumentation to concern scepticism about knowledge of other minds: 'The sceptic's view is logically incompatible with the operation of the ordinary language rules ...' (Chihara/Fodor, 1965, p. 402). Compare Cook on the behaviourist alternative to Cartesianism: 'What this [supposing 'pain' refers to behaviour] would fail to account for, of course, is my pity or concern for them [other people]' (Cook, 1969, p. 127).

However, the argumentative strategy against the Cartesian never claimed to move beyond the confines of the actual; indeed this was almost a defining mark of ordinary language philosophy. But in order to be developed into an argument against the possibility of a private language, there would have to be an appeal to claims, or principles, concerning the nature of language as such.

Consider Malcolm's suggestion as to how the reductio of the notion of a private language should be constructed: 'Postulate a "private" language; then deduce that it is not a *language*' (Malcolm, 1954, p. 537). An argument of this sort would involve analyzing the very concept of language and showing that somewhere beneath appearances lies an essential requirement for publicity. However, as a platform from which to build this kind of case against private language, the conservative appeal to ordinary language did not fare well. Cook, for instance concluded nothing particularly

---

[15]   See, also, Malcolm's treatment of §§244–55 in Malcolm (1967).

important about the essential nature of language. Instead the appeal to use created a picture of language as a set of more or less loosely connected language games, with certain recurrences in vocabulary, but with each word having a contextual meaning only. A viable argument against private language *in principle* could not be construed along these lines.[16]

Looking back, it is possible to see that the in-principle argument being sought here required recourse to fundamental analysis within semantics. Semantics was an expanding subject around 1970, and this growth would soon foster renewed attention to Wittgenstein's philosophy. The main field of interest in ordinary language philosophy, however, was the philosophy of psychology, not the philosophy of language – the nature of pain rather than the nature of the language with which we typically react to the experience of pain. It was through philosophical psychology that the ordinary language approach clarified the privacy issue.

---

[16] This drawback was, it seems, generally recognized in the early 1970s. Interestingly, it seems to have ensured that some quite profound accounts of *Philosophical Investigations* received less serious attention than they merited merely because they bore the label 'ordinary language philosophy'. Deserving of special mention here is von Savigny's discussion in (1969), which made several points that were, in point of fact, repeated by later writers in connection with §§243–315. See also Holborow (1967).

PART III
Language within Philosophy

Chapter 8

The Problem with Private Ostensive Definitions

The gradual emergence, during the 1960s, of the notion that the Reductio Argument and similar arguments relied on a combination of verificationism and memory scepticism threatened the very idea of a cogent private language argument. This threat, I think it is fair to say, was never more than a threat. Although the attempts to frame an argument against the possibility of a private language mentioned here were more or less directly modelled on argumentative moves that commentators claimed to have unearthed in *Philosophical Investigations*, the accusation that Wittgenstein himself relied upon verificationism or memory-scepticism was not prevalent.[1] There was still hope that Wittgenstein had been on the right track. Quite a few philosophers maintained their interest in the argument, and the lack of any published response to Thomson and others with similar claims should not lead one to assume the opposite.

One reason why the reaction time was so long was that it would have to be derived from reconsidering the relevant sections in *Philosophical Investigations* itself. No secondary interpretations proved suitable as foundation for further advancements. The process was furthermore extended because the reactions which came in the early 1970s, depended their interpretations on arguments in *Philosophical Investigations* which they read from sections outside §§243–315 and views on language which were only implicitly assumed in here. In other words, new fuel for the discussion was again found within Wittgenstein's authorship and it is therefore no surprise that it was presented by two philosophers, Anthony Kenny and Peter Hacker, who had independently provided some of the first thorough examinations of *Philosophical Investigations* since Pitcher's influential book of 1964. Pitcher's book, for all its merits, left readers in the dark about several of the sections in Philosophical Investigations focusing on private language.

8.1 Approaching Philosophical Investigations Anew

The first serious alternative to the verificationist reading of the Reductio Argument was presented in an article by Anthony Kenny in 1971.[2] Among the

---

[1]   Some can be found; for example, Mundle (1966) and Donagan (1966).

[2]   Kenny (1971), printed in Jones (ed.) (1971) and in a slightly altered version in Kenny (1973), Ch. 10. Several sympathetic presentations of arguments similar to the Reductio Argument can be found in the late 1960s, but none provided a serious alternative to a verificationist account. See, for example, von Savigny (1970), p. 71.

merits of Kenny's paper was the fact that it described the underlying structure of *Philosophical Investigations* §§243–315. Kenny suggested that §§246–52 argue that others can know my pain, and that §§253–5 argue that others can have my pain, and that therefore ordinary sensation language is not a private language. So when, in §256, Wittgenstein restates the private language hypothesis first set out in §243, he proceeds by considering 'pseudo-pain', a sensation satisfying the requirements for being spoken about in a private language, and the real kernel of the private language argument is then found in §258 and following sections (Kenny, 1971, p. 216). Kenny also argued that Wittgenstein presents three arguments against any proposed private language, each of which is more or less strongly associated with a key section, §§258, 265 and 270, respectively. The same structure was recognized by Hacker, but he regarded §§246–55 as mainly concerned with the consequences of the definition in §243 (Hacker, 1972, p. 222). Such an exegesis made possible a more systematic approach to Wittgenstein's argumentation than had been identified earlier on, and gave the argument a clear focus that had been implicit at best since Malcolm's review of *Philosophical Investigations* in 1954.[3] Another novelty was the separation of the argumentation belonging to these sections. Thus these new interpretations communicated the picture of Wittgenstein's argumentation as a thorough examination, considering the issue from different angles and blocking the escape routes for a proponent of a private language. It presented a picture of Wittgenstein proceeding systematically.

Malcolm's Reductio Argument, by contrast, is not a resume or explication of an argument Wittgenstein had given in *Philosophical Investigations*, but is better described as a recollection of certain assumptions which are criticized by Wittgenstein. It was unclear from which sections Malcolm derived his premises, but §258 and §265 are quoted during the presentation of the argument, and they were no doubt regarded as crucial by Malcolm (Malcolm, 1954, p. 532). Kenny argued that these sections discuss independent proposals.

The argument Kenny described condensed into §258. However, the details which supposedly freed this argument from verificationist assumptions were by no means easy to make out. Consider Charles Marks's account of Kenny's interpretation, given in 1975 (Marks, 1975, p. 151–2). A diarist fixes his attention on a particular sensation and decides to call sensations like this '*S*'. Some time later, the diarist classifies a sensation as *S*. We enquire what is meant by '*S*'. The diarist might say, 'By "*S*" I mean *this*', while gesturing towards his current sensation. Now Marks quotes Kenny's rebuttal of such an attempted identification: '"This is *S*" is not a genuine proposition capable of being true or false; for what gives it its content is the very same thing as gives it its truth: the significance of the predicate is supposed to be settled by the reference of the subject' (Kenny, 1971, p. 219). So appealing to his current sensations would not help the private language speaker confer meaning on '*S*'.

For Marks, Kenny's argument could only be sustained by relying on some version of verificationism. Kenny's claim that 'This is "*S*"' could not be false was denied by

---

Marks, because he failed to see that it was an ostensive definition *introducing* a term into a language (Marks, 1975, p. 154). Had it been such an ostensive definition, it might well have been incapable of falsity, but since it was uttered *after* the original introduction, Marks thought the predication might very well be false:

> The present argument will work only if one assumes that the private language speaker's earlier ostensive definition did not introduce '*S*' into the language and that his reminder of what '*S*' means must, contrary to his intention, itself introduce '*S*' into his private language. Both of these assumptions are question begging. (Marks, 1975, p. 154)

One could, perhaps, preserve the lack of falsity for a non-introducing ostensive definition on the basis that the private language speaker could not know when his self-scribing statements involving 'S' were false, but such an argument would seem to depend on the verification principle (Marks, 1975, p. 165). Marks's point here was that Kenny's only valid argument would have to be construed along the following simple lines: since the claim 'This is "*S*"' cannot be verified, it is meaningless and so incapable of falsity. From this he concluded that Kenny had not managed to show that Wittgenstein's argumentation was free of reliance on the verification principle.

Marks's interpretation of Kenny was coherent in the sense that the verification principle could indeed yield an argument against a private language, but he had misunderstood Kenny's emphasis on ostensive definitions.

Kenny was best interpreted as making the assumption Marks characterizes as question-begging in the passage quoted above. Kenny had opened his article with a section on ostensive definitions, stressing a point Wittgenstein makes early in the Blue Book and again in *Philosophical Investigations* §§27–35: ostensive definitions presuppose an understanding of the role in language of the word which is supposed to be defined.[4] Kenny's argument here referred back to *The Blue and Brown Books* (pp. 16–17). Suppose I wish to explain to you the meaning of the word 'Toff'.[5] I do this by pronouncing the word while pointing towards a pencil. To catch on, you need to know in advance whether I intend the word to refer the pencil itself, its colour, its size, and so on. In other words, you need to know the place in language the word occupies. So ostensive definitions cannot be fundamental, or primary, when it comes to teaching and understanding intersubjective language. Against this, the proponent of a private language might hold that he can use a private analogue of the training that makes a public language possible. It is this possibility that is ruled out in §§243–315. As Kenny says:

> What the later discussion does, in effect, is to show that in the case of the private ostensive definition there *cannot* be any analogue of the background which is necessary if public ostensive definition is to convey meaning. (Kenny, 1971, p. 207)

Whether he begged the question or not, Kenny had argued '... that the private language speaker's earlier ostensive definition did not introduce "*S*" into the language'. The

---

[4]   Kenny (1971), pp. 206–7. Kenny does not seem to have distinguished the Wittgenstein of *Philosophical Investigations* from that in the Blue Book.

[5]   Wittgenstein used 'Toff' as example here.

soundness of the contrary assumption was something that Marks had paid only cursory attention to.

According to Kenny, Wittgenstein's consideration, in §258, of the problem of endowing a predicate, '*S*', with a private meaning can be summarized as follows. We are to suppose that I want to keep a diary about the occurrence of a certain sensation. In fact the word 'sensation' is misplaced here, as Wittgenstein points out in §261. We cannot allow a word in a private language to be given a descriptive definition via words from our public language – i.e. the language in which 'sensation' belongs – without dismantling its privacy. Given that no descriptive definition can be involved, we are left with ostensive definitions; so, with an ostensive purpose, I concentrate my attention on the sensation and at the same time write '*S*' in my diary. To refute the idea that this ceremony could in any way confer meaning on '*S*', Kenny imagined the situation later on, when I claim to recognize a sensation as S, saying aloud 'This is "S" again'. What reply could I make to the question 'What do you mean by "S"?'. The answer, and its refutation (which Kenny associated with §258), appears in the following passage, part of which has already been quoted in connection with Marks's discussion:

> If the private language speaker says 'By "S" I mean *this*', gesturing, as it were, to his current sensation, then it is clear that 'This is S' is not a genuine proposition capable of being true or false; for what gives it its content is the very same thing as gives it its truth: the significance of the predicate is supposed to be settled by the reference of the subject. 'Whatever is going to seem right to me is right', therefore; and 'that only means we can't talk about "right"' (*Inv.* 258). (Kenny, 1971, p. 219)

Marks seems to have either overlooked or disregarded Kenny's view, expressed here, that 'This is "S" again' is analytic and therefore incapable of being true or false (Kenny, 1971, p. 221). In the sentence the word 'this' is defined with reference to 'S' and vice versa. It follows that the original private ostensive definition did not introduce 'S' into the language. The verification principle was not invoked for the simple reason that there was no earlier meaning-giving act to verify.

Peter Hacker published a similar interpretation of §258 shortly after Kenny (Hacker, 1972, p. 235). The naturalness with which ostensive definitions are employed in our ordinary explanations creates the illusion that they can, of themselves, provide all the necessary means of concept-acquisition: 'Hence we are under the illusion that one could always "pick out" the sensation pain from one's stream of consciousness and name it. But "picking out" already presupposes that we possess the concept and so cannot serve to explain our acquisition of it.' (Hacker, 1972, p. 235). So to explain one's understanding of a concept by invoking ostension is to presuppose a frame of reference, not to provide it.

According to Kenny and Hacker, the imaginary proponent of a private language could still maintain that the private situation provides means of establishing a criterion of correctness analogous to public ones. To cover all the possibilities, Wittgenstein had not ended his argumentation in §258. Unlike Malcolm, Kenny and Hacker who saw §265 as dealing with a proposal that had not been considered in §258. Hacker's characterization was the most explicit one: where §258 had dealt mainly with concept acquisition, §265 dealt with *possession* of a concept. His explanation of why concept possession was not possible followed the ideas presented in §265: 'For a private linguist, as we have seen, possessing a concept is akin to having a mental filing cabinet in which exemplars are correlated with labels. This functions as a mental dictionary, providing a subjective justification for the use of a word' (Hacker, 1972, p. 236). The guiding idea here is that the use of a word 'S' is correct, when its denotation shares certain relevant features with the memory sample associated with 'S'. When the private language speaker is in doubt about whether a word is being used correctly, he can produce the memory-sample and make the necessary comparison. Hacker argued that such an attempt to establish a sense of correctness would not work, but his arguments had striking affinities with the argument shown by Thomson to depend on verificationism and memory scepticism. For instance, the checking procedure could not work because:

> The memory mechanism must produce the right memory correlation. But not only is it impossible for the private linguist to distinguish a correct sign-exemplar correlation, but, given the privacy of the exemplar, it is impossible in principle to distinguish a correct from an incorrect correlation. (Hacker, 1972, p. 236)

Hacker appeared to assume that, at some point in the future, a Wittgensteinian theory of meaning without verificationist elements would be available to support this kind of argument. He thought, presumably, that criteria would be crucial in this endeavour; but until the position was fully set out, some form of covert verificationism was bound to be suspected.

Marks took Kenny's interpretation of §265 to be similarly vulnerable. He claimed that '...verificationism is avoided only by the assumption of epistemic principles which either beg the question or entail scepticism about memory' (Marks, 1975, p. 151). Kenny, on the other hand, clearly thought that his analysis of Wittgenstein avoided such questionable assumptions. He denied that verificationism was in play (Kenny, 1971, p. 221), and he also rejected the notion that his case relied on memory scepticism. He acknowledged that verificationist and memory-sceptical interpretations were prevalent among critics of arguments against private language; and he noted that these critics might have been encouraged by advice Wittgenstein had given in Part II of *Philosophical Investigations*: 'Always get rid of the idea of the private object in this way: assume that it constantly changes but that you do not notice the change because your memory constantly deceives you' (Wittgenstein, 1953, p. 207). But he claimed that a misunderstanding was involved here (Kenny, 1971, p. 217). Kenny's claims turned out to be right, but this would have been very hard to see in the climate of the time.

Kenny imagined the situation in which the private language speaker, some time after framing his ostensive definition, claims of a sensation that it is S. What can he say, now, when asked: 'What do you mean by "S"?' In §258 the case was considered in which he utters 'By "S" I mean *this*', while gesturing to his current sensation. In §265 an alternative possibility is considered. Marks presents this alternative by suggesting that the private language speaker might say that

> (1) ... by 'S' he means 'sensations' of the same kind as the one involved in his original ostensive definition. (Marks, 1975, p. 152)

Kenny sets the answer out slightly differently:

(2) ... by 'S' I mean the sensation I named 'S' in the past. (Kenny, 1971, p. 219)

The difference in wording is important. In (1) the original ostensive definition points to a sensation, an S-exemplar, and subsequent uses of 'S' correlate with this exemplar through memory; an excellent memory will ensure that each time the private language speaker is asked about the meaning of 'S' the S-exemplar will come into his mind.

In (2) the original ostensive definition is not a success, the necessary background not having been provided, and this means that, in fact, no sensation was named 'S' in the past. So 'S' cannot be correlated with an S-exemplar as it is in (1). All that is left is the memory of a sensation that was at some point in the past named 'S'. It is vital to notice that there is no inconsistency here: it is perfectly possible to maintain that in the original ostensive definition no sensation was named 'S' *and* at the same time hold that there is a memory of a sensation that was named 'S' in the past.[6] In Kenny's argument, it is the latter of these which is correlated with 'S'. It is just this proposal that Kenny sees Wittgenstein as arguing against in §265.

Some doubt might remain about whether this is an accurate account of Kenny's argument. However, apart from his remarks about memory-scepticism, ostensive definitions, and the purpose of the sections on private language, the account is supported by at least two other remarks Kenny makes. First, he explains that the correlated objects are memory-samples of private objects, not exemplars:

> We are supposing that I wish to justify my calling a private sensation 'S' by appealing to a mental table in which memory-samples of private objects of various kinds are listed in correlation with symbols. (Kenny, 1971, p. 218)

Secondly, immediately after this he points out that there is just the memory, or, as he calls it here imagination, and not anything which it is a memory or an imagination *of*:

> But as this table exists only in the imagination, there can be no real looking up to see which sample goes with 'S', i.e. remembering what 'S' means. (Kenny, 1971, p. 219)

Given this important difference between (1) and (2), it is clear that Marks failed to identify the position against which Kenny was arguing.

Proceeding with the argument we find, in fact, further indications of Marks's misunderstanding. According to him, the question that was problematic for the private speaker was: 'Is it possible that he *misremember* that 'sensation'?' (Marks, 1975,

---

6   Perhaps a graphic representation would be useful here. The correlation in (1) can be represented like this: 'S' → S-exemplar , where a good memory allows the subject to ascertain that the curved arrow is continuous; forgetting the meaning of 'S' would be represented by a discontinuous arrow. Contrast this with the drawing of the correlation in (2): 'S' → memory of a definition of 'S'. Here memory could play the almost same role with regards to the arrow as in (1), but in (1) misremembering could be symbolized by the arrow leading to a T-exemplar, for instance. This option is not available in (2).

p. 152, my emphasis). Accordingly he faces the following dilemma (Marks, 1975, p. 155). If he says that misremembering is *not* possible, then 'S' means whatever memory occurs to him in connection with 'S', and whatever seems right is right – an intolerable situation bearing in mind the final remark of §258. If, on the other hand, he says that it is possible, then he does not know what 'S' means. Acceptance of the second horn of this dilemma could be defended by Marks by appealing to §265 but seemed to rely on memory scepticism.

In Kenny's version the question was: 'Now, is it possible that the *wrong* memory might come at his call?' (Kenny, 1971, p. 219, my emphasis). This generates a dilemma with a slightly different second horn. The first horn is intact: if it is not possible for the wrong memory to come at his call, then 'S' means whatever memory occurs to the private language speaker. Hence we are left with the situation, described in §258, that whatever seems right is right. If, on the other hand, it is possible for him to call up the wrong memory, then the alleged private language speaker does not know what he means. For if he can think that 'S' should be correlated to the memory of the sensation which he named 'T' in the past, he has misunderstood what is involved in correlation with the mental table.

The differences between Kenny's and Marks's arguments are subtle, but they are enough to show that Kenny's argument can be sustained without invoking memory-scepticism or verificationism. In Kenny's argument there is no memory-scepticism in play, because there is nothing for the memory to be about, and hence nothing to forget or misremember. Equally, the argument is not verificationist: there is no question of 'This is "S" again' being meaningless, because the reference of 'S', the memory of the sensation which was named 'S', cannot be known. What the argument does seem to exploit, in order to discard the first horn of the dilemma, is the principle Kenny claimed it did, namely: that a proposition must be capable of truth or falsity (Kenny, 1971, p. 221). If whatever seems right is right, then there is no place for an incorrect use of the word; consequently statements involving the word cannot be false.[7]

In contrast with Malcolm, Kenny did not treat Wittgenstein's argumentation as a straightforward reductio ad absurdum of the idea of a private language. It was not that one deduced from the assumption of a private language that it was not a language (Malcolm, 1954, p. 537); there was not, on this approach, any conceptual inconsistency for the argument to exploit. Rather Kenny took Wittgenstein to be developing a general pattern of thought that shows how attempts to construct a private language might be discarded.

So far we have considered and rejected two attempts to show how such a language might be maintained. We now turn to a third suggestion. In contrast with the other two, this suggestion had already been considered in its essentials in Kenny's 1966 article. Since it utilized similar ideas as the previous suggestions, I will not repeat these: certain premises are taken for granted here. Furthermore, I will not consider Marks's criticism. Although understandable, it is misguided. I shall look only at

---

[7]   Even when it is explicated, this kind of argument is not easily projected on to Hacker's §265 argumentation. I believe that his argument *does* involve verificationism or memory-scepticism, though I will not attempt to justify this claim.

Kenny's argumentation, and at the connection to §293 and §304. Hacker saw this connection and accordingly provided a better interpretation of these sections than the one given by linguistic behaviourists.[8]

We are, then, to consider a similar course of action as in the previous cases up to the point at which we enquire after the meaning of 'S'. We now find the private language speaker giving a new explanation:

> [3] 'S' refers to the private sensation I have found to be correlated with my blood pressure rising.[9]

The immediate attraction of this explanation is that it seems make it possible to misidentify the sensation. This, of course, is necessary if we are to avoid the situation in which whatever seems right is right. The scenario in which the private language speaker has discovered that whenever he has a particular sensation the manometer shows that his blood pressure rises is introduced by Wittgenstein in §270. Kenny's explanation of why Wittgenstein denied that this would exclude a situation in which whatever seems right is right is, however, enigmatic; he sacrificed clarity for compactness.

Suppose, then, that the private language speaker does indeed find a correlation between the private sensation and his blood pressure. How could Wittgenstein deny that a mistake has occurred, when the private language speaker says 'S' and then finds that his blood pressure has not risen? According to Kenny, Wittgenstein did not say this situation was impossible. Instead he denied '... a would-be intermediate step between having the sensation and judging "Now my blood-pressure is rising", a step which would consist in recognizing the sensation as a sensation of a particular kind, and remembering that a sensation of that kind indicated a rise in blood-pressure' (Kenny, 1971, p. 220). This was too succinct for most readers.

To clarify this 'would-be intermediate step', we can begin by referring to the sensation, whose status is in question, as X. Suppose now that the private language speaker experiences X. He must now (1) remember that X is correlated with a rise in blood pressure. Can he misremember here? If he cannot, then X will be defined as the sensation which occurs when his blood pressure rises; but this would conflict with the hypothesis that X is a *private* sensation. Consequently, it must be the case that he can misremember that X is correlated with rise in blood pressure.

Also, however, (2) he must recognize that X is the sensation which he refers to when uttering 'S'. Can he misrecognize or misidentify here? If he cannot, then whatever seems right will be right. So it must be the case that he can fail to recognize that X is referred to by 'S'.

It is (1) and (2) that make up the 'would-be intermediary step' – i.e. both recognizing X as an S and remembering that X is correlated with rise in blood pressure. It is this scenario, appealing to a public phenomenon in order to make misidentification possible, which Kenny calls a mere show: 'Misidentification here would not matter,

---

[8]   See Section 6.4.

[9]   This is based on a suggestion of Kenny's: 'The third possibility is that the private language speaker correlates his use of "S" with a public phenomenon', Kenny (1971), p. 220. Contrast with Marks (1975), p. 152.

provided that I both misidentified the kind of sensation *and* misremembered what kind of sensation indicated the blood-pressure rise' (Kenny, 1971, p. 220).

Kenny's conclusion was that X could only be genuinely misidentified as an S if it stood for the sensation occurring when there is a rise in blood pressure, but that '... if it does, then there is no room for the intermediate step, and "S" is not the name of a private object but a word in a public language' (Kenny, 1971, p. 220). Again one might wonder whether the conclusion might have been more readily understood if it had been presented as a dilemma: *either* the private language speaker cannot misrecognize X as the reference of 'S' (in which case there is no language), *or* he cannot misremember that X is correlate with a blood pressure rise (in which case it is not a private sensation). Kenny concludes that X is not a private sensation.

Neither Marks nor Hacker managed to identify this kind of argument when they considered §270 and Kenny's article. Despite this, Hacker considered the situation in which a man constantly misremembers what the word 'pain' means in his private language although he uses the word in a way that is in keeping with the usual symptoms and presuppositions of pain. In the above account, this possibility arises when the private language speaker constantly both misrecognizes and misremembers in the 'would-be intermediate step'. Remarkably, Hacker interpreted Wittgenstein's rejection of this scenario by referring to the section immediately after §270, but there is absolutely no doubt that this section is a comment on §270:

> Here I would like to say: a wheel that can be turned though nothing else moves with it, is not part of the mechanism. (§271)

So even though Hacker did not recognize the argument in §270, he still managed to arrive, to some extent, at its conclusion.

These approaches of the early 1970s made possible a new understanding of later sections of *Philosophical Investigations*. These sections could only be understood in part, and sporadically, in the linguistic behaviourist's interpretation. Neither Kenny nor Hacker engaged in a systematic treatment, but I will mention Kenny's remarks on §293, the beetle-in-the-box example. These remarks provide a very different understanding from that given by, for example, Pitcher's work in 1964. Both writers believed that the beetle is intended to represent, or symbolize, a sensation such as pain, but Kenny denied that Wittgenstein had in any way accepted the irrelevance of the sensation itself for language. Instead he maintained that Wittgenstein here gave '... one formulation the idea that it is acquaintance which conveys meaning: it is only one's own pain that one is acquainted with, so it is only from one's own case that one knows what pain is' (Kenny, 1971, p. 208). Such an idea is in conflict with views Kenny had shown Wittgenstein to have held on ostensive definitions. Consequently, the claim, closing §293, that if we construe the grammar of the expression of sensation on the model of 'object and designation' the object drops out of consideration as irrelevant and was not meant to be read as a premise in a *modus ponens*,the conclusion being that the sensation itself would play no part in sensation language. Insetead it was part of a *modus tollens* whose conclusion Kenny explains as follows: 'the model of "object and name" which we are to reject is the idea that a speaker understands a name by being acquainted with its bearer.' (Kenny, 1971, p.208)

8.2 The Change of Focus

According to Kenny, Wittgenstein's principal target had been this 'object and name' model of language acquisition, a model representing acquaintance as an essential part of the learning of language:

> ... others may teach us what words mean, but they must do so by putting us in a position where we ourselves can become acquainted with the object which is the meaning of the word to be learnt (*Inv.* 362). (Kenny, 1971, p. 206)

By identifying this model as the target of the argument, Kenny broke with earlier accounts, since these usually followed Malcolm in regarding Cartesianism as the main focus of Wittgenstein's attack. Of course, the 'object and name' model – which I will refer to below as 'Platonism' – had been recognized as problematic even by Malcolm (Malcolm, 1954, pp. 530–1), but Malcolm tended to connect the difficulties with Cartesianism. So, for instance, in his editorial introduction to the book in which Kenny first presented his account O. R. Jones wrote:

> The Cartesian assumes that words for sensations and feelings come to have the meaning they do in much the same way as words for things like chairs and tables acquire meaning. There is just one difference. In the case of sensations and feelings all public features, including the behaviour and observable circumstances of the person who has the sensations or feelings in question, will be irrelevant so far as the meaning of the word is concerned. (Jones (ed.), 1971, p. 15)

What Kenny had done by focusing on the act of introducing words was essentially to lead the discussion away from the philosophy of psychology towards the philosophy of language. He had changed the core application of the argument.

Wittgenstein's case against Platonism, as Kenny interpreted it, did not rest on verificationist assumptions (Kenny, 1971, p. 221). Marks had argued that Kenny could not make a cogent argument without some form of verificationist premise, but he failed to fully appreciate the argumentation Kenny had extracted from *Philosophical Investigations*. The fault here lay to a large extent with Kenny: the logic of his account of the argument was at crucial points very hard to decipher and distinguish from a verificationist account.[10]

Rather than arguing that the content of an initial act of meaning giving could not be tested, Wittgenstein had argued that no initial such act had taken place. A crucial step here is taken in §§27–35 – that is, before Wittgenstein raises questions about the possibility of a private language in §243. In these sections Wittgenstein discusses the idea that the essential procedure for learning what another speaker associates with a word is to encounter the object to which the speaker applies that word while

---

[10] Another work in which Kenny was saddled with verificationism was Candlish (1980); see also Candlish (1998).

hearing the word uttered – the procedure of ostensive definition. Kenny's rejection of this idea consisted in pointing out the multiplicity of connections between word and object that could be generated in this situation: 'But the ostensive definition will not suffice by itself, because it can always be variously interpreted' (Kenny, 1971, p. 206). This argument applied to public as well as private ostensive definitions. Kenny believed, however, that the private language speaker could not be refuted so easily:

> A private language, he might maintain, might be learnt from private sensations not by bare ostension but by some private analogue of training in the use of words. This suggestion shows that the critique of the primacy of ostensive definition does not render superfluous the later explicit discussion of private languages. (Kenny, 1971, p. 207)

But when he turned to §§258ff, Kenny omitted to consider the anticipated comparison with 'the training in the use of words'. There was no appeal to the way in which we actually learn a language. What Kenny in fact did was to consider the following possible reply to §§27–35: 'It might be true that private ostension could not build a bridge between word and the sensation felt, but something did happen and the word was made to stand for something!' According to Kenny, it was this insistence that the private ostension would still have some semantic significance that made discussion of the possibility of a private language necessary. Essentially, then, between Kenny's argument and an argument against private ostension there was only a slight difference in emphasis; but there was still a difference.

The view that in §§243–315 Wittgenstein extends his earlier criticism of *public* ostension to embrace *private* ostension gained wider acceptance during the 1970s. We considered one version of this view when we examined Hacker's analysis of §258 (Hacker, 1972, pp. 234–5). In another commentary, presented in 1978, Dummett referred to the private language argument as '... Wittgenstein's argument against the possibility of a private ostensive definition'. Dummett took this argument to be, as he put it, incontrovertible.[11]

Before 1970, however, this way of viewing matters had been at best implicit in the work of critics and expositors of Wittgenstein's thought. The novelty of Kenny's approach was to zoom in on the ostensive act and ask for its criterion of success. This undermined the earlier tendency to think of ostension as an adequate foundation of meaning – the easy assumption that one could simply point at an object, or some aspect of it, when one was asked for the meaning of a term.

8.3 Overcoming Verificationism

The adoption of Platonism and the privacy of sensations, together with the Cartesian picture, yield a private language. It ensures that it is impossible for me to be acquainted with other people's sensations and for them to be acquainted with my sensations. But privacy is a hallmark of the Cartesian picture of the mind, which

---

[11] Dummett (1978), pp. xxxii–xxxiii; see also Dummett (1978), p. 452. Other advocates of something like this view included Pears (1970), Goldberg (1971), Hallett (1977), Baker (1981), Armstrong (1984) and Baker/Hacker(1984).

had been criticized since the Second World War on both sides of the Atlantic, and so one might think that rejection of Cartesianism would be enough to remove the temptation to accommodate a private language. However, motivated, as it is, by empiricist concerns, Platonism leads to the belief that a private language is primary and the foundation on which our common language is erected. It promotes a picture of words standing for ideas in the mind of the speaker which, as Hacker says, can be found in vivid detail in Locke's *An Essay Concerning Human Understanding* (Hacker, 1972, pp. 224–9).

What is the motivation behind Platonism? There is, on the one hand, the naturalness with which we employ ostensive definitions in ordinary conversation. We do constantly single out objects, or aspects of objects, by pointing to them or, to ourselves, by assiduously directed concentration. This pre-philosophical picture is detectable in the story of Adam's naming the beasts in the garden of Eden. It becomes something like a doctrine in the Augustinian view of language that Wittgenstein describes in the opening paragraphs of *Philosophical Investigations*.

There is, however, a deeper intuition behind Platonism, one with a more theoretical origin. It is the intuition that we, in philosophy, are required to identify a foundation on which epistemological enquiries, systematized in empirical science, can proceed; and that since justifications ultimately run towards what is observed, it is here, in observation, that the foundation should be located. This epistemological impetus, which ultimately leads down to private language, might even be said to possess a certain primacy compared to the one proceeding from the Cartesian mind. In the *Meditations* it is the search for certainty that leads Descartes to cogitatio.

Moving forwards in history, we can see that it was the 'epistemic order of objects' that guided Carnap's insistence on a solipsist foundation in *The Logical Structure of the World* in 1928 and on the unrevisability of *The Unity of Science*'s protocol language. Ideally, the construction ensures that a knowledge claim cannot be justified unless it is conceptually tied to what is given in observation. At the same time, the construction provides an explanation of how language connects to the world. This is the empiricist motivation for adopting Platonist semantics.[12] Underlying the threat posed by privacy that Carnap faced in 1932 was the Platonist semantics of words being tied to observed 'entities'.

It can be seen, then that there is a deep intuition that the vantage point, and the ultimate basis, of our knowledge about the world must also be the ultimate basis of the meaning of our words, the starting place for meaning.

The demonstration of the inadequacy of private ostension had implications that were at once profound and far-reaching. Crucially, it undermined the traditional Platonist conception of language as a mirror of reality established by a mental act of association. This rejection of Platonism has an immediate impact on the

---

[12]   Compare McDowell (1994), p. 6: 'We could not begin to suppose that we understood how pointing to a bit of Given could justify the use of a concept in judgement – could, at the limit, display the judgement as knowledgeable – unless we took this possibility of warrant to be constitutive of the concept's being what it is, and hence constitutive of its contribution to any thinkable content it figures in, whether that of a knowledgeable, or less substantially justifiable, judgement or any other'.

argumentation in Thomson's construal of the Reductio Argument. There, the verification requirement (the third premise) is treated as an extra requirement on top of what is in fact a Platonist construal: the private association between sign and sensation is rejected, not because it is incapable of connecting them, but because the private situation cannot provide an effective check that there is constancy in the employment of the relevant terms. Understanding, here, is modelled as knowledge of the initial situation, and knowledge requires justification. The tendency to equate understanding and knowledge of meaning is unfortunate, because it motivates the Platonist picture of meaning as some kind of entity of which it is possible to have knowledge.

Plainly, the rejection of private ostensive definition in Kenny's account avoids verificationism. More than this, however, it queries the service into which Thomson presses verificationism in her version of the Reductio Argument. Rather than relying on the verification principle, the later argument is a criticism of the deeply felt intuition which it expresses.

Nevertheless, it was alleged that a form of verificationism had been employed in Kenny's argumentation. It is indeed hard to deny that Kenny's formulations involved ambiguities that made it possible to interpret them that way, but as the examination of his arguments above has shown, there was a subtle difference.

Instead of holding that the truth or falsity of an empirical statement at least needs to be within the reach of possible verification, Kenny had embraced the principle that a proposition needs to be capable of both truth and falsity. He called this the Bipolarity of Propositions (Kenny, 1971, p. 221). Why was this not satisfied in cases like 'This is E'?[13] The answer is: because '... what is supposed to give it its content is the same as what is supposed to give it its truth' (Kenny, 1971, p. 221). The private language speaker had used the very same statement to describe the meaning of 'E' and to speak about the state of the world, and this could not be done.

Apparently Kenny thought the argument would be more convincing if it rested simply on the idea that whatever gives a sentence its truth cannot at the same time give its content. However, his argumentation actually involved an ingenious employment of the Wittgensteinian distinction between empirical statements, explaining the way in which the world is furnished, and grammatical statements, explaining the meaning of words. In the example given in §258, 'This is E' needs to function as an empirical and grammatical proposition at the same time, and as a consequence it can do neither. In connection with a grammatical proposition, explaining the meaning of 'E', we need an independent account of what *this* is; otherwise the sentence becomes incapable of being false. But since this can only be given by repeating the sentence (saying something about what is present), the sentence must be an empirical statement; and if it is an empirical sentence, we can only evaluate whether it is true or false by having an independent account of what 'E' means. Alas, this can only be given by saying 'This is E'. On neither construal, then, was 'This is E' capable of being false. This was why Kenny called it analytical.

Of course, this argument requires us to assume that statements of each category, empirical and grammatical, are capable of being false. Implicitly, Kenny made this

---

[13] This was the explanation Kenny had discussed in connection with §258.

assumption. He said that statements in both categories were propositions (Kenny, 1971, p. 213). He also linked propositions with a capacity for falsity: 'A proposition must contain the possibility of its truth, but *no more than* its possibility: hence there are no such things as analytic propositions ...' (Kenny, 1971, p. 221).

In this way Kenny distanced Wittgenstein's ideas from a mistaken reliance on the analytic-synthetic distinction. The thought that statements of logic and mathematics, together with statements that spell out meaning relations, are *analytic* in the sense of being true purely in virtue of their meaning, and the connected thoughts that it is senselessness to suppose that they are false, and that they provide no information about the world, were avoided. This distinction had been severely criticized by Quine in the early 1950s (Quine, 1951), and the criticism had become widely accepted.[14]

Kenny did not explain his understanding of the empirical-grammatical distinction. It is clear, however, that there were ways in which the two distinctions – analytic-synthetic and empirical-grammatical – diverged. Where analytical statements explaining the meaning of terms hold true in virtue of meaning alone, Kenny seemed to think that grammatical statements might be thought of merely as second-order descriptions of the use we make of the relevant expressions. As such they would be false if they failed to describe this use correctly. Secondly, analytical statements had the form of equivalences, whereas grammatical statements were allowed a much wider significance. For instance, the sentence 'I know when I am in pain' was held to be grammatical statement explaining the use of first-person pain ascriptions.

These differences meant that the empirical-grammatical distinction would not be directly vulnerable to Quine's criticism. Hence it was capable of supporting Kenny's arguments without relying openly on verificationism; but even so, the argument against private ostension still stands.

8.4 The New Role of Language in Philosophy

Kenny's attack on private ostensive definition removed the verificationist label from Wittgenstein's argument. Not only did he decouple Wittgenstein's case against private language and the verificationist outlook, but, at the same time, he turned the case into a criticism of verificationism. Underlying this advance was the fact that Kenny's account was more powerfully focused on the basic requirements of language than before. To recapitulate, the mistake about language he wanted to expose was '... the belief that words can acquire meaning by bare ostensive definition' (Kenny, 1971, p. 205). Before passing on to the problems inherited by philosophical theories in which this mistake is made, I will briefly indicate how radical this result is in contrast with previous efforts.

Apart from work dealing with Wittgenstein's private struggles in the 1930s, discussion of privacy has been largely located within two streams of philosophical enquiry. Both found inspiration in Wittgenstein's writings – one in the *Tractatus*, the other in *Philosophical Investigations*. Philosophers representing both the Vienna Circle and ordinary language philosophy had pronounced that investigating language

---

[14]   See, for example, Hacker (1996b), p. 265, and Burge (1992), p. 6.

would be a cardinal task of philosophy. In this sense, both assigned language a primary role within philosophy. The result, however, of this assignment, as can be seen in the privacy discussions examined in the chapters above, was not so much an interest in the mechanisms of language, and the general principles underlying it, but rather that language became a tool for deriving results in other areas. Language was, for the most part, a means and not an end.

In the Vienna Circle the focus on language was motivated by a recognition that knowledge claims in science had to be intersubjectively communicable and thus expressible in language. Likewise, Cook, in 1965, displayed little interest in the question of how sensation terms refer. His study of sensation language was a means to achieve a better understanding of the nature of psychological phenomena. Advocates of both approaches regarded the study of language as a way of disarming metaphysical theories like Cartesianism. In contrast with this, Kenny argued that the case against private language could deliver results, not about an area of discourse, but about the medium – about language itself.

It is worth considering whether Kenny's argumentation could have been developed within the above frameworks. The verificationism originating in Carnap's philosophy was one of Kenny's targets. Hence the positivist framework was not one in which the verificationist version of the private language argument would readily be replaced with a verificationism-free argument against private ostensive definitions. From the perspective of the ordinary language philosopher, however, it was possible to accommodate Kenny's results more readily. Thus, for instance, the interpretation of §§243–315 provided by E. von Savigny in a book explicitly characterizing Wittgenstein as an ordinary language philosopher involves essentially the same points as Kenny had made (von Savigny, 1969, pp. 54–9). But by the early 1970s ordinary language philosophy of the kind presented above in previous chapters had lost its impetus. The 1972 book in which Cook's article 'Solipsism and Language' appeared, *Wittgenstein: Philosophy and Language* (Ambrose & Lazerowitz (eds), 1972), was one of the last to, in effect, represent the 'school'.

Part of the reason for this decline was the conception of language that was inherent in ordinary language philosophy and so crucial a part of its methodology. That conception could not serve as foundation for a vibrant and serious philosophy of language as its tasks were being formulated in the 1970s. In a programmatic article published in 1976, Michael Dummett queried several aspects of the 'ordinary language is all right' view of language. One criticism he made was that the strategy of ordinary language philosophers of approaching and explaining the uses of sentences one by one failed to take in account the interconnectedness of sentences. He remarked that the ordinary language approach '…would fit a code of signals, the significance of each of which has to be learned separately, but not a language' (Dummett, 1975, p. 444). Instead of trying to understand the competence of a language user, advocates of the ordinary language method virtually took it for granted. Secondly, and more importantly, they failed to distinguish contextual from literal meaning:

> Anyone not in the grip of a theory, asked to explain the meaning of a sentence like ... 'I know I am here', would be disposed to begin by distinguishing what the sentence literally said from what, in particular circumstances, someone might seek to convey by uttering

it; but, from the standpoint of the orthodox 'ordinary language' doctrine, only the latter notion was legitimate – *it* was what constituted the 'use' of the sentence ...' (Dummett, 1975, p. 445)

The standpoint from which these criticisms were made was one according to which the cardinal task of philosophy of language was to develop a 'general account of language', one clarifying '... those principles, regulating our use of language, which we already implicitly grasp' (Dummett, 1975, p. 442). In particular, what came to be known as 'the creative power of language' – i.e. the ability to generate, from a finite set of words, a potentially infinite number of distinct sentences – needed to be explained. Given these aims, ordinary language philosophy, which seemed to conceive of language as a set of loosely connected language games, was no foundation to build from. It would have to be abandoned.

So the philosophical frameworks which, until the 1970s, had accommodated the private language argument were gradually and inevitably replaced, and with this evolution Wittgenstein came to occupy a less central role. However, although the argument against private ostensive definitions was strongly associated with Wittgenstein's name, as had been all 'private language arguments' since 1953, the waning of Wittgenstein's influence did not make the argument obsolete. In some circle's, it is true, questions about the possibility of private language became less relevant. Thus, for example, following Quine's attack on Carnap's 'Philosophy as the Logic of Science' in his 1951 article 'Two Dogmas of Empiricism', the view that philosophy is continuous with science – a view that almost in its essence located the possibilities of a private language outside its confines – had become dominant in the United States. This notwithstanding, however, the privacy issue remained both alive and controversial. In holding private ostension to be impossible, one seemed to concede the accuracy of a logical or linguistic behaviourist account of sensations. Did acceptance of the argument not involve the sacrifice of the idea that what ultimately decides the status of pain ascriptions is the pain itself?

It was probably these worries that lay underneath Strawson's claim that:

> It *is* part of what is now fashionable to call our general *theory* of the world that we regard other people as subject to roughly the same range of sensations as we are painfully or joyously or indifferently aware of in ourselves; and it is in no way contrary to reason to regard ourselves – as in any case we cannot help doing – as justified in certain circumstances in ascribing to John a particular state of feeling which we cannot in the nature of the case experience ourselves, and his being in which is therefore, if such is the standard invoked, necessarily verification-transcendent. (Strawson, 1976, p. 19)

Two frameworks in which the argument against private ostension figured in the 1970s are threatened by Strawson's dismissive comment. One is the debate that Strawson had talked about: the question whether, in a general theory of meaning, sentence-meaning should be construed *anti-realistically* in terms of assertibility conditions or *realistically* in terms of truth conditions. Strawson argued that the very nature of sensations demanded a realist account of sensation language employing truth conditions; without that, he said, the intelligibility of the discourse could not be preserved. In his reply, Dummett swiftly refers to Wittgenstein's argument:

Strawson here unblushingly rejects that whole polemic of Wittgenstein's that has come to be known as 'the private-language argument'. On Strawson's view, I know what 'pain' means from my own case: ... it is I who then invested the word with the meaning that it henceforth had in my language by means of a private ostensive definition, saying to myself, 'It is *this* that the word "pain" stands for'...
Strawson contents that this view is 'part of what is now fashionable to call our 'general *theory* of the world'. If this is so, it is only in a sense in which 'our' general theory of the world does not have to be true, and there is no compulsion to believe it. (Dummett, 1978, pp. xxxii–xxxiii)

In this debate between the anti-realist and the realist – in, that is to say, these attempts to understand the relations between assertibility, meaning and truth – the private language argument was claimed by the anti-realists. It would, however, become very much more than an ally, or support, when a new debate about rule-following began to emerge in earnest in the 1970s and 1980s. This debate is examined in the Chapter 9.

Wittgenstein's private language argument also played a role in the continuing attempt to build a theory of language incorporating the notion of a 'criterion'. Criteria had been discussed a great deal in connection with privacy since the publication of Malcolm's 1958 article. Roger Buck, for instance, in spite of his heavy criticism of Malcolm, regarded the notion of a criterion as fundamental:

If I am talking, using a language, there must be criteria for the words I use. This is the nature of words, language. If I can't use a word wrongly, misidentify something, then there is no point in claiming to have identified it rightly. (Buck, 1962, p. 190)

In this approach criteria are a feature of language in general. The impossibility of a private language is shown by applying the notion of a criterion to a particular area of discourse, subjecting it to general constraints on language. It emerges that private language is impossible because 'There are here *no criteria* which can explain getting it right or wrong, and as right or wrong turn out to be without sense, so does the idea of identification (or misidentification) of inner experiences' (Buck, 1962, p. 190).

It was insights of this kind that fostered the hope, in the 1960s, that a systematic theory of language could be founded on the criterial relation, and the model for the construal was conceived as being the relation between sensations and their expression. Wittgenstein's well-known §580 aperçu – 'An "inner process" stands in need of outward criteria' – was often cited in this connection.

In the early 1970s the criterial doctrine was connected with anti-realist semantics by writers such as Hacker.[15] I shall not describe this development, although it is worth mentioning in passing that frequent reference was made, by those who pursued it, to *Philosophical Investigations* §§243–315. As a putative solution to the problem that had bothered Strawson, the criterial view – the belief, that is to say, that meaning should be ultimately explained with reference to criteria – had a relatively short life. Some of the more genuinely Wittgensteinian criterial proposals that appeared during this short period will be touched upon in Chapter 10.

---

[15] Hacker (1972), p. 302. Other writers making the connection were Baker (1974) and Wright (1978).

Chapter 9

The Rule-following Considerations

It is fair to say that Kenny's interpretation of the private language argument, described in the previous chapter, was not generally adopted in the 1970s. Marks's interpretation came closer to capturing what most writers at this time took to be Wittgenstein's argument. The picture of §§243–315 which nonetheless began to form in the early 1970s was one of an argument freed of dependence on verificationism and memory-scepticism.[1] Two insights into the private language argument are prominent here; and both attach significance to points made in *Philosophical Investigations* made before §243.

One insight has already been considered, since it was itself an essential component in Kenny's interpretation: the idea that ostensive definition is not the ultimate bridge between language and reality. Kenny's point had been that if private ostension is the only means of constructing a private language, then its possibility is shown to be impossible by §§27–35 and §§243ff combined. The second insight took the notion of rule-following to be the central issue in *Philosophical Investigations* and the discussion of the possibility of a private language to be secondary. The latter discussion was regarded in the context of this insight merely as a part – albeit a hugely important one – of a general critique of meaning. The main exponent here was Saul A. Kripke, whose account appeared in print in his *Wittgenstein on Rules and Private Language* in 1982 but had been widely known since it was first presented at a conference in London, Ontario, in 1976.[2] According to Kripke 'the private language argument' was '... principally to be explicated in terms of the problem of "following a rule"' (Kripke, 1982, p. vii), the discussion of which was located in *Philosophical Investigations* in sections leading up to §202, where the possibility of private rule-following is denied. It is this approach, and in particular Kripke's pursuit of it, that I shall focus on in this chapter, since it was extremely influential in the early 1980s and continues to be so. Again, as always, one is tempted to say that *Philosophical Investigations* was the source from which new vigour entered discussions about the possibility a private language.

---

[1]   However, McGinn (1984), p. 48, and Craig (1982) take Wittgenstein's arguments to rely on a verificationist approach. Wright (1980), p. 29, also sticks with this interpretation.

[2]   See Kripke (1982). Kripke had in fact published his views a year earlier in an article in Block (ed.) (1981), but Kripke (1982) offers a fuller treatment of the issues. As an indication of the extent to which Kripke's views were known in the late 1970s, it might be pointed out that Holtzman and Leich (eds) (1981), which appeared in 1981, is a compilation of papers presented at a symposium discussing, among other things, Kripke's views. In 1976 Kripke remarked that he had had many of his ideas on Wittgenstein and rule-following for more than a decade: see Cavell (1979), p. xvi.

The end of Chapter 8 described general changes in the early 1970s in the way in which questions about language entered philosophical discussion; philosophers essentially became more concerned with the nature of language than they had been before. This new approach formed the context of the rule-following debate. There was, however, another transition at some point in the 1970s, a transition in which Kripke's and Kenny's interpretations of Wittgenstein were involved. Kenny and Kripke both took §243ff to be closely tied to other parts of *Philosophical Investigations*, and this became the general attitude towards *Philosophical Investigations* and §243ff. In essence, the assumption was that there are some general ideas flowing through the whole book. Not only did this make the discussion of Wittgenstein's view of private language more comprehensive, in so far as his ideas were now being located before §243, but it also became important to say what role one held §243 to play in the advocacy of these general ideas, and how one conceived the book's overall structure.

Simplifying matters somewhat, one might characterize the situation before 1970 as one in which *Philosophical Investigations* was more or less understood as being a compilation of loosely connected, but fundamentally self-contained discussions, one of these being the discussion of a private language. The unifying factor, if there was one, was the method employed in all these discussions – a method whose description was concentrated around §§124–8, which contained remarks on philosophy as therapy. This approach seemed appropriate given that Wittgenstein had, in his preface, characterized the book as a collection of 'sketches of landscapes … made in the course of … long and involved journeyings' (Wittgenstein, 1953, p. vii). Hallet's companion to *Philosophical Investigations*, which appeared as late as 1977, is a qualified case of the 'sketches' approach. He compares the composition of *Philosophical Investigations* to maps, and philosophy to city centres:

> Now were the city laid out like central Manhattan, an orderly description in general terms would be possible. But how would one describe the center of London or Rome? Could anything systematic or coherent result? Would there be chapters? A solution I have seen is a book of aerial photos, so arranged that the overlapping and continuity could be noticed as one passed from page to page, though the series sometimes broke off so as to take up again at a different point in the city or come back over the same terrain from a different direction. Such is the plan Wittgenstein adopted in the first part of the *Investigations* and in individual sections of Part Two, and the sort of discontinuity he sometimes found forced upon him. (Hallett, 1977, p. 45)[3]

In effect, the new approaches of the late 1970s denied this kind of discontinuity and claimed that Wittgenstein had been much more strategic in building up his argumentation. At once, this made it necessary to consider the relation of §243ff to the discussion about rule-following which preceded it.

Among the leading opponents of Kripke's interpretation of Wittgenstein on rule-following were Peter Hacker and Gordon Baker, who had together launched a major exegesis of Wittgenstein's *Nachlass* in order to uncover Wittgenstein's intentions

---

[3]   See also Fogelin (1976), p. 95; compare §203.

in *Philosophical Investigations*.[4] However, on the issue of the relationship between Wittgenstein's discussions of rule-following and private language, Gordon Baker, taking §243ff to be concerned with private ostensive definition, seemed in 1981 to agree to an extent with Kripke: 'That argument [against the possibility of a private language], far from being an autonomous critical theory, is an application of certain morals drawn from considerations of rules and rule-following to a particularly educative realization of the Augustinian picture' (Baker, 1981, pp. 43–4). However, Baker could not bring himself to say that §243ff did not ventilate any essentially new results. This was Kripke's conclusion:

> In my view, the real 'private language argument' is to be found in the sections *preceding* §243. Indeed, in §202 *the conclusion is already stated explicitly*: "Hence it is not possible to obey a rule 'privately': otherwise thinking one was obeying a rule would be the same thing as obeying it." I do not think that Wittgenstein here thought himself as *anticipating* an argument he was to give in detail later. (Kripke, 1982, p. 3)

Consequently for Kripke §243ff was a special case of more general considerations to be found in the sections discussing rules and rule-following. In Kripke's view, these considerations constituted '... perhaps the central problem of *Philosophical Investigations*.'[5] Against this, Baker and Hacker used their expert knowledge of Wittgenstein's *Nachlass* to show that in the original manuscript from which Wittgenstein retrieved §202, the relevant passage occurs *after* the exposition of the private language argument.[6] Additionally, they pointed out that §§201–3, which Kripke considered the pivotal point of the book, had not even been included in the intermediate version of *Philosophical Investigations* Wittgenstein had prepared (Baker and Hacker, 1984, p. 11). Exegetically then, at any rate, if the point of the exegesis is to elucidate Wittgenstein's intentions, Kripke's claim was dubious.

---

[4] Their analytical commentary, which deals only with the first part of *Philosophical Investigations*, comprised four volumes: Baker and Hacker (1980), Baker and Hacker (1985), Hacker (1990) and Hacker (1996a).

[5] Kripke (1982), p. 7. A word about terminology might be appropriate here. I have previously referred to §243–315 as the interval traditionally viewed as containing Wittgenstein's remarks on private language, and I will stick to that. The writers I discuss here, however, mostly leave out the right delimiter and refer simply to §§243ff. When I present and discuss these views I will adopt this notation. Furthermore, a tendency to speak of 'the private language argument' without qualification emerges in the work I shall be discussing. Usually this label refers to Wittgenstein's argumentation in §§243ff, and it is implicitly assumed that the interpretation of these paragraphs is more or less fixed. This can be seen repeatedly in McDowell (1984), for example. I will also adopt this terminology in so far as I think it unlikely that the context permits ambiguity. Thus, when I speak of 'the private language argument' I shall be referring to Wittgenstein's argumentation in §§243ff, whatever it might be. By contrast, when I speak of 'the rule-following considerations' I shall be referring to the main line of thought in §§143–242, whatever that might be. Finally, when I discuss particular interpretations of Wittgenstein's argumentation against private language, I shall either use italics or mention the name and article in which the argumentation is found.

[6] Baker and Hacker (1984), p. 21. The relevant manuscript was MS 129 (in G. H. von Wright's indexation), which is reprinted in Wittgenstein (1993), pp. 480–507.

Kripke did have some reservations about attributing the entirety of his argument and conclusion to Wittgenstein, and he explicitly disavowed any aim of providing a detailed exegesis of Wittgenstein's text (Kripke, 1982, p. 2). He claimed to be dealing with the sections in the interval §§143–242, but he focused on the sections preceding §§201–2 because his conclusion was stated here. Because of this, his interpretation of the 40 sections occupying §§202–242 in terms of the rule-following considerations was somewhat unclear, as was his handling of the transition to the discussion of private language. Perhaps in anticipation of exegetical criticism, he remarked that he had concentrated on the logic of the argument; he remarked that the most appropriate way to think of the argument might be as 'Wittgenstein's argument as it struck Kripke' (Kripke, 1982, p. 5). Below, I will often simplify matters and say, or imply, that Kripke advocated the considerations being examined. It should borne in mind throughout, however, that Kripke in fact denied that he was presenting his own views (Kripke, 1982, p. 5).

9.1 The Problem of Following a Rule

The bearing of Kripke's argument on the possibility of a private language is rather indirect, since his argument has considerably wider scope: in the argument, a sceptical paradox concerning understanding gives rise to a sceptical solution, which happens to rule out the possibility of a private language. The sceptical conclusion or paradox to which Kripke saw Wittgenstein's thoughts leading was a radical one:

> ... there is no fact about me that distinguishes between my meaning a definite function by 'plus' (which determines my responses in new cases) and my meaning nothing at all. (Kripke, 1982, p. 21)

This conclusion was, of course, meant to apply *universally* to ascriptions of meaning, not just to the particular word 'plus' or to mathematical discourse. Accordingly, it would have implications for the private language problem.

In order to derive such a conclusion about meaning from considerations about rules, Kripke made use of an analogy between rules and meaning – an analogy which had been used by Malcolm in 1954 and which derived ultimately from Wittgenstein. Roughly, the analogy was that the mechanism that makes the addition rule determine a correct result when one is computing sums is comparable to the way in which the meanings of words determine particular uses.[7] The identification of the content of one's understanding of a word with a rule is intuitive, because we tend to think of the way in which one understands a word or expression as determining *infinitely* many applications or uses. When I associate a certain meaning with a word, this determines, so to speak, unique applications of the word in the future. The important thing here is that when I understand the word, and thereby become capable of applying it in the future to infinitely many new cases, my understanding defines a *norm* or *standard* relative to which my applications of the word can be measured.

---

[7]   See, for example, McDowell (1984), p. 257 for the naturalness of the analogy. See also Baker (1981), pp. 46–9 and Armstrong (1984), p. 50.

Similarly the addition rule determines an infinite set of ordered triples of numbers which are correct applications of the addition rule. Accordingly, the comparison of meanings to rules respects the familiar idea that in order for a word to have a meaning there should be a distinction between correct and incorrect uses of it.

Kripke's central example was addition. He asked: What fact about me makes it true that I referred to the addition rule when, in the past, I used the word 'plus'? What is it for me to have grasped a rule according to which 125 is the correct answer to $68 + 57$, if it so happens that I have never actually applied the rule to calculate that particular sum? How can it be ruled out that I was not guided, in my previous calculations, by the 'quus' rule:

$$x \text{ quus } y \quad = \quad x + y \text{ , if } x,y < 57$$
$$= \quad 5 \text{ otherwise (Kripke, 1982, p. 9)}$$

If none of my previous applications have been to numbers greater 56, they will not reveal whether I have used the plus or the quus rule. In fact, for any finite list of applications, there will always be infinitely many functions that accord with that list.

What else can I appeal to in order to justify the claim that I meantaddition, and was not applying the quus function, when I said 'plus' in the past? Clearly, it is not an answer to this question to give details of the general procedure, or instruction, I have applied in all my previous uses of 'plus'. Even if I can state the recursion rules for addition – (x), (x+o=x) and (x+y' = (x+y)') – it will remain true that they too can be interpreted in infinitely many ways. The formulation of a general procedure does not by itself determine its interpretation, and my finite many previous applications are consistent with infinitely many interpretations of this general procedure; so we have come no closer to an answer. Even if we assume that I have unlimited cognitive capacities, the problem remains that anything I mention to justify my insistence that I meant this function rather than that one in my past applications must itself be subject to interpretation.

We can now see that the problem Kripke had presented as one concerning past applications of rules actually applies to our present and future use of words and expressions as well:

> When we initially presented the paradox, we perforce used language, taking present meanings for granted. But now we see, as we expected, that this provisional concession was indeed fictive. There can be no fact as to what I mean by 'plus' or any other word at any time. The ladder must finally be kicked away. (Kripke, 1982, p. 21)

Meaning, understood as a standard that determines the correctness of our use of words, turns out to be illusory.

Before capitulating to this conclusion Kripke considers possible ways of saving the notion of meaning. One group of responses appeals to the notion of a *disposition*. Thus to mean addition by 'plus' is to be disposed, when asked for any sum 'x+y' to give the sum of x and y as the answer. It is a dispositional fact about me which differentiates between correct and incorrect uses of words (Kripke, 1982, p. 23). Although more sophisticated explanations invoking the notion of a disposition were available, Kripke's contention that dispositions failed to do justice to the normative element in meaning and rule-following applied to them all. The problem, he contended, was that a dispositional account fails to capture the normativity of meaning; it can only explain what a person is disposed to answer, not what he *ought* to answer. Wiping out that distinction, we are vulnerable to Wittgenstein's mocking rebuke, expressed in §258 among other places, that 'whatever is going to seem right to me is right. And that only means that here we can't talk about right' (Kripke, 1982, pp. 23–4).

The other approach Kripke considered involved attempts to identify meanings with introspectable mental states of some kind, perhaps a mental picture. But Kripke pointed out, along Wittgensteinian lines, that such pictures would not fare any better than a verbal explanation since they also could be interpreted in infinitely many different ways; nothing determinate or normative was captured here (Kripke, 1982, p. 42). For example, I cannot explain my grasp of the concept *green* by saying that my use of 'green' is always accompanied by a certain mental image, or sample, which I bring to mind and which determines my applications of the term (Kripke, 1982, p. 20). My previous applications are consistent with an infinite number of images coming to mind. One image is consistent with an infinite number of differing future applications. Here we can see that Kripke's scepticism does not rely on any behaviouristic assumptions: '... whatever "looking into my mind" may be, the sceptic asserts that even if God were to do it, he could still not determine that I meant addition by "plus"' (Kripke, 1982, p. 14). The issue is therefore primarily ontological; we are asking what fact it is about someone's mental state that constitutes him meaning one thing or another. But there was an epistemological condition which any candidate would have to satisfy, namely: that it must be possible to show how someone in possession, as it were, of that fact could appeal to it in order to justify his use (Kripke, 1982, p. 11).

In fact, as Kripke remarked in conclusion:

> If there really were an introspectable state, like a headache, of meaning addition by 'plus' (and if it really could have the justificatory role such a state ought to have), it would have stared one in the face and would have robbed the sceptic's challenge of any appeal (Kripke, 1982, p. 51).

Given the failure of these attempts to locate a fact which would render meaning ascriptions determinately true or false, the radical conclusion applying to all discourse follows:

> There can be no such thing as meaning anything by any word. Each new application we make is a leap in the dark; any present intention could be interpreted so as to accord with anything we may choose to do. So there can be neither accord, nor conflict. This is what Wittgenstein said in §202. (Kripke, 1982, p. 55)[8]

---

8   Notice that the scope of this conclusion is considerably wider than it is in the formulation quoted at the beginning of this section. Kripke assumed that scepticism about meaningful discourse would spread to global meaning-scepticism. This seems reasonable, for if 'By "X" I mean Y' has no truth conditions, nor does 'X is green'.

According to Kripke, Wittgenstein accepted, in this conclusion, the claim that meaning was not to be construed in terms of facts or entities, but he also insisted that we could nonetheless speak about accord and conflict.

Kripke presented his conclusion as a radical form of scepticism about meaning that renders the notion of meaning, and hence language, unintelligible and impossible if accepted in full. But he also thought that Wittgenstein had presented a solution which, if successful, would avoid the self-defeating conclusion that all language is meaningless. According to Kripke, the cornerstone of Wittgenstein's solution was located in the idea that an account of sentential meaning should be given in terms of assertibility conditions instead of the traditional truth-conditional account. This change in the basic semantic notion described a major difference between the early and the later period in Wittgenstein's philosophy. In the *Tractatus* the idea had been that 'To each sentence there corresponds a (possible) fact. If such a fact, obtains, the sentence is true; if not, false' (Kripke, 1982, p. 71). The sceptical paradox renders this view untenable; Wittgenstein had therefore replaced it with a view in which sentential content is to be explained in terms of assertibility and in which the function of stating truths about the world is replaced by a 'utility' function:

> Wittgenstein replaces the question, "What must be the case for this sentence to be true?" by two others: first, "under what conditions may this form of words be appropriately asserted (or denied); second, given an answer to the first question, "What is the role, and the utility, in our lives of our practice of asserting (or denying) the form of words under these conditions?" (Kripke, 1982, p. 73)

Appropriate answers to these two questions will endow an assertoric 'form of words', and ultimately any words, with meaningfulness.

The primary challenge is, then, to discover the assertibility conditions of a sentence – to answer what Kripke represents as Wittgenstein's first question. It is here that the impossibility of a *private* language is revealed. In connection with any assertoric sentence, such as '68 + 57 = 125', we might ask for its assertibility conditions when considering an individual in isolation (Kripke, 1982, pp. 87–8). Bearing in mind the sceptical conclusion, it should be obvious that any attempt to justify the claim that 125, and not 5, is the answer the individual *ought* to arrive at in making the calculation will be in vain, as will be any attempt to justify asserting the above sentence. Ultimately, the only 'justification' the individual seems to be able to offer is that 125 is the answer he is inclined to give; the above sentence is merely the one he is inclined to assert. But this is at odds with the demand that in meaningful discourse there should be a distinction between 'seems correct' and 'actually correct'. Consequently, we are forced to conclude that no substantive content can be given to the idea of a person in isolation meaning something in his use of words (Kripke, 1982, p. 89).

Fortunately the situation is different when the person is allowed interaction with a community, or even just one other person. In a community of two people who have been given the task of computing the above sum, each person will produce the answer he is inclined to give. Hence there will be not only the answer which seems correct to each individual, but also the answer they can both agree on. This means that one person can justify his answer, not only appealing to his inclinations, but by saying that he could bring the other person to agree with him; and this means in turn that a community can respect the distinction between 'seems correct' and 'correct', because there is a difference between the answer a person's inclinations dictate and the answer that person agree about with others (or most people, or experts) in the community.

This, according to Kripke, was the way in which Wittgenstein preserved our ordinary talk about meanings. However, despite the apparent harmony here, the objectivity usually ascribed to ordinary discourse, at least by philosophers, was missing from Wittgenstein's sceptical solution, for this conclusion conceded that the sceptic's negative conclusion could not be answered:

> There is no objective fact – that we all mean addition by '+', or even that a given individual does – that explains our agreement in particular cases. Rather our license to say of each other that we mean addition by '+' is part of a 'language-game' that sustains itself only because of the brute fact that we generally agree. (Kripke, 1982, p. 97)

The appearance of meaningful discourse, then, could only be preserved in a community in which individuals happen to agree on most applications of words. Kripke pointed out that Wittgenstein's account should not be confused with one in which 'assertibility' is identified with the response the community is disposed to give. Such an account would incorporate a notion of objectivity that would fall victim to the sceptical paradox:

> What follows from these assertability conditions is *not* that the answer everyone gives to an addition problem is, by definition, the correct one, but rather the platitude that, if everyone agrees upon a certain answer then no one will feel justified in calling the answer wrong. (Kripke, 1982, p. 112)

According to Kripke, this platitude was Wittgenstein's sceptical solution.

9.2 The Kripkean Private Language Argument

How did these results affect the private language problematic? Kripke's had aimed to show that the question posed in §243ff about whether a private language was possible was preceded not only in the structure of *Philosophical Investigations*, but also substantively by another question facing anyone confronted with the sceptical conclusion: 'How can we show *any language* at all (public, private, or what-have-you) to be *possible?*' (Kripke, 1982, p. 62). It then turned out that the answer Wittgenstein had given to this question involved essential reference to a community; and according to Kripke it was this component of the solution which rendered private language impossible. In Kripke's view, the purpose of §243ff was not to present new insights, but rather to cement the conclusions about meaning drawn earlier by applying them to sensation discourse:

The sceptical conclusion about rules, and the attendant rejection of private rules, is hard enough to swallow in general, but it seems especially unnatural in two areas. The first is mathematics ...
Now another case that seems to be an obvious counterexample to Wittgenstein's conclusion is that of a sensation, or mental image. Surely I can identify these after I have felt them ...
(Kripke, 1982, pp. 79–80)

So the sections following §243 merely go over the same considerations again, but in connection with a particular case; a sceptical paradox about sensation discourse is formulated. Kripke summarized his view of the argumentation found in these sections the following way:

In particular, this point applies if I direct my attention to a sensation and name it; nothing I have done determines future applications (in the sense of being uniquely *justified* by the concept grasped). (Kripke, 1982, p. 107)

The point of the 'private language argument' was not to rule out a private language, but to show us, or remind us, that general considerations about rule-following apply to sensation discourse.[9] The argumentation here was really a special case of the earlier demonstration that nothing in the mind could fix a particular interpretation and therefore meaning. §§243ff demonstrate that even when the subject matter is sensations, i.e. entities within the mind, a mental image cannot dictate its own unique interpretation.

In this picture, the essence of the argument is located earlier in *Philosophical Investigations*. The argument is part of a more general plan to weed out a natural, intuitive conception of language in general. It does not directly rule out a private language, but the sceptical solution does, since it excludes a person in isolation from genuine language use; reference to a community is essential.[10] For Kripke, then, all the details of a private language argument, some of the argumentation for the sceptical paradox and the sceptical solution, were in place before §§243. The 'Kripkean Private Language Argument' was just a part of the rule-following considerations, and not even a corollary of them; and Wittgenstein's positive views about language were part of the private language argument.

The distinctive feature of the Kripkean Private Language Argument is the structure it assigns to *Philosophical Investigations*. Since Kripke took §§243ff to be rehearsing parts of the sceptical paradox, he did not take these sections to embody a new, independent argument against the possibility of private language. Nor did he engage in detailed treatment of these sections – and of course this made sense, since he took them to be repeating points made earlier in the book. But although his analysis of §§243ff – the historical focal point of the private language debate – was barely developed, the influence and value of Kripke's more general analysis should

---

9   Compare Baker and Hacker (1984), p. 22.
10   See Kripke (1982), pp. 87–8, discussed in the previous section. More will be said about Kripke's use of the word 'isolation' later, but, if anything, it rules out private language in the sense used so far, i.e. language which of necessity would be intelligible to one person only.

not be underestimated. First of all, he provided a clear account of the sections of *Philosophical Investigations* on rule-following, and these sections had been rather obscure to previous interpreters.[11] Moreover, in describing the sceptical solution, his account detailed Wittgenstein's positive views on meaning. In this respect his views were presented with clarity, where others might be accused of a certain obscurity.[12] Secondly, Kripke's work again placed the interpretation of *Philosophical Investigations* at the top of the agenda in linguistic philosophy, albeit while relegating the private language issue to a more peripheral role. This time the question was about what essentials a general theory of linguistic meaning should incorporate, and about whether the central notion should be truth or assertibility. This comes through in the following passage, where Paul Boghossian introduces a survey article about the rule-following considerations:

> On Kripke's reading, the passages on rule-following are concerned with some of the weightiest questions in the theory of meaning, questions – involving the reality, reducibility and privacy of meaning – that occupy centre-stage in contemporary philosophy. (Boghossian, 1989, p. 507)

Discussions about rule-following and its wider implications continue today; a substantial number of articles on the subject are published each year. This is not the right place to enter into this debate. What I want to do in the next few sections is to focus on the period when the 'Kripkean' debate was most intense, the first half of the 1980s, and to ask whether the Kripkean Private Language Argument can be ascribed to Wittgenstein. In particular, I shall ask what reason we have, if any, to suppose that Kripke captured the essential point of *Philosophical Investigations* §§243–315.

9.3 Making Room for the Community

Whether the Kripkean argument can be ascribed to Wittgenstein is an important question, particularly since the argument contains a positive, albeit disillusioning, account of language – an idea about what language *is*. One is tempted to ask: Was the sceptical solution the motivation underlying Wittgenstein's dictum that meaning would reveal itself in use? What I want to argue in the next couple of sections is that Kripke's sceptical solution was the consequence of a framework Wittgenstein rejected: that is, Wittgenstein articulated the sceptical paradox, but did not embrace the sceptical solution. It follows from this that the Kripkean Private Language Argument is not Wittgenstein's but the product of a particular agenda.

To begin with, observe that the sceptical solution is a desperate answer to the question facing anyone who has ceased to believe that a straight solution to the

---

[11] For example, notice the absence of any treatment of these sections in Hacker (1972) and Kenny (1973).

[12] I shall not be concerned with these matters, but see, for example, McDowell (1984), pp. 272–6, and Baker and Hacker (1984). For accusations of obscurity see Boghossian (1989), pp. 543–4, on McDowell, and Sartorelli (1991) and Williams (1991), pp. 164–7, on Baker and Hacker.

sceptical paradox is possible: 'How can we show *any language* at all (public, private, or what-have-you) to be *possible?*' (Kripke, 1982, p. 62). As Kripke presents it, the sceptical solution is an attempt to show how it can *appear* that there is a distinction between 'seems correct' and 'correct'; it is an attempt that accepts not only the sceptical paradox but also the sceptical conclusion, that there is no meaning. In other words, if it is necessary for meaning that there be a genuine distinction between false and true, then the sceptical solution is a 'no meaning' account of language. Since no norms are attached to expressions, the only thing one can do is to observe what happens when people converse. This conclusion follows directly from the logic of the argumentation in Kripke's book.[13] Instead of thinking of language use as an activity governed by norms, Kripke even says that we should think of it as being grounded in responses one 'is inclined to give' and in 'feelings of confidence' (Kripke, 1982, pp. 88–91).

On the other hand, it seems reasonable to insist that Wittgenstein had appealed to a practice and a community:

> And hence also 'obeying a rule' is a practice. And to *think* one is obeying a rule is not to obey a rule. Hence it is not possible to obey a rule 'privately': otherwise thinking one was obeying a rule would be the same thing as obeying it. (§202)

Kripke's solution seems to reflect the importance Wittgenstein had assigned to such notions. Furthermore, although there were several other interpretations of Wittgenstein at the time Kripke wrote, each emphasizing the importance of practice and community in slightly different ways, none of them were clear alternatives. I will briefly consider two influential contributions which helped to shape the debate (albeit to a lesser extent than Kripke's approach) as it developed from the early 1980s. These contributions are Crispin Wright's *Wittgenstein on the Foundations of Mathematics* (1980) and John Mcdowell's paper 'Wittgenstein on Following a Rule' (1984).

Around the time Kripke's interpretation of Wittgenstein began to be absorbed, Wright presented an interpretation of Wittgenstein's philosophy of mathematics. Wright's analysis centred on issues about rule-following that Kripke had focused on.[14] The close relationship between Wittgenstein's views on meaning and mind, on the one hand, and his views on mathematics, on the other, had been noticed by Kripke. The latter, of course, derived his paradox using the addition rule as an example; he had even planned a subscript about Wittgenstein's view on mathematics.[15]

---

[13]   Kripke's account of the sceptical solution is not univocal. On the one hand, he holds it to be a 'no meaning account', but in the remarks from Kripke (1982), p. 73, quoted above in Section 9.1, he seems to say that we can still attach certain assertibility conditions to a sentence even if these are fairly unusual and counterintuitive.

[14]   Wright (1980) was based on lectures given in Oxford 1974–77.

[15]   Kripke (1982), p. vii. Construing the rule-following considerations as '... perhaps the central problem in the *Philosophical Investigations*', Kripke (1982), p. 7, makes the relationship to Wittgenstein's views on mathematics rather natural, because a similar discussion about rules is found in Section VI of Wittgenstein (1956).

Being mainly concerned with Wittgenstein's remarks on the foundations of mathematics, Wright did not directly engage in exegesis of *Philosophical Investigations* §§243–315. However, he did refer to these passages as '...concerning the idea of a private rule of language' (Wright, 1980, p. 36). According to Wright, Wittgenstein's point here was that a rule could not be followed privately, because '... I have no way of making a distinction between seeming to myself to be using "S" correctly and really doing so' (Wright, 1980, p. 28). In fact §§243–315 served as a substantial part of some of the argumentation Wright attributed to Wittgenstein, even though he did not explicitly refer to them later when he rehearsed '... the bearing of the rule-following considerations upon the whole idea of investigation-independence ...' (Wright, 1980, p. 216).

The target in Wright's work was similar to Kripke's; but where the latter had talked about rules, Wright discussed 'patterns of application'. The notion of investigation-independence captures the idea that to grasp the meaning of a word is comparable to grasping a pattern of application which requires a determinate verdict in previously unconsidered cases.

Wright started from the private case. Suppose that we wish to respect the idea that the meaning of a word is comparable to a pattern extending, of itself, indefinitely. We might then conceive the idea that learning the meaning of a word is a matter of 'cottoning on' to this pattern: the pupil forms a hypothesis, an inspired guess, about the pattern of application which the teacher tries to get across (Wright, 1980, p. 216). From here we might form a picture of a community of speakers as a congruence of idiolectic patterns: 'each of us knows of an idiolectic pattern of use, for which there is a strong presumption, when sufficient evidence has accumulated, that it is shared communally' (Wright, 1980, p. 217).

In order to subvert this picture of language, Wright considered the question whether a speaker could know what conformity to his idiolectic pattern required, i.e. which of his applications of a word would accord with his idiolectic understanding. The negative answer he gave to this question was, in essence, based on Wittgensteinian reservations 'concerning the idea of a private rule of language', although this might have been stated more clearly. Commenting on the situation in which a pupil forms a hypothesis about the meaning of a word that we, the teachers, try to get across, Wright wrote:

> *We* cannot tell whether he implements his hypothesis [his idiolectic pattern] correctly, that is, whether his expectations here really are consonant with the interpretation he has on our treatment of, say, the samples we gave him; and *he* cannot provide any basis for a distinction between their being so and its merely seeming to him that they are. (Wright, 1980, p. 217)

Consequently, a community would be necessary for language, because understanding would somehow have to be shared:

> ... There cannot be such a thing as first-person privileged recognition of the dictates of one's understanding of an expression irrespective of whether that understanding is shared. (Wright, 1980, p. 217)

Respecting this conclusion, the temptation now, Wright noted, would be to locate investigation-independence in the pattern which the community seems to follow in its applications of a given word; but since there is a precise parallel between the individual following an 'idiolectic' pattern and the community following an 'idiolectic' pattern, the above considerations will apply once more in the latter case. Hence, the idea of meaning as an investigation-independent pattern must be rejected, and the only notion of correctness an individual can deploy is one involving his applying words in accordance with the applications others in his community are disposed to make (Wright, 1980, p. 220). For the community, however, there is no standard.

These considerations led Wright to interpret Wittgenstein's continued reference to practice and a community as an indication that he had embraced *communitarianism*: the view that correct application of an expression is located in the totality of the community's actual dispositions. This view, however, is not a viable alternative to Kripke's account. In fact Kripke had explicitly avoided such a view in characterizing his sceptical solution, because it would fall prey to a form of the sceptical paradox: an infinite number of rules are consistent with 'the totality of the community's actual responses'.[16]

So although Wright ended up with a position very close to Kripke's sceptical solution, his position was different enough to be exposed to the sceptical paradox, and Wright offered no alternative escape route. Assuming Wittgenstein had been consistent in his application of the sceptical paradox, he could not have been a communitarian.

John McDowell developed his views largely in response to the arguments of Kripke and Wright. Kripke and Wright had pointed out that they were acting only as advocates for Wittgenstein's views, but McDowell's own views were to a large degree identical with those he attributed to Wittgenstein.[17]

In McDowell's interpretation, the idea Wittgenstein attacked in formulating the sceptical paradox was one according to which one's understanding of a word is separate from, and dictates, the applications one makes of the word. The problem the sceptical paradox brings forward is that nothing we could claim the understanding to reside in would successfully fulfil that purpose, because, whatever it is, it could be interpreted in infinitely many different ways. The decisive notion here was that of *interpretation*. When we are asked what could constitute one's understanding of an expression

> ... we tend to be enticed into looking for a fact that would constitute my having put an appropriate *interpretation* on what I was told and shown ... (McDowell, 1984, p. 229)

Having derived the paradox from *Philosophical Investigations*, Kripke had taken Wittgenstein to accept its conclusion; but McDowell suggested that Wittgenstein

---

[16] Kripke (1982), p. 112. The term 'communitarian' was Boghossian's name for the position Wright attributed to Wittgenstein. See Boghossian (1989), p. 534.

[17] Wright (1980), p. vii, expresses some disagreement with Wittgenstein. McDowell did not directly state his sympathy with the views he was attributing to Wittgenstein, but he clearly thought Wittgenstein's views viable. See, for example, McDowell (1984), p. 242.

held the view that a misunderstanding leads us to think of understanding as some kind of interpretation. On this view, the sceptical paradox is intended to make us realize, with Wittgenstein, '... "that there is a way of grasping a rule which is *not* an *interpretation*"' (McDowell, 1984, p. 229). This idea offers an escape from a dilemma in which one horn is occupied by the sceptical paradox and the other horn saddles us with a 'mythology' according to which following a rule, or applying a word according to one's understanding, is pictured as the operation of a 'super-rigid yet ethereal' machine. In the mythology, the meaning of an expression somehow contains all its applications. The sceptical paradox makes the second horn of the dilemma untenable, thereby leading us to the other horn, where it is conceded that meaning is impossible. Kripke was wrong to suppose that Wittgenstein describes a way in which the first horn can be occupied. Instead Wittgenstein had rejected the idea, underpinning *both* horns, that understanding was an interpretation (McDowell, 1984, p. 231).

McDowell pointed out that Kripke's sceptical solution would represent a dubious construal of Wittgenstein's views, because in §201, immediately after stating the paradox, Wittgenstein explicitly says that it rests on a misunderstanding. Moreover, Wittgenstein goes on to say that the paradox shows

> that there is a way of grasping a rule which is *not* an *interpretation*, but which is exhibited in what we call 'obeying a rule' and 'going against it' in actual cases (§201).

These remarks had been conveniently avoided in Kripke's quotations.[18] McDowell, by contrast, took them literally: Wittgenstein had denied that understanding should be construed as some kind of interpretation; and his answer to the question of how there could be understanding without interpretation had been that obeying a rule is a practice, a regular use, a custom (McDowell, 1984, p. 239): 'it is precisely the notion of communal practice that is needed, and not some notion that could equally be applied outside the context of a community' (McDowell, 1984, p. 254).

However, on the question of how the notion of communal practice would single out the correct interpretation from the infinite set – how it would offer a straight solution to the sceptical paradox – McDowell was remarkably unclear. He appeared to believe that Wittgenstein wanted us to stop asking for justifications:

> By Wittgenstein's lights, it is a mistake to think we can dig down to a level at which we no longer have application for normative notions (like 'following according to the rule'). (McDowell, 1984, p. 242)

McDowell suggested that we should resist the temptation to enquire after 'bedrock ... of how things are at the deepest level at which we may sensibly contemplate the place of [meaning] in the world'. Apparently Kripke and Wright had gone too far in pursuit of justification, but McDowell offered no explanation of why this was so.

---

[18]   This discrepancy was pointed out by several scholars; see, for example, Malcolm (1986), p. 155 and McGinn (1984), pp. 67–8.

It would appear, then, that McDowell had come closer to the real Wittgenstein than Kripke, because he had taken Wittgenstein's rejection of the paradox into account. But in taking this course, McDowell saddled Wittgenstein with mysticism.

9.4 The Sceptical Paradox and the Picture Theory

I have now presented three important contributions to the debate about rule-following and understanding in its initial phase. Their significance can hardly be doubted. For example, in Boghossian's summary of the debate, published in 1989, these three accounts supply positive solutions to the rule-following problematic.[19] It was argued in the previous section that neither Wright nor McDowell offers a viable solution to the sceptical paradox. Wright's version of the rule-following argument is vulnerable to the paradox, and McDowell's version fails to provide a penetrable account of the way in which Wittgenstein could avoid the paradox. Although, helpfully, it does draw attention to the fact that he rejected it. Apparently, then, Kripke's sceptical solution, the 'no meaning' account, describes the only position Wittgenstein could have consistently held.

I now want to elaborate on Wittgenstein's remark, made at the end of §201 and quoted above, that '... there is a way of grasping a rule which is *not* an *interpretation*, but which is exhibited in what we call "obeying a rule" and "going against it" in actual cases'. I will claim that the relevant assumption is one that Wittgenstein rejects. If this is right, Kripke's sceptical solution does not provide a framework for sound exegesis of §§243–315. I will also claim that the assumption in question is shared by both parties in the debate about whether a theory of meaning should have assertibility or truth as its fundamental notion – a debate to which Michael Dummett and Hilary Putnam, among others, have contributed.

Let us begin by isolating the assumption. The initial challenge leading to the sceptical paradox is one of finding a unique interpretation of a meaning statement: 'By "plus" I mean addition.' This is interpreted as the problem of finding the entity the speaker singles out in his understanding of the term. All of the attempts rejected during the derivation of the sceptical paradox essentially tried to fix meaning by isolating a particular objective fact: this fact was either the reference of the word ('By "green" I mean *this*') or fixated reference ('By "green" I mean what I am disposed to call green'). Such accounts of meaning make no mention of the fact that language is a medium of communication. It may empirically true that we require some kind of communicative setup to learn a language, but the fundamental assumption is that the primary nature of language is to correspond. You learn a language by learning what the individual words correspond to in the world; you gain knowledge of a rule for application. Using a word correctly means obeying the rule.

Having acquired this knowledge, you can use language for communication. Now what I suggest is that we read Wittgenstein, and §202 in particular, as rejecting this assumption. That is, we assume that, in the context of language use, 'obeying a rule' means, roughly speaking, communicating successfully via language:

---

[19]   Boghossian (1989); see also Hale and Wright (eds) (1997), Part II.

And hence also 'obeying a rule' is a practice. And to think one is obeying a rule is not to obey a rule. Hence it is not possible to obey a rule 'privately': otherwise thinking one was obeying would be the same thing as obeying it. (§202)

Ultimately, language is a tool for communicating, and communication requires some degree of agreement between the participants about how to use a word. You can define a word's meaning in whatever way you like, but it will only be what is common to your definition and your interlocutor's understanding that gets across.

This means that a fundamental norm guides all discourse, namely: that you should use words in a way that makes communication a success. You should therefore use words consistently, or if there is a change, all parties should be made aware of it. And this norm is primary in the sense that if the use of words in a given context fails to live up to it, language will not perform its distinctive role. Accordingly, the meaning of a word derives from this norm: the meaning of a word is what it refers to in such a way that its use in communication makes communication a success. But this means that reference cannot be learned outside the actual discourse in which it is used, or without a grasp of the customs governing its use.

By contrast, there was, underlying the sceptical paradox, a particular conception of the nature of language – one that Wittgenstein had embraced in his early days, but vehemently attacked in his later works. On this conception, the primary purpose or nature of language is to correspond to something else, to *picture* the world. Only when this correspondence is established can language be used for communication. So Wittgenstein might have agreed with Kripke that the sceptical solution is the only viable answer to the sceptical paradox within a framework which takes the picture theory for granted. He came, however, to reject this framework; indeed, it was by developing the sceptical paradox that he had intended to expose its Achilles heel.

From a systematic, and even an exegetical, point of view these remarks are far too brief. The point I wish to get across is that Wittgenstein and Kripke had rather different perspectives: Wittgenstein did not embrace the sceptical solution, and it follows from this that the Kripkean Private Language Argument cannot be attributed to him. Despite its clarification of the sceptical paradox, Kripke's account does not provide a framework within which a sound analysis of §§243–315 can be developed. The last word in the private language debate had not been said.

The real force of Kripke's interpretation of Wittgenstein can only be appreciated by paying attention to the debate of which it is a part. The picturing conception of language was a *fundamental* element in the project of providing a theory of meaning *independently* of the communicative aspect of language which Dummett, among others, had argued was the fundamental task in philosophy of language. First, the idea was that the primary notion of meaning is that of literal, or cross-contextual, meaning.[20] It is a direct implication of this idea that communication that always occurs in a context, or is relative to a background, is to be ignored. Secondly, and more importantly, the key idea was that what is meant by a word is to be derived from what someone understands by it, or from what he knows, perhaps implicitly: 'A model of meaning is a model of understanding, i.e. a representation of what it is

---

[20]   See the Dummett quotation on p. 133.

that is known when an individual knows the meaning' (Dummett, 1973, p. 217). This is a competence that can manifest itself without making any reference to a practice of communicating; the relevant knowledge can be possessed without being used in acts of communication. So Kripke's book was in effect a heretical contribution to the debate about whether speaker-meaning should ultimately be accounted for in terms of truth conditions or assertibility conditions.

It is also fair to say that Kripke played an important role in the development of the private language argument of §§243–315, despite the disclaimer entered earlier. To begin with, he presented his argument with such clarity and power that for many readers his book was the first successful attempt to make sense of Wittgenstein's ideas.[21] Many philosophers still view what they would call 'the private language argument' through a Kripkean lens.

A second reason why Kripke's book played an important role in developments in attitudes to the private language argument is that it helped to bring Wittgenstein's thought to a wider audience. We have already seen that Wittgenstein's thinking had an important bearing on the discussion of whether meaning is best construed in terms of truth conditions or assertibility conditions. It also appeared, once again, in the work of sociologists.[22] Consider, for instance, Bloor in 1997:

> Perhaps the most notable recent sociological reading, and one that has been at the centre of much controversy, is Saul Kripke's brilliant *Wittgenstein on Rules and Private Language* (1982). Although Kripke expresses reservations about the truth of Wittgenstein's conclusions, he has no doubt about the importance of his arguments, or their sociological character. (Bloor, 1997, p. 7)

Thus it was through Kripke's clear and heretical writings that Wittgenstein became the central philosophical inspiration for the 'strong programme', a programme querying scientific positivism advanced by David Bloor and Barry Barnes.

---

[21]   See, for example, McGinn (1984), p. vii, and Koethe (1996), p. xi. Even today, Kripke's book is for many students a way into Wittgenstein's later work, introducing §§243–315 through the rule-following considerations.

[22]   Peter Winch introduced Wittgenstein's ideas on following a rule into social science in 1958; see section 5.5.

Chapter 10

Revisiting *Philosophical Investigations*

Philosophical Investigations set the stage for debate about the possibility of a private language in 1953. Ever since then it has been at the centre of that debate. The evolution of the private language debate was, and still is, intimately tied up with developments in the interpretation of *Philosophical Investigations*. Wittgenstein's thoughts have been so central to the debate that there is a sense in which most articles in previous chapters have served a dual purpose, illuminating both whether a private language is possible and why (and in what sense) Wittgenstein thought it was not. Clear as it might be that the interpretation of Wittgenstein is logically separate from the truth about private languages, the issues have been remained very close. By and large, developments and refinements in the private language argument have led to developments and refinements in our understanding of Wittgenstein.[1]

Since 1990s, however, there has been a move towards a more purely scholarly, historical approach to Wittgenstein's work, including his treatment of private language. More than ever before specialist academics working the history of ideas now separate Wittgenstein scholarship from current, substantive debates in the philosophy of language and mind. Wittgenstein has entered the pantheon of great philosophers, and his writings are accorded increasingly serious exegetical attention, in the manner of classic texts. Indeed, it might be said with some justice that, in so far as there is an ongoing discussion about private language today, this revolves around the interpretation of §§243–315 and their role in Wittgenstein's philosophical work – a discussion which also draws extensively on the immense Wittgensteinian *Nachlass*.

Separation of the exegesis of *Philosophical Investigations* from contemporary debates has resulted in a better climate for a proper understanding of both the book and Wittgenstein in general. Looking back, it is striking that, despite the immense efforts described in the previous chapters, little in the way of consensus emerged about what is going on in §§243–315 between 1953 and the mid-1980s. Some disagreement might well have been expected, of course: the relevant sections are remarkably, notoriously, open to interpretation, and the aim in the secondary literature has often been to explicate what Wittgenstein *did not* write or left only a limited trace of in *Philosophical Investigations*. Wittgenstein did not explicitly identify his target. Nor did he describe, in a straightforward way at any rate, the conclusions to be drawn from his argumentation. This meant that the scope for interpretation was, and is, considerable.

But even where attention was confined to the text – to questions merely about what Wittgenstein *did* write – the period produced no consensus. Several attempts to

---

[1]   Compare Bloor (1997), p. ix.

describe and explain the text have been unsuccessful in establishing an authoritative version of Wittgenstein's argumentation. This is not to say that there have been no interesting, well thought-through attempts at exegesis. Nor is it to deny that that the range of what are thought to be possible ways of interpreting the key sections in the private language argument has narrowed. The point is rather that no *one* attempt has come to be regarded as the correct way to understand Wittgenstein's argumentation against a private language. No interpretative orthodoxy has developed.

Interpretative agreement is even rarer when we turn to questions about Wittgenstein's wider philosophical purpose in arguing against private language, and to issues raised by the role of the private language argument in the overall argumentation of *Philosophical Investigations*. Is Wittgenstein, for instance, discussing language in general, sensation language in particular, or perhaps even sensations as such, independently of language in the relevant sections? Since the sections themselves offer no univocal answers, the general attitude towards *Philosophical Investigations* and Wittgenstein's philosophy becomes important, and here the experts of today depart in different directions. In truth, several different accounts of Wittgenstein's thought can be, and have been, backed by substantial textual evidence. Wittgenstein's works as a whole are important sources in the interpretative endeavour, but it must be acknowledged that the situation is a long way short of being one in which agreement on all fronts has begun to prevail.

This subject – the proper interpretation of Wittgenstein's philosophy and the role of the private language argument in it – is, in effect, the focus of professional philosophical discussion of private language at present. Emerging from this wider discussion, however, is an elaborate and convincing account of many of the details of the argument adumbrated in §§243–315. Although there are still small disagreements over some details, a considerable number of once contentious issues are resolved in recent interpretations.[2] It has become possible to focus on the text.

Thus one thing that has now been established beyond doubt is that *Philosophical Investigations* is a very systematic book. It consists of compressed material, certainly, and it is the product of Wittgenstein's continued efforts, as he writes in the preface, to present his material so that '... the thoughts should proceed from one subject to another in a natural order and without breaks' (Wittgenstein, 1953, p. vii). To arrive at this result, Wittgenstein produced no fewer than five versions of the text between 1936 and 1946; and although he ultimately felt that he had failed to attain his goal, one should not be too ready to believe that the book is an album of philosophical remarks, as Wittgenstein says in the preface.[3]

---

[2]   By 'current interpretations' I mean those that represent the most serious claims to understand Wittgenstein's argumentation. These should not be confused with the most common interpretations, which I think are probably those considered in the Chapter 9. Many philosophers do, I think, take Kripke's interpretation to be the most plausible of those available.

[3]   Wittgenstein (1953), p. vii. The five editions of Part I of *Philosophical Investigations* have now been published together in Wittgenstein (2001). See Hacker (1990), pp. 12–14, for an account of the history of §§243–315.

These points apply to §§243–315. This interlude is dense with philosophical thought, and because Wittgenstein develops his thoughts in dialogue with an interlocutor, his style becomes argumentative throughout. In his responses Wittgenstein is assembling a 'private language argument'.

With this in mind, and with recent scholarly work in hand,[4] we can begin to work our way towards an authoritative version of the particular sections in §§243–315 that have, historically, played a dominant role in the argumentation, mainly because Wittgenstein seems here, perhaps more openly than elsewhere, to be proceeding argumentatively in first making an assumption and then deriving certain conclusions from it. These are §258, §265, §270 and §293. They have been focal points of the previous chapters. They have also received special attention in much recent work on *Philosophical Investigations*.

10.1 The Memory-Criteria Argument

In the many published efforts to clarify Wittgenstein's views on privacy, §258 is the single most discussed section of *Philosophical Investigations*. Despite the fact that this section opens by introducing a new stage-setting, its train of thought flows quite naturally from the sections preceding it. The issue is introduced in §243. Contemplating the possibility of monological languages, Wittgenstein raises the question whether one can imagine a language describing one's immediate, private sensations, the consequence being that the language would be intelligible to no one other than its solitary speaker. The following sections then argue that our sensations are not private in any sense in which they could serve as the entities described in the private language.[5]

In §256 the conclusion to be drawn from these investigations is stated: we are not immediately led from our ordinary (gewöhnliche) sensation language to the idea of a private language, so we still lack a foundation for the private language; actual sensations are not private in the required sense. In an immediate development of this observation the suggestion is raised that we might arrive at privacy of the required sort if we separate sensations from their natural expressions: 'And now I simply *associate* names with sensations and use these names in descriptions' (§256).[6] Since this is the suggestion which triggers the considerations that follow in §258, it should be emphasized that to start with Wittgenstein assumes that there is a genuine sensation here of the kind that can be named in this associative manner. This assumption is criticized in §261.

In §257 Wittgenstein points out that the associative construction is very far removed from our ordinary sensation language, but at the same time he admits that

---

[4] I have focused on Candlish (1998), Canfield (2001), Hacker (1990) and von Savigny (1988). In my opinion these works can make the strongest claim to have interpreted Wittgenstein correctly.

[5] See Chapter 7 for detailed treatment.

[6] The passage equivocates on the question whether it is Wittgenstein himself or the interlocutor who makes this suggestion; but this question is in any case unimportant, since there is no doubt that it is a suggestion of which Wittgenstein disapproves.

a language of this kind, if it could be constructed, would be private. We should, however, be aware that we have achieved our result too easily, because when we ordinarily say 'He gave a name to his sensation' we think of definition by ostension, and this is best viewed as an intra-linguistic definition, 'I will associate *this* with the name "pain"'. This conclusion was derived in §§27–35.[7] But since we are not working within the confines of ordinary language, the proponent of a private language needs to show that his act of association can deliver what is demanded for a definition.

At this point the interlocutor – the proponent of the possibility of a private language – is not challenged to show that private ostension involving association can succeed where public ostension has failed. Rather he must show that the association can provide the setting which ostension, public or private, builds upon. It is for this purpose that the suggestion initiating §258 is invoked. The first sentences set the stage: suppose I, a speaker of a shared language, wish to keep a diary about the recurrence of a certain sensation. For this purpose I associate a sensation with a sign 'S' which, given the circumstances, will function as a descriptive expression[8] and whose meaning will be private. By the privacy requirement 'S' cannot be given a verbal definition, since this would make it a word in our ordinary, public language. If this were not the case, we would have to enquire for the meaning of the signs in the definition. Also by the privacy requirement 'S' cannot be defined by ordinary ostension. Although it is non-verbal, it requires the stage-setting I am trying to provide (§§27–35).

Given these limits, the interlocutor still suggests that one might employ something analogous to ostensive definition – namely, conduct in which I say, or write down, 'S', while I concentrate my attention on the relevant sensation, thereby impressing on myself the connection between sign and sensation. It is this suggestion for fixing the meaning of 'S' that Wittgenstein considers in the following, complicated remarks. The first move is to focus on the consequence of the above ceremony. If this ceremony is supposed to fix the meaning of 'S' (and this is indeed the purpose of a definition), then the meaning of 'S' is the connection I have impressed on myself. The text here is notorious. The statement that '... in this way I impress on myself the connexion between the sign and the sensations' makes it sound like an already existing connection is impressed, but if that is the case the immediately following question should be: What is that already existing connection? Instead, however, the idea is that it is the connection between sign and sensation that is impressed, or brought into being: 'But "I impress it on myself" can only mean: this process brings it about that I remember the connexion *right* in the future' (§258). In other words, if the meaning of 'S' is constituted by the connection impressed on myself between sign and sensation, then, for any sensation x, my criterion for 'S' referring to x is that I remember correctly that 'S' refers to x.

This, however, is a bogus criterion. In the present case I have no criterion for remembering correctly, since that presupposes that I understand what I am supposed

---

[7]   See p. 221.

[8]   I use the term 'expression', which can be taken to refer to both words and sentences. Strictly speaking, 'S' functions as a one-word sentence in the tentative private language, but it will nevertheless be convenient to say things such as 'This is S' in which 'S' is used as a word.

to remember, and so the right-hand side of the conditional above does not make sense. I can only have a criterion to the extent that I *seem* to remember correctly, but then 'S' will refer to x whenever I have the impression that 'S' refers to x. Having no criterion for what 'S' refers to and what it does not, we will not have succeeded in endowing the sign with any meaning.

Before digging deeper into these structured thoughts, we should consider §265. Here Wittgenstein considers the suggestion, made by the interlocutor, that a criterion for remembering correctly might be found in memory. Might we not have a criterion saying that I remember that 'S' refers to x when, and only when, my belief that 'S' refers to x is supported by a clear memory that 'S' does indeed refer to x.

The interlocutor attempts to fortify his suggestion with an analogy: Could I not appeal to a clear memory in order to justify my dim memory that 'S' refers to x, just as I can appeal to a table in my memory to justify my instinctive translation of the word 'T' into 'U'? Against the interlocutor Wittgenstein points out that he should be clear about what he can do when. We should distinguish the following. 1) If the table in my memory exists outside, or independently of, my memory, then the clear memory of the table in which 'T' is translated into 'U' can justify my translation of 'T' into 'U'; but 2) if the table exists only in my imagination, then my clear memory of the table in which 'T' is translated into 'U', can justify only the fact that I *imagine* that 'T' should be translated into 'U'. It is the latter of these which is analogous to the situation with 'S'. My clear memory that 'S' refers to x can justify my *thinking* that I remember that 'S' refers to x, but not the fact that I *do* remember. As happened with the suggestion in §258, we are left with the problem that one cannot remember something one does not understand. Obviously, this goes for a clear memory as well as for a dim memory.

10.2 Strategic Clarifications

The analysis just given sufficiently clarifies the structure of Wittgenstein's argument in §258 and §265, I believe. In preparing it I was influenced by an earlier analysis offered by Eike von Savigny in his commentary to *Philosophical Investigations* (von Savigny, 1988, pp. 305–9 and 303–16), although von Savigny envisages a considerably more linear and argumentative structure than I have.[9] But my analysis merely recounts the essential progression of Wittgenstein's thought. In view of this, several connected points are worth making.

For one thing, the wide acceptance of the meaningfulness of ordinary language should be noticed: every sign definable by ordinary means is part of ordinary language, and the argumentation scrutinizes not the parts of ordinary language that concern sensations, but a language putatively beyond its confines. However, in order to formulate the setting assumed by the private speaker, Wittgenstein has to discard the principle that everything defined by means of ordinary language is part of that language, because 'S' supposed refers to a 'certain sensation', a term in ordinary

---

[9]   Focusing exclusively on §258, Canfield (2001) presents a generalized version of the above.

language. It is this initial reduction of the demands, leaving a contrived and artificial notion of sensation behind, that Wittgenstein mocks in §261: 'What reason have we for calling "S" the sign of a *sensation*? For "sensation" is a word of our common language, not of one intelligible to me alone' (§261).

It is also important to emphasize that Wittgenstein is not arguing against private ostensive definitions.[10] The suggestion that he is, which was considered in Chapter 8, has in recent times gained a foothold through Peter Hacker's detailed 1990 commentary.[11] Leaving aside the details of his somewhat flighty remarks on §258, Hacker essentially argues that a private mental ostensive definition fails to establish a connection between sign and sensation, and that consequently there is no criterion for remembering the connection correctly (Hacker, 1990, pp. 118–20). His argument against the supposition that '... we are trying to mimic, *in foro interno*, the procedure of giving it ['S'] a use by an ostensive definition employing a sample' (Hacker, 1990, p. 119), is similar to the one employed earlier in *Philosophical Investigations* to show that ostensive definitions presuppose stage-setting. But, in fact, Wittgenstein's strategy is to argue that a connection was established in the initial private act of ostension, but that it failed to establish a criterion for subsequent use.

The account Stewart Candlish gives makes this contrast clearer.[12] Candlish is suggesting not only that, in §258, the proponent of private language utilizes a procedure analogous to ostension, but also that this procedure actually produces a lasting connection – a connection, that is to say, that the private linguist impresses on himself in such a way that he remembers it correctly (Candlish, 1998, p. 149). So far so good: it seems that I have managed to establish a meaning-conferring connection between 'S' and the sensation. Imagine now, however, that I subsequently feel the 'S' sensation and ask myself 'What do I mean by "S" on the second occasion?' (Candlish, 1998, p. 153, my translation). According to Candlish, Wittgenstein at this point considers and rejects two, as it were, nearby answers the private speaker might give. The answer he imagines Wittgenstein rejecting in §258 is '... that by "S" is meant nothing other than the same (kind of) sensation that I now have' (Candlish, 1998, p. 153, my translation). Wittgenstein's two-sentence rejection of this answer at the end of §258 is now decompressed by Candlish. He observes that fact-related claims presuppose a distinction between truth and falsity. This again presupposes a distinction between the origin of meaning and the origin of the truth of the claim. But in the present case the sensation serves both these purposes, so we should not conceive of 'S', uttered or written down in a diary the second time, as a factual claim, but rather as another ostensive-like definition of 'S'.

In all essentials, this is the interpretation Kenny had presented as long ago as 25 years earlier, and Candlish acknowledges as much (Candlish, 1998, p. 152).

---

[10] von Savigny (1988), p. 305, and Candlish (1998), p. 147, both support such an interpretation.

[11] Hacker (1990). See p. 236 for a list of writers who found this kind of argument in *Philosophical Investigations*. Recent advocates, besides Hacker, include McGinn (1997), p. 131 (only §258), and Glock (1996), p. 312.

[12] See Candlish (1998). Candlish presented a similar interpretation of Wittgenstein (and Kenny, on which see below) in Candlish (1980).

Nonetheless, because he misinterprets Kenny, Candlish fails to see that when he turns to *Philosophical Investigations* §265 and §270 he describes an argument that differs, once again, very little from Kenny's. Given this, I will not repeat myself further and present the rest of Candlish's argument.[13] It is worth noting, however, that from a purely exegetical point of view, Candlish's account is suspicious. For despite his stated intention of staying close to the text (Candlish, 1998, pp. 143 and 160), it requires considerable good will to identify the above argument in the text of §258. Moreover, neither Candlish nor Kenny makes use of the notion of criterion – a notion so obviously crucial to the argument of the succeeding section. And they construe §265 as presenting a new attempt to justify the connection between 'S' and the sensation. In fact it is an attempt to elaborate the suggestion made in §258.

I should emphasize that these problems are mainly exegetical. The interpretation I presented earlier can be translated into an account like Candlish's with a few certain plausible assumptions. Consider the bogus criterion on page 1: For any sensation x, my criterion for 'S' referring to x is that I remember correctly that 'S' refers to x. On this bogus criterion, I would remember the impressed connection correctly every time I seem to remember it correctly. The reference of 'S', or what I mean by 'S', will be every sensation I honestly and sincerely call 'S'. We have now arrived at the suggestion Candlish considers in connection with §258. With these explications, then, the sort of account given by both Candlish and Kenny might be looked upon as one capturing the essentials of Wittgenstein's line of thought in §258. Given this, it might be claimed to state more clearly the reasons why the putatively private language fails.

From this perspective, Candlish's account is more easily differentiated from Hacker's. The latter argues that nothing happens in the initial ostension at (to deploy some useful variables here) t_1. Hacker therefore presents his refutation in relation to that moment in time. In Candlish's version, on the other hand, it is granted that the private language speaker impresses on himself a connection between sign and sensation at t_1. It is about this connection that Wittgenstein's remarks: "'I impress it on myself" can only mean: this process brings it about that I remember the connexion *right* in the future' (§258). It would seem, then, that Hacker has failed to register adequately Wittgenstein's willingness to grant his opponent the impressed connection. Having said that, we should emphasize, however, that the refutation is ultimately inevitable in both cases, for it turns upon events at a later time, t_2, when 'S' is subsequently used.

What this shows is that despite their apparent differences, several accounts in recent years capture the essentials of Wittgenstein's argument, but that those who, like Hacker, conceive of the argument as one directed against private ostensive definition should not be counted amongst these. This is not to say that Wittgenstein's ideas do not conflict with the idea of private ostension; as we have seen, such ostension is opposed in 'Notes for the "Philosophical Lecture"' (MS 166).[14]

---

[13]   At least, in the way Kenny's account, in Kenny (1971) and Kenny (1973), is construed in Chapter 8. Reference to the mistaken interpretation of Kenny can also be found in Canfield (2001), pp. 387–8.

[14]   See Section 4.1.

Candlish's and Kenny's accounts set out the presuppositions they ascribe to Wittgenstein clearly. In Candlish's version it is acknowledged, first, that fact-related claims presuppose a distinction between truth and falsity; and second, that any distinction between truth and falsity will presuppose a further distinction between the origin of the meaning and the origin of the truth of the claim.[15] We have already seen that the exegetical evidence for Candlish's and Kenny's interpretation of §258 is rather weak. So also with these claims: Candlish does not say where Wittgenstein made the claims; and apart from referring to Wittgenstein's earliest writings on logic (Wittgenstein, 1961, pp. 188–208), Kenny mentions only §279 in *Philosophical Investigations* and §536 in *Zettel*.[16] Worse, so far as the soundness of the argument is concerned, both writers seem to take the claims to be so obvious that neither elaborates them further. But even if we *are* dealing with innocent assumptions here, we should be told why we can safely accept them.

Both of these circumstances encourage more confidence in the exegetical probity of what I shall be calling the 'Memory-Criteria Argument'. Confidence in the argument's cogency, however, requires the use of criteria in the argumentation to be rendered at least as inconspicuous as the principles employed in Candlish and Kenny's version. For this reason I shall now consider the notion of a criterion employed in the Memory-Criteria Argument in detail.

10.3 The Demand for Criteria: Language Essentials

'Criterion' is the decisive notion in §258: it is the demand for a criterion that ensures 'S' is not a term in a private language. Wittgenstein, however, seems to take criteria for granted here. He explains neither why a criterion is required, nor what he employs the notion for. In this section I shall attempt to fill this gap in Wittgenstein's argument. I shall not attempt to explain in exhaustive detail what Wittgenstein associated with the notion. Nor will I describe how he used it in different contexts. I shall concentrate on the role it is supposed to play in §258. In the Blue Book, which contains the most detailed presentation of the notion offered by Wittgenstein, he contrasts criteria with symptoms. The latter are characterized as '... a phenomenon of which experience has taught us that it coincided, in some way or other, with the phenomenon which is our defining criterion' (Wittgenstein, 1958a, p. 25). This suggests that a criterion is criterial by necessity and definition, and also something by which one can explain one's use of words – for example, one's use of 'angina'.[17] These remarks give a helpful, if only rough, indication of the way in which Wittgenstein employed the terms 'criteria' and 'symptom'.

Instead of digging more deeply into the general issues here, I will concentrate on the role the notion of a criterion is supposed to play in the argumentation in §258. However, one thing that emerges from a study of Wittgenstein's general

---

[15]   Candlish (1998), p. 153; but see also Kenny (1971), p. 221.

[16]   Kenny (1971), pp. 221–2.

[17]   Wittgenstein (1958a), p. 25. For a detailed examination of Wittgenstein's use of the term, see Hacker (1990), pp. 545–71. Note that Hacker's views here differ considerably from those found in Hacker (1972).

use of the term is that a the notion of a criterion, as Wittgenstein understands it, differs somewhat from the semi-specialized, quasi-logical notion employed in the 1960s and 1970s.[18] It is also important to notice, looking at Wittgenstein's general employment of the term, that although criteria can be used in describing the relation between a sensation and its expressions,[19] Wittgenstein does not restrict them to that relationship. In fact he mentions a number of things which require criteria and might serve as criteria.[20] In §258 the demand for a criterion for remembering correctly is invoked, not simply because we are dealing with sensations, but because we wish to endow a sign with meaning. It is meaning that requires a criterion of correctness in the first place, and it is because we fail to produce a genuine criterion for the use of 'S' that the private language fails. Hence we should acknowledge that Wittgenstein is concerned with the requirements of language. He does not rest his demand for criteria on his conception of sensations [130].

Given that his demand for criteria rests on his conception of language, it is necessary to explain why Wittgenstein thinks criteria are needed in §258. Why should a criterion be needed when 'S' refers to x? The traditional answer here is that criteria, or a criterion, is required by knowledge: the private language speaker needs to ascertain for sure whether 'S' refers to x. But this approach clearly points towards some kind of verificationism. The weaker explanation, in the sense of being less substantial and controversial, Wittgenstein seems to give is that the need for a criterion is simply inherent in the notion of a description. This, at any rate, is all that is required for his argument to succeed. For a sentence to have the status of a description, which is the status intended for 'S', it must have a standard of correctness: it must be make sense to distinguish between what it describes correctly and what it describes incorrectly. The criterion simply marks that difference. Likewise conflating 'seems right' and 'right' will wipe out any independent notion of correctness.

To be sure, the weak explanation makes it less obvious why the criterion stated will not do the job, but the problem here, again, is semantic and not epistemic. The problem is not that the memory of what 'S' refers to is too weak a foundation for the demanded distinction, but that the criterion itself is senseless. The memory-criterion is ineffective because it both presupposes that '"S" refers to x' makes sense *and* at the same time is meant to guarantee that it does. A necessary condition of the correctness of the memory that 'S' refers to x is that 'S' *does* indeed refer to x; but it was that connection which we set out to establish, so we cannot presuppose it. So although Wittgenstein is not concerned with the inadequacy of memory, he does make a point about memory – namely, that it has to make reference to something beyond itself in order to make sense.

Here Wittgenstein's lack of interest in justification and concentration on meaning becomes clear. Thus when, in §258, he requires a criterion for remembering correctly, he is simply demanding *sense*. He does not take that to coincide with a demand for

---

[18] Hacker (1990), p. 546. For a list of features ascribed to criteria in Hacker (1972), pp. 283–310, and for a rejection of these, see Wright (1984).

[19] See, for example, §580 ('An "inner process" stands in need of outward criteria'), on which many accounts of the criterial position were modelled.

[20] See Hacker (1972), pp. 285–6, for references to Wittgenstein's diversity of use.

justification in beliefs about, or for knowledge of, memory. In the final sentence of §258 the situation that makes no sense is 'remembering correctly' and not 'knowing that one remembers correctly'.[21] Memory, then, has to make reference to something beyond itself, to what is remembered, if it is to make sense. When it does this it can serve as a criterion; it does not require, additionally, to be justified by something beyond itself for this purpose.

It can be seen, then, that Wittgenstein's demand for criteria is in fact driven by rather trite standards of correctness without which words become mere sounds: if an expression is a description, it should at least make sense to say that it describes one thing and not another. Likewise a memory requires that of which it is a memory to make sense.

What now becomes of 'S', given these clarifications? Two possibilities present themselves. Since the stage-setting the private speaker imagines cannot satisfy the above requirements, we should not conceive of 'S' as a descriptive term in a private language. We can instead think of it, or better, its use, as expressing the speaker's impression of the presence of a private sensation; for this is all it can be when the criterion for 'S' referring to x becomes the impression of a memory that 'S' refers to x. But now 'S' has the status of a public expression of a sensation.[22] If, however, we wish to stick to the unintelligible criterion, Wittgenstein suggests that we might alter our conception of what a private language involves: 'And sounds which no one else understands but which I *"appear to understand"* might be called a "private language"' (§269).

This account of the role of criteria in §258 is very close to the one Canfield offers.[23] Both von Savigny and Hacker, who employ the term frequently but do not explicitly defend the use of criteria in §258, seem to hold similar views.[24] General agreement can also be found that we are primarily discarding the possibility of a private language, but opinions differ over the implications Wittgenstein takes this impossibility to have. Addresal of that last question will be postponed until later, because here much depends on one's conception of what is argued in *Philosophical Investigations* §270. §270 should therefore be considered first.

10.4 The Manometer-Beetle Argument

§265 supports the stage-setting suggested in §258, so there is a natural temptation to compose a single argument from the two sections. Combining §270 and §293 into a single argument, as I propose to do, is less natural, since they make converse points about private identification. According to von Savigny:

---

[21] Compare Canfield (2001), p. 387.

[22] Compare what might be said to have been justified in §265 above.

[23] See especially Canfield (2001), pp. 384–91, but also Canfield (1996).

[24] See von Savigny (1988), p. 308, and Hacker (1990), pp. 545–70. The, in some circles, influential Cavell (1979) also emphasizes the importance of criteria, but he opts for a more phenomenological and existential reading of §§243–315. It is not clear to me how his criterialism is essentially distinct from verificationism.

> In PU [*Philosophical Investigations*] 270, a concrete use of 'S' as expression of a certain sensation experience is described and shown *that identification has no role within this pattern of use*. Here [§293] with the aim of refuting it, it is assumed that "Beetle" is used to identify the contents of the box and from this shown that *the identification role in this practice is excluded.* (von Savigny, 1988, p. 344, my translation)

I think this connection is both genuine and strong enough to warrant consideration of §270 and §293 in conjunction.

The two sections have not normally been connected, apart from it being observed that both are about privacy. Hacker, for instance, treats them in separate sections.[25] Again, following Kenny, Candlish conceives of §270 as presenting a third attempt by the proponent of private language, following those made in §258 and §265, to establish his position. He suggests that the final sentence of §269 – 'And sounds which no one else understands but which I *"appear to understand"* might be called a "private language"' – presents a situation in which we seem to have a private language: he speculates that apparently unintelligible signs are here used in accordance with a private meaning behind the publicly accessible circumstances. §270 then is interpreted by Candlish as feeding on this apparently private meaning:

> That suggests another chance for the proponent of the private language idea: Perhaps the private speaker can endow "S" with a meaning by attaching it to a publicly accessible phenomenon?[26]

This acknowledges that a transition to ordinary sensation language has occurred in §270, but it fails to reflect the fact that Wittgenstein is speaking here about a genuine sensation. This contrasts strikingly with the contrived, artificial example in §258. Both von Savigny and Hacker recognize this, and they therefore regard §270 as only loosely connected with §258. They suggest that where, in §258, Wittgenstein was talking primarily about a private language, he is now addressing the question whether sensations are ascribed to oneself by means of a private identification.[27]

I will follow the von Savigny and Hacker approach below. I concede that Kenny and Candlish present a possible, and perhaps more perspicuous, interpretation. I suggest, however, that because of their oblique focus on 'artificial' sensation rather than genuine sensation, they fail to draw the right conclusions at this point.

In §270, then, Wittgenstein's interlocutor has realized that the tentative establishment of criteria does not make genuine private understanding possible; the private speaker cannot endow the sign 'S' with meaning, so a private understanding of sensation terms is impossible. Taking this point on board, might it still not be that we identify sensations and ascribe them to ourselves because of recognition? It is this suggestion which is discussed in §270.

---

[25] In Hacker (1990), p. 207, Hacker points out that §293 elaborates a suggestion made in §272 on the real problem with private experience, but he does not further suggest a connection. Compare Hacker (1990), p. 237, which regards §293 as pursuing the point made in §271.

[26] Candlish (1998), p. 159, my translation. Compare Kenny's suggestion, quoted on p. 230.

[27] von Savigny (1988), p. 319, and Hacker (1990), p. 133.

Suppose I discover that whenever I have a particular sensation my blood pressure rises, and that using 'S' as sign for the relevant experience I write 'S' in my diary according to some documentary purpose I happen to have. So 'S' refers to a private, genuine sensation which is correlated with a rise in blood pressure. Perhaps after several tests confirming the correlation between the sensation and a rise in blood pressure, I might abandon the indefinitely articled '*a* private, genuine sensation' and say that 'S' refers to the impression, or sensation, that my blood pressure rises.[28] Even more abruptly than in §258, Wittgenstein here progresses from the stage-setting to a compressed argument for the important conclusion that

> ... now it seems quite indifferent whether I have recognized the sensation *right* or not. Let us suppose I regularly identify it wrong, it does not matter in the least (§270).

Although, as I say, the correctness of Candlish and Kenny's construal cannot be ruled out,[29] I suggest the following is going on here. It is natural to think that 'S' is written in the diary in response to some kind of recognition. Do I not recognize a sensation as 'S' because I identify it as the one I had previously when I ran through the tests with the manometer? If we suppose that the concept of identification plays a role here, then misidentification should make sense. Again it should be noticed that it is *semantic* issues that are currently being addressed: there is no suggestion that misidentification should be possible, only that it make sense. Furthermore, the misidentification cannot rest on the possibility that I write down 'S' without a rise in blood pressure occurring. For 'S' would then refer, not to the sensation, but to the actual rise. So the following possibilities are left: either (a) that a mistake occurs whenever I have the impression that my blood pressure rises, but I do not notice it – however, in that case I would not have the impression; or (b) that I do not have the impression that my blood pressure rises, but think I have – however, if I think I have an impression, then I have it. Each of these suggestions therefore fails to make sense of the idea of misidentification, and so also of identification. Neither (a) nor (b) ensures that mistakes are intelligible. But if mistakes are unintelligible, the concept of identification plays no role; every sensation I describe using 'S' will be S.

The remaining sentences in §271 elaborate this point. The idea that we identify sensation is merely a consequence of the conception of sensations as private objects, and this conception is now also threatened by the above argumentation. This is the background to Wittgenstein's remark about the 'knob' which is a mere 'ornament'. Wittgenstein's interlocutor construes this remark as a colourful statement of the conclusion that the sensation has become irrelevant and launches two reservations: first, why should we now call S a sensation? Might it not be something else which prompts me to write 'S'? Second, why a unique type of sensation? Could 'S' not describe a set of sensations? Wittgenstein answers both of these concerns is by referring to the way in which 'S' is used in practice.

---

[28]   This kind of definition of 'S' would violate the conditions for private language set down in §258. For Candlish and Kenny, such a remark would be problematic, but here we need not be concerned about this, because I am dealing with a genuine sensation.

[29]   Wittgenstein's construal of the setting for the argumentation here does, however, suggest a different interpretation from that offered by Candlish and Kenny.

The conclusion is that one does not ascribe sensations to oneself by exploiting a previous identification; identification makes no sense here. This again points to another conclusion – one that Wittgenstein states only metaphorically at this point, but which is set out literally in §271, namely: that sensations should not be conceived of as private objects. In Hacker's apt terminology: 'The 'private object' is only a free-wheeling cog in the mechanism of a genuine language' (Hacker, 1990, p. 6).

If §270 states that we do not ascribe sensations to ourselves in ordinary sensation language by drawing on previous identifications, §293 might be viewed as contemplating the question: What if we did do that? The original motivation for §293, however, is not that question, but instead a suggestion, raised some ten sections earlier, about how we learn sensation language:

> That I recognize that there is something there (in me) which I can call 'pain' without getting into conflict with the way other people use this word? (§283)[30]

This introduces the idea, scrutinized by Wittgenstein in §293, that '... it is only from my own case that I know what the word "pain" means'.

§293, with its 'beetle in the box' remarks, is one of the most eye-catching sections of *Philosophical Investigations*. It comprises three paragraphs, the first of which presents the motivation for the enquiry and findings set out in the remaining two. The first paragraph is short. Suppose I know only from my own case what 'pain' means. If everyone speaks about the same kind of thing as I do when talking about pain, it follows that everyone should know only from their own case what pain means. But is there now any reason to think that everyone speaks about the same kind of thing? It is a negative answer to this question that Wittgenstein elaborates in the rest of the section by comparing pain on this model to a beetle in a box.

Suppose each of us knows what pain is from his own case alone. This is like supposing that everyone has a box, with something in it, into which no one else can look, and that everyone refers the thing in the box as a 'beetle'. Then it might be that everyone had something different in the box, or even that the contents of boxes constantly change. In this case, there is no reason to assume that all the boxes have the same content. This is a well-made point, but Wittgenstein's main interest is not in the fact that we would, or should, remain sceptical about the contents of other boxes, but that it would be *irrelevant* to common use of 'beetle' what was in the box, because the boxed thing we call 'beetle' plays no part in that use. Or conversely, bringing the argument here into contact with §270: if each of us identified the presence of a 'beetle' by reference to his own box, we would not arrive at a common use for the word.

In connection with pain, the point becomes that on this model the pain itself, the private object, drops out of consideration and becomes irrelevant to our public language. So the interlocutor ends up being caught in the very situation he sought to avoid by speaking about private objects; and it is he who should be worried about questions of the kind raised in §270. Questions such as: 'And what is our reason for

---

[30] Hacker (1990), p. 206, and von Savigny (1988), p. 341, both acknowledge this connection.

calling "S" the name of a sensation here?' Broadening the perspective, Wittgenstein's wider point in setting out these considerations is that we should reject the initial suggestion and give up thinking that one knows only from one's own case what pain means, an idea he goes on to mock in the sections following §293. This point should also lead us to reconsider theoretical assumptions lying behind the 'own case' approach, including the model of sensation language envisaged in §283.

The above argumentation connects beautifully with that of §270. As in §270, the contrast between pain as a private object recognized by private identification and ordinary sensation language is discussed; and both sections argue that the one precludes the other. §270 mainly concerns identification of sensations and §293 mainly concerns sensations as private objects, but both sections develop so as to cover both issues. In fact, although 'private object' readily describes the situation with sensations in §293, the closest Wittgenstein himself comes to this characterization is in calling sensations 'objects'. The word 'private object' is not used, although §§294–295 speak about a 'private picture'.[31] The word 'object' in the above argumentation, then, should not be taken too literally as meaning some kind of specific entity. Rather it should be understood with reference to 'identification' and criteria. That is, an 'object' is whatever is identified by criteria, and a 'private object' is whatever is identified by private criteria. This leaves considerable scope for various interpretations of 'object' and points towards the generality the considerations here have usually been regarded as having. Therefore, although §270 and §293 appear to discuss different notions of identification and of the private object, they are closely related.

In so far as §270 relates to §258 (as many commentators have thought), the change of subject in §270 is one of Wittgenstein's more successful attempts to proceed from one subject to another in a seamless way;[32] but it must be accepted nonetheless that from §270 and onwards Wittgenstein's main concern is the idea of sensations as private objects. This is the main target both of the 'Manometer-Beetle Argument' and the intermediary sections in which Wittgenstein treats other aspects of the idea. §288, for instance, argues against the supposition that we could imagine a pain that was totally isolated from its expression. But Wittgenstein also seeks to identify, and undermine, the motivation behind this idea of sensations as private objects – as he does in §283 and §297.

10.5 Wittgenstein's Target

The Manometer-Beetle Argument is not primarily concerned with the possibility of a private language. It is mainly directed against the idea of a private object. Hence, in so far as Wittgenstein presents a private language argument, it is located in §§256–

---

[31]   The only section in *Philosophical Investigations* that makes mention of a 'private object' is found in Part Two (Wittgenstein, (1953), p. 207), and the use there in no way conflicts with the characterization below. Both Hacker (1990), pp. 206–8, and Canfield (2001) employ the term.

[32]   In the preface to *Philosophical Investigations*, Wittgenstein had stated this as one of his intentions. See Wittgenstein (1953), p. vii.

69 and takes the form of the Memory-Criteria Argument. As with the Manometer-Beetle Argument the name here suggests a more unified structure than is actually offered. Accordingly, we might speak with some justification of private language arguments, or, perhaps more correctly from an exegetical angle, of a passage of private language argumentation evolving over a range of sections. So the Memory-Criteria Argument is Wittgenstein's private language argument. But what is its relation to the Manometer-Beetle Argument? Here we touch upon the question what Wittgenstein intends to demonstrate in §§243–315, and that question is controversial.

Von Savigny takes §§256–69 to contain the essentials of Wittgenstein's treatment of privacy. In his interpretation, *Philosophical Investigations* §§1–315 argues for the following thesis 'about meaning'.

> That someone by an expression, by an action, by a picture and so on means something (means something by it), does not concern him alone. It consists more in that the pattern of his individual behaviour is encapsulated in the community to which he belongs. (von Savigny, 1988, p. 7, my translation)

Being a part of this general argument, §§243–315 argue, according to Von Savigny, that a private language is impossible by dealing concretely with sensation language, and this is mainly established in §§256–69. The sections after §270, like §§246–55, have the purpose of making that result more convincing [130]. So von Savigny's interpretation suggests that we should concentrate on the Memory-Criteria Argument.

Hacker, on the other hand, takes the thinking of §§243–315 to represent an attempt to establish the untenability of a certain picture of the mind:

> Its global target is a misconstrual of our concepts of experience, of the nature of the mental and its relation to behaviour that is pervasive in philosophy. (Hacker, 1990, p. 19)

So even though he acknowledges that this involves discarding an associated conception of language (Hacker, 1990, p. 16), Hacker takes Wittgenstein to be concerned primarily with sensations and the mental realm in general – or, in the above terminology, with the 'private object'.[33] Canfield also regards the rejection of a private object as more fundamental than the rejection of a private language (Canfield, 2001, pp. 378–80), while Candlish seems satisfied to note merely that Wittgenstein rejects both private language and private object[34].

I do not have any conclusive way of settling this question about Wittgenstein's primary concerns, but I shall indicate why I find the view of Hacker and Canfield more plausible. First, when, in §243, Wittgenstein introduces the question about a private language the privacy of the language is a consequence of the privacy of the

---

[33]   The phrase 'private object' then comes to stand for the common element in the collection of philosophical views which Hacker takes Wittgenstein to be undermining. In a footnote (Hacker (1990), p. 16) Hacker mentions, as examples, Descartes, Hume, phenomenalists, central state materialists and contemporary functionalists.

[34]   Candlish (1998), pp. 145–6. Note that neither Canfield nor Candlish consider §§272ff.

speaker's sensations; without the privacy of sensations the question about private language would not arise. Wittgenstein also implies that the notion of a private object is the more basic topic leading to discussion of a private language in his 'Notes for "Philosophical Lecture"'. There he notes the train of thought behind the idea of a private language: 'The private object. The naming of the private object. The private language. The game someone plays with himself.'[35] His strategy, then, is to move backwards through this chain of ideas, raising doubts. Hence the argumentation against a private language is not only intended to show the essential publicity of language, but also to remove the motivation for the idea of a private object. It is the philosophical temptation to posit a private object that motivates the idea of a private language. From this angle, the Manometer-Beetle Argument is more fundamental for Wittgenstein than the Memory-Criteria Argument, because it deals with a kind of privacy that comes to mind more intuitively and is therefore more reluctantly abandoned. Even when the impossibility of a private language has been admitted, one wants to hang on to the idea of a private object.

In interpreting the Manometer-Beetle Argument as an attack on a more fundamental notion of privacy we are not obliged to treat it as an argument concerning language. Consequently, we should stick to the conclusion that the Memory-Criteria Argument is Wittgenstein's private language argument. The Manometer-Beetle Argument does, however, play a role in the argumentation that amounts to more than merely being located in its surroundings. It is generally recognized that Wittgenstein's treatment of the idea of a private language involves the whole of §§243–315, and even if we are concentrating on language, we should invoke sections beyond §§256–69. This becomes obvious when we enquire about the misconceptions involved in the idea of a private language, the target of the Memory-Criteria Argument. Let me explain what I mean by looking at this enquiry in more detail.

Some conclusions about language, drawn from the Memory-Criteria Argument, do not concern the fact that we are dealing with sensations. Generally speaking, the argumentation makes the point that a single gesture, or word-introduction, cannot endow a word with meaning. This point is discussed early on in *Philosophical Investigations*, most notably in §§27–35, but Wittgenstein is not merely repeating the lesson in a private forum: by this point, the private language speaker has taken into account that merely fixing one's attention while pronouncing 'S' will not of itself establish a connection between word and object.[36] Rather Wittgenstein argues that even an established connection – or impressed connection – cannot be meaning-constituting. Two misconceptions give the private language speaker the impression that what he has done is enough to constitute meaning. Both turn out to be mistaken on closer scrutiny:

---

[35]   Wittgenstein (1993), p. 447. Note that in contrast with his approach in *Philosophical Investigations*, Wittgenstein here speaks about 'the private object'. Compare the remark on p. 305.

[36]   Of course, this is the picture portrayed in accounts which regard Wittgenstein as attacking the notion of private ostensive definition.

1. Memory is not the faculty by which the constancy of meaning is secured. Instead memory presupposes meaning if it is to make sense.
2. The infallibility by which a speaker employs a term cannot be just assumed; this would involve conflating 'right' and 'seems right'. Rather, we require a criterion of correctness with which we, and he, can measure the infallibility of his use.

These are, I think, the important lessons to be drawn from the Memory-Criteria Argument. However, these misconceptions turn on the idea of how we might construe a private language. They do not directly concern its motivation. Given this, the Memory-Criteria Argument might merely lead the private language speaker to look for new ways to construct a private language.[37] In other words, the Memory-Criteria Argument does not become convincing on its own. Wittgenstein needs to remove its source, and the most dominant motivation for a private language, which is the idea of sensations as private objects. Until he removes that idea, and corrects the corresponding conception of sensations, the idea of a private language is unlikely to disappear.[38]

So we are drawn to consider the motivation behind a private language. Why would we think that sensations are private objects? From a philosophical perspective it is true that 'the inner-outer picture of the mental' which '... has dominated philosophy since Descartes' (Hacker, 1990, p. 15) leads in that direction. Hacker might be right that several philosophical views promote such a picture.[39] But to regard Descartes as the villain here would be to confuse matters, because we do not get the idea that we sometimes speak about private objects from Cartesianism. Rather, it is because we speak in the way we do that Cartesianism is appealing. Our fundamental motivation lies in a misconception in our ordinary ways of speaking about sensations, where we construe talk about pain on the model of talk about objects. Several sections in §§243–315 suggest as much, most notably §304:

We have only rejected the grammar which tries to force itself on us here.

> The paradox disappears only if we make a radical break with the idea that language always functions in one way, always serves the same purpose: to convey thoughts – which may be about houses, pains, good and evil, or anything else you please.[40]

It is not that Wittgenstein takes our sensation language to be defective. His point is rather that, guided by a false picture of how language functions, we are led to think that a sensation is some kind of object we become acquainted with. So our tendency

---

[37]   Although one might doubt whether any genuinely new ways remain to be found.

[38]   Both von Savigny and Hacker defend this interpretation. The disagreement above turns on Wittgenstein's primary focus – i.e. on whether, primarily, Wittgenstein is making a point about language or about the mind.

[39]   Hacker (1990), p. 16, but also p. 27. Other works in which the general philosophical applicability of Wittgenstein's argumentation is stressed are Stern (1994), p. 553, and Canfield (2001), p. 380. Candlish (1998), p. 146, mentions a 'Cartesian soul', while McGinn (1997), p. 117, focuses on William James.

[40]   Others are §§289, 291, 292. See also 317.

to think private language is possible derives from our thinking of sensations as private objects, which again is motivated by a false picture of language. It is only by removing these misconceptions, or straightening them out, that we shall finally come to see that the ascription of a private language is unnecessary. In this broader perspective, the Manometer-Beetle Argument is the more fundamental, because it undercuts the motivation for a private language by getting rid of the idea of a private object.[41] Once again, in the course of a detour through the nature of mental entities, our attention is directed towards language: the private language is motivated by the private object, which is motivated by a mistaken conception of how language functions, its grammar.

10.6 The Notion of 'Use'

The previous section described the negative conclusions Wittgenstein seeks to establish in §§243–315. I defended the view that these sections include points about both language and the mind, a view held by most contemporary experts. I will now turn to the positive conclusions. In order not to go too far off track, however, I will concentrate mainly on the conclusions about language and, where possible, ignore those concerning sensations and the mind in general.

One writer who takes §§243–315 to contain an argument for a general thesis about language is von Savigny. On his interpretation, the sections up to §315 or so show that for an action like an utterance, or gesture, to mean something it must be embedded in a social context.[42] This separates his ideas from the general trend, which is towards the view that Wittgenstein's later work is essentially free of philosophical theses. Methodological factors may be in play here. Von Savigny's approach to *Philosophical Investigations* is unconventional, because he concentrates exclusively on that text and views it as self-contained. Put bluntly, he intends, not to uncover Wittgenstein's thoughts, but the book's content [130]. Perhaps surprisingly, this takes him in a direction other than that travelled by the majority of commentators, who seek for the most part to uncover Wittgenstein's overall intentions. With this aim, the majority of commentators have concluded that Wittgenstein does not offer any theses in the traditional philosophical sense. Indeed he displays hostility towards the kind of theory building that has been the aim of much traditional philosophy. His deflation of traditional philosophical views does not result in an alternative systematic theory. It is guided by attention to particular examples and the actual workings of language.

Marie McGinn is explicit about this:

> We must, therefore, resist the attempt to sum up, or to state philosophically exciting conclusions, and allow instead for a series of clarifications to take place in which 'the philosophical problem ... completely disappears' (PI 133). (McGinn, 1997, p. 29)

----

[41]   von Savigny (1988), p. 283, Hacker (1990), p. 27, and Canfield (2001), p. 380, all identify conflations of ordinary language as the source of the motivation.

[42]   von Savigny (1988), p. 7. The passage is quoted above, on p. 307.

From this interpretative stance we shall look to Wittgenstein's later work in vain for positive conclusions. Others are less quietistic and allow Wittgenstein to have some positive views. Hacker, for instance, takes Wittgenstein to offer clarifications of certain central concepts. Referring to his own examination of the sections before §243, he points out that '... it has been argued earlier that the meaning of a word is not an object of any kind, but rather is given by an explanation of meaning, and an explanation is a rule for the use of a word' (Hacker, 1990, p. 21). This, at least on its face, fails to square with McGinn's insistence that Wittgenstein's views cannot be expressed in general theses or formulae.

Although there is dispute over the degree of Wittgenstein's 'anti-philosophical' tendencies, there seems to be general agreement that §§243–315 offers mainly negative conclusions about language; this goes even for von Savigny and Hacker.[43]

In my view, the claim that Wittgenstein does not offer any positive conclusion about the nature of language in §§243–315 is accurate.[44] However, reading through *Philosophical Investigations* one cannot but conclude that certain notions have a certain centrality and are used in positive description of what language is. 'Use' (§43), 'custom' (§198), 'practice' (§202) and 'technique' (§150) fall into this category.[45] I will not attempt to explain in detail what Wittgenstein meant by these terms. That would involve discussing a number of early sections in *Philosophical Investigations* and the clarification of other notions like 'language game' and 'form of life'. However, I do believe that the Memory-Criteria Argument illuminates some important aspects of Wittgenstein's use of these words, and I now wish to say something about this. I shall concentrate on §§243–315. The remarks I make will also provide a deeper insight into assumptions operating behind the Memory-Criteria Argument. Methodologically, then, I adopt an approach which, like Canfield's, involves digging more deeply into the argumentation in order to uncover Wittgenstein's fundamental assumptions rather than taking a step further and searching for the conclusions or consequences Wittgenstein draws from the argumentation.

Allow me to again draw attention to the use of a criterion in §258. It has already been remarked that it is the demand for a criterion that the private language fails to satisfy in the Memory-Criteria Argument. Criteria provide a standard of correctness that meaning requires; they provide a notion of sameness through which two different uses of an expression can be compared. Given the importance of the notion, we should notice the wide range of criteria Wittgenstein seems to allow. From the treatment in §258 alone, it seems that, even if their verifiability can be doubted, sentences that are recognized as being meaningful can serve as criteria endowing a problematic expression with a meaning. For example: My criterion for 'S' referring to x is that x is a sensation with no natural expression. Such a criterion would make 'S' an expression in our shared language, because the criterion is publicly meaningful. Despite the fact that 'S' refers to private phenomena, a speaker's understanding of

---

[43]   See the table of contents in von Savigny (1988), and Hacker (1990), p. 16.

[44]   Where sensations and other mental phenomena are concerned, I am not so certain.

[45]   Wittgenstein does display an aversion to any kind of technical jargon; he also uses these words in other places with less emphasis. Other terms that should be mentioned here are 'application' (§11), 'function' (§11) and 'role' (§50).

'S' could still be checked, because we could enquire after his criteria for using it. If we wished to do so, we might further enquire after the criteria for his understanding of the expressions which make up his criterion for 'S'.[46]

Wittgenstein says in §258 that we are not allowed to give a verbal definition of our putatively private sign 'S', since that would make it a sign in a public language. But he does allow the private language speaker to verbally identify criteria that are non-verbal. Without this allowance the private language thesis could not be considered or even stated. Accordingly, the private language speaker states the criterion that is meant to endow 'S' with meaning: My criterion for 'S' referring to x is that I remember correctly that 'S' refers to x.[47]

Here it looks as though the private language speaker satisfies the above requirements and gives a non-verbal criterion in verbal terms; but only for a moment, because it rapidly becomes evident that the criterion that is meant to secure the meaningfulness of 'S' at the same time presupposes its meaningfulness. The apparent availability of the criterion rests on a misconception about memory. Memory cannot store meaning at the most basic level, because it presupposes it. Although memory will not provide the necessary foundation for meaning, the private language speaker's suggestion should lead us to realize that something akin to memory will, in an important sense, have to do the job. To the private language speaker, that is, memory is the only route by which to secure meaning. Certainly, any notion replacing memory as the foundational criterion will have to deal with that requirement.

One inclination at this point is to invoke the notions of 'practice' and 'custom' to which Wittgenstein appears to assign considerable significance around §200. I think there is no little truth in the suggestion that Wittgenstein could use these notions to replace memory at the foundation of meaning. On the other hand, they might have too much social content. Where they have not been taken to be self-evident and in no need of explication,[48] they have been interpreted, like Kripke's account, as referring to a social context.[49] Here the usual strategy is to locate the standard of correctness with reference to community.

It is important to see that if the only genuine support for meaningfulness is offered by notions, like 'practice' and 'custom', which make essential reference to a community, then we cannot take §§243–315 to deliver any genuine insight into the nature of language. For then the impossibility of a private language would have been established by Wittgenstein *before* the extended discussion presented in §§243–315 (as the Kripkean Private Language Argument suggests). Wittgenstein does make the point that language is a social affair, a means of communication. However, he does not do this in §§243–315, but rather in discussing rule-following in §§142–243; and this discussion does not decide the possibility of a private language in advance,

---

[46] The use of 'private' here, applying to 'sensations whose presence a person can choose to keep secret', does count among the uses Wittgenstein allows. See, for example, §246 (the last sentence) and §248.

[47] From p. 288.

[48] I think Baker and Hacker (1984) and Bloor (1983) take them in this way.

[49] See Chapter 9.

because it does not exclude *any* language not satisfying the relevant demands.[50] The view that Wittgenstein does not consider this to be the main lesson of §§243–315 is further supported by the fact that he does not use the notions 'practice' and 'custom' here. In §§243–315 he does not mention practices or customs at all.

Instead I suggest we revert to certain notions of which Wittgenstein makes extensive use in §§243–315, namely: 'use', 'function' and perhaps also 'purpose'.[51] What underlies these notions is not an essential appeal to a society, but rather the idea that language is a functional activity – an activity interacting with the world and not just a detached description of it. 'World' here means everything outside language. It is important to notice here that Wittgenstein is employing terms like 'use' and 'function' in an extremely broad sense, because he takes ordinary language to be meaningful. Indeed a function exists so long as one can explain how the world would look if the sentence was true. Thus, for example, 'Copernicus smiled a lot as an infant' possesses criteria and is meaningful. These criteria, however, are most likely to be verbal. We might therefore enquire after the meaning of the criteria, which again might be stated verbally. One is here reminded of Wittgenstein's remark: 'These things are finer spun than crude hands have any inkling of' (Wittgenstein, 1956, VII, §57). At some stage, however, we will have to explain our use of words by going outside language and making a connection with the world. In other words, in connection with a word, a verbal criterion for meaning may always be available, but when this criterion is compared with the way in which the speaker uses the word, it is the latter standard of correctness which decides whether he has employed the term correctly.[52]

So, fundamentally, the standard of correctness resides in the purpose for which an expression is employed. This explains the necessity for a standard of correctness and criteria: it must make a genuine difference in use, understood in a broad sense, whether you employ the term or not. Hence beneath the demand for a criterion in §258, and indeed beneath the general demand for criteria, we find notions like 'use' and 'function' which permeate the treatment of other issues in *Philosophical Investigations*.

Returning to the situation in §258, these remarks do, I think, help to explain why 'S' fails to become an expression describing a certain private sensation. The failure is, of course, a direct consequence of the missing criterion, or of the fact that the alleged criterion is meaningless. But we can now see why it is necessarily meaningless. The key lies in the observation that 'S' is a 'language starter'. This means that, although we have described the criterion for 'S' by using words, it is not

---

[50] The connection between §§142–242 and §§243–315 is intricate. It involves the question whether an infant Crusoe could develop a language. I cannot follow that issue here, but see Canfield (1996).

[51] 'Use' figures in §§246, 247, 257, 261, 262, 288, 289, 290, 288 and 293; 'function' in §§260, 274, 280 and 304; and 'purpose' in §§246, 257 and 304. Their significance varies. Thus §257 does, I think, contain a rather trite use of the term 'use', but it puts 'purpose' to significant use.

[52] Compare Canfield (2001), p. 386, on the infant Crusoe: 'If we choose to say that such a person has language our criterion will have reference to *consistent behaviour of a certain kind*' (my emphasis).

verbal. For we lack a meaningful private language in which the criteria can be stated in a way analogous to the case involving the sentence 'Copernicus smiled a lot as an infant'. So the criterion for 'S' is a genuine use criterion: it connects directly to the world, and consequently the failure to provide such a criterion resides in the fact that the private language speaker has no use whatsoever for 'S'. In Wittgenstein's words:

> For a note has a function, and this 'S' so far has none (§260).

The central lesson of the Memory-Criteria Argument is that *no* use can be provided for an expression in the surroundings imagined by the private language speaker; and this result does not figure anywhere before §243.[53] Nowhere in this line of thought has Wittgenstein excluded the possibility of an infant Robinson Crusoe inventing a language for himself for some purpose – perhaps, for keeping track of the ebb and flow of the tides. Hence Crusoe is a potential speaker. Equally central (although it is made in other places in *Philosophical Investigations*) is the observation that we can give a verbal definition, or provide a verbal standard of correctness for some expression, immediately. We can instantly assign 'S' meaning by using language, and after this we might rely on memory or written documentation if need be, to maintain the meaning. If the standard of correctness for an expression is provided by use, however, that standard will have to emerge through use; and if that is the case, we will be in no position to separate defining instances from statements made by the expression in the way the private language speaker imagines.

I conclude that even if we cannot use the term 'use theory' to designate Wittgenstein's position, because that position is not a hypothetical construction of the kind susceptible to empirical scrutiny, Wittgenstein *is* guided by a 'use idea' of language. This use idea is shaped in the discussion of meaning that Wittgenstein returns to again and again throughout *Philosophical Investigations*. It therefore cannot be clarified fully by examining Wittgenstein's treatment of a private language – nor would I claim for a moment that it has been properly explicated in the present work. This, however, should not obscure the main purpose of this section. The intention was not to give a comprehensive treatment of Wittgenstein's notion of use, but to show that the fundamental ideas guiding his treatment of private language pervade *Philosophical Investigations*. Underlying Wittgenstein's treatment, then, there is a certain systematicity.

---

[53]   Even though it is foreshadowed in §202.

Chapter 11

Private Language Arguments, Wittgenstein and Contemporary Philosophy

Eighty years have passed since the Vienna Circle's endeavours to divide philosophy into the meaningful and empirical, on one side, and the meaningless, unproductive metaphysics conducted by intuition, on the other. During this period the character of philosophy has changed dramatically, and it will probably never again look as it did in the 1920s. The developments we have followed in the preceding chapters were a leading source of the turbulence and drama that characterized twentieth-century philosophy.

My main concern has been to understand the evolution of argumentation against the possibility of a private language, and in particular to trace the way in which that argumentation was connected with, and reflected, the ideas and agendas that spawned it in different periods. In this epilogue I will change the focus slightly. Instead of trying to understand the changes that occurred, I will attempt to get clear about where, exactly, this strand has led us to today. Many contemporary philosophers refuse to accept the kind of radical naturalism in philosophy of mind and language that has been advocated by, among others, Millikan and Dennett. I shall suggest that this refusal is well explained by a more basic reluctance to accept the conclusions Millikan and Dennett draw from Wittgenstein's writings on the possibility of private language. Wittgenstein's tireless striving for liberation from the need for a private language is relevant, in contemporary philosophy of mind and language, then, in the battle over naturalism.

The climate has changed in the last ten to fifteen years. Ever since the publication of *Philosophical Investigations*, if not earlier, the debate about the possibility of a private language has been intimately tied to Wittgenstein's name. It would be perfectly accurate to describe the preceding chapters as following one strand in the story of the way in which Wittgenstein influenced and changed twentieth-century philosophy.

Today Wittgenstein's name figures less frequently in philosophy of mind and language than it used to. This is not to say that interest in him has diminished – quite the contrary. A constant flow of books about *Philosophical Investigations* is maintained by Wittgenstein scholars. And with the now large amount of published material from Wittgenstein's *Nachlass*, historians of ideas continue to speculate on the developments that occurred in Wittgenstein's philosophy during his stay in Cambridge and, even further back, on the way in which the new ideas drew upon results and insights that can be found in the earlier *Tractatus*. In this literature, work on the private language argument, as found in §§243–315, is especially abundant.[1] And, of course, it should not be forgotten that Wittgenstein's thought continues to be applied to wider philosophical topics, and indeed non-philosophical topics in fields such as sociology. It is nevertheless true that in substantive philosophy of mind and language, Wittgenstein has now become a historical character.

The possibility of a private language is, then, no longer a popular topic in contemporary philosophy of mind and language. It has taken up a peripheral position on the philosophical agenda as new problems and questions have appeared. As the account of the discussion of private language arguments given in Chapter 10 partly shows, genuinely penetrating accounts of the private language argument have focused on Wittgenstein as a historical character. The question 'Could there be a private language?' is increasingly addressed within the confines of the interpretative enquiry 'What did Wittgenstein think about private languages?' In so far as advances in the substantive issues raised by private language are still being made, those advances generally occur within literature whose chief focus is Wittgenstein's work.

The influence of Wittgenstein's work on contemporary philosophy of mind and language, although wide-ranging, is often subtle. There are two types of Wittgensteinian today, one might say: those who discuss his work and those who have internalized some of his distinctive conclusions. Many in the second group could be referred to as third-generation Wittgensteinians, because their access to Wittgenstein's legacy was mediated. Leading mediators were Gilbert Ryle, in Oxford, and Wilfrid Sellars, in Pittsburgh. In this way, although Wittgenstein's arguments are not debated much today, a relatively clear divide can be drawn in contemporary philosophy of mind and language by asking philosophers whether they think positively or negatively about those arguments. Obviously, there continue to be substantial disagreements among those whose attitude is positive, but I would suggest that most would go along with the revisionary conclusions reached in the Memory-Criteria Argument and the Manometer-Beetle Argument. This is the true legacy of *Philosophical Investigations* §§243–315.

Here is bold statement of these conclusions. In the rule-following considerations examined in Chapter 9 a sustained attack on a particular conception of the nature of the normativity of meaning is presented. Normativity is an essential property of meaning and understanding: it is the property in virtue of which it is possible for an expression to be false or misrepresent, and hence in virtue of which it is possible, also, for an expression to be true or represent accurately. If our use of language is not subject to norms, the notion of meaning disappears.

Wittgenstein attacks the idea that the meaning of an expression can be found outside the context of its use and still determine correct use. In §201 Wittgenstein summarizes the results of his investigations: 'This was our paradox: no course of action could be determined by a rule, because every course of action can be made out to accord with the rule.' Here the conclusion reached is that every use of an expression can be made to accord with the meaning of the expression. If this is so, the possibility of falsity, and so normativity, disappears.

---

[1]   See Hutchinson/Read (2005) for an overview of some of the schools of Wittgenstein exegesis that have emerged.

The Memory-Criteria Argument extends this conclusion to the 'private' domain – a domain in which one would appear to have full control. Whereas §201 summarizes an argument showing that any application can be made to accord with a rule, §258 demonstrates that it is impossible to bring use of a private term out of accord with its initial definition. The result, however, is the same as it was in the public scenario: the demand for normativity, that criteria should determine correct use, cannot be sustained in the context of private definition. This conclusion is further elaborated in §265. There is no way of assessing '... whether my present usage agrees with my past usage, whether I am *presently* conforming to my *previous* linguistic intentions' (Kripke [80], p. 12), because in fact my previous usage determines nothing. The general conclusion is that meaning is not conferred on a word simply by a corresponding object, whether that object is public or private. So one cannot first determine, or stipulate, the reference of a word, and assume that this will impose norms on use; reference can only be determined within use.

The Memory-Criteria Argument lays the foundation for the Manometer-Beetle Argument. In the latter Wittgenstein uses the conclusion of the former to query the relevance of the private experience or object – an object whose presence we might feel to be necessary to justify claims about our experiences. The idea dispelled is that we are somehow confronted with something immediately given whose content we identify, and that since identification can go wrong, this conception explains the meaningfulness of mental terms and expressions. The negative conclusion Wittgenstein reaches is that identification plays no role in use (§270), and that even if we insist that sensations are identified, they are irrelevant for the meaningfulness of sensation terms (§293).

Many philosophers still find these conclusions about the normativity of meaning and the nature of sensations provocative. They do so because they discard what we are naturally led to in thinking and theorizing about language and the mental.

Kripke, for instance, in his influential and important account of the rule-following considerations, could not quite embrace its conclusions:

> What had previously seemed to me to be a somewhat loose argument for a fundamentally implausible conclusion based on dubious and controversial premises now appeared to me to be a powerful argument, even if the conclusions seemed even more radical and, in a sense, implausible than before. (Kripke, 1982, p. 1)

In a way this autobiographical remark nicely summarizes what is probably a common view of Wittgenstein's arguments today. That is, many philosophers today would go along with the idea that those arguments are compelling and have no clear refutation. But the fact that Wittgenstein opposes intuitive and plausible views without leaving a clear view of the alternative has also lead many to the conclusion that something has gone awry here.

The positions Wittgenstein attacks are dear to philosophers. Normativity is essential to the idea that linguistic and mental items can have, or be directed upon, particular and determinate contents, and hence be capable of truth and falsity. This is the respect in which such items stand out and qualify as something other than mere elements in causal structures. In view of this, some observers acknowledge the seriousness of Wittgenstein's considerations about normativity, conceding that these considerations need to be addressed at some point:

> This is a topic of the greatest difficulty. It constitutes perhaps the most major challenge facing twentieth-century philosophy (Wright, 1987, p. 29).[2]

While others are less humble and bolder:

> If the Mentalese story about the content of thought is true, then there couldn't be a private language argument. Good. That explains why there isn't one. (Fodor, 1998, p. 68)

Quite a few philosophers today take up one of these positions, or a variant of one of them. The conclusion of the Manometer-Beetle Argument has mostly been taken to concern linguistic meaning. The notion that private experience is '… ornament, not connected with the mechanism at all' (Wittgenstein, 1953, § 270), has either been judged to be so openly wrong that Wittgenstein could not have meant it literally but merely meant to make a point about language, or interpreted as an attack on specific historical doctrines like Cartesianism or phenomenalism. The popularity of the concepts of qualia and phenomenal consciousness can be read as a refusal, by a large sector of the philosophical community, to fully embrace the Manometer-Beetle Argument.

Some philosophers of mind and language, however, have embraced Wittgenstein's negative conclusions and seen them as a way out, as the breaking of a spell. The focus of these philosophers has been on the constructive project of moving beyond Wittgenstein, of building on the foundation laid by him.

Wittgensteinians of this later sort have often sought to explore and develop Wittgenstein's emphasis on practice and use, on rules that are implicit in practice. They have tried to show how these notions are essential to a proper understanding of the normativity of meaning. As Robert Brandom succinctly puts it, the idea here is that 'semantics must answer to pragmatics' (Brandom, 1994, p. 83). That is, the 'theoretical point of attributing semantic content to intentional states, attitudes, and performances is to determine the pragmatic significance of their occurrence in various contexts' (Brandom, 1994, p. 83).

From this perspective Wittgenstein's arguments had the effect of demonstrating the futility of putting semantics before pragmatics, representation before use, in normative theory. An awareness of that futility permeates Robert Brandom's *Making it Explicit*, a book in which deep investigation into the nature of language and social practices of rational agents is carefully conducted. Brandom's approach is explicitly rationalistic. It involves the idea that there must be 'norms all the way down'. Brandom insists, moreover, that norms '… (in the sense of normative statuses) are not objects in the causal order' (Brandom, 1994, p. 626). Ruth Millikan, on the other hand, has developed Wittgenstein's legacy in a naturalistic direction. For her, Wittgenstein's emphasis on the primacy of use, and on the idea that we should look at the function of a word to determine its meaning, receives a much more precise interpretation: '"Meaning", in the most basic sense, simply *is* function; it is what I have called

---

² See also Wright (1992), Ch. 6.

"proper" or "stabilizing" function ..., or, very roughly, what Sellars called "survival value"' (Millikan, 2005, p. 90). Millikan embeds the notion that meaning is, first and foremost, determined by the effects of an item, and only secondarily by reference, in a natural-selective framework. It is no coincidence that she begins her influential *Language, Thought, and other Biological Categories* by suggesting that we develop Wittgenstein's analogy between words and tools (Millikan, 1984, p. 1).

Despite considerable differences in the theoretical frameworks offered by Millikan and Brandom, both of these philosophers have learned a key lesson from Wittgenstein about what the normativity of meaning requires. Each has then taken on the task of trying to understand normativity as a genuine phenomenon. By contrast, Daniel Dennett has suggested that we understand meaning ascriptions as part of a particular kind of perspective one can adopt on complex systems: the so-called intentional stance (Dennett, 1987). To him, our ascriptions of content or meaning essentially require distinctive analysis, but he has been somewhat unforthcoming on the question whether the elements postulated in this stance have a genuine grounding, probably as a result of his rather dismissive attitude to philosophical theorizing.

Much more could be said about all three of these constructive projects – each of which, of course, has important sources of inspiration other than Wittgenstein. It would misleading not to mention Sellars and Quine here, for example. At any rate, what the projects share is a willingness to take on board Wittgenstein's conclusions on rule-following and private language and move beyond, or build on, them. In this sense Wittgenstein's arguments have been absorbed by contemporary philosophers and have become foundational.

Those who are sceptical about this foundation – and some are, of course – are confronted not only by the considerations Wittgenstein himself adduced, but also by more recent independent work in a similar vein. Ruth Millikan, for instance, has argued for the negative conclusion Wittgenstein reached in the Manometer-Beetle Argument:

> The belief that the intentional contents of one's explicit intentions are 'given' to consciousness is just one strand of a tangle of entrenched beliefs which I have called 'meaning rationalism'... Meaning rationalism, in its various forms, has gone unquestioned in the philosophical tradition to such a degree that, to my knowledge, no arguments have ever been adduced to support it. However, a large portion of Wittgenstein's *Philosophical Investigations* is devoted to an attempt to *dispel* the notion that what one intends, especially when one intends to follow a rule, is given in what appears before consciousness. And a considerable portion of the Wilfrid Sellars corpus is built on the motif that *nothing* is, epistemically, given to consciousness.
>
> My intention is to kill meaning rationalism *dead*, and then beat on it (Millikan, 1993, pp. 28–9 and 12).

It is not hard to sense the frustration here.[3]

Even more explicitly, and with perhaps greater dedication, Daniel Dennett has sought to expose modern manifestations of the fallacies Wittgenstein warned against.

---

3   See also the epilogue of Millikan (1984).

At the end of his influential *Consciousness Explained*, which contains several chapters on resolving 'the traditional paradoxes and mysteries of consciousness' (Dennett, 1991, p. 17), Dennett writes:

> Several philosophers have seen what I am doing as a kind of redoing Wittgenstein's attack on the 'objects' of conscious experience. Indeed it is ... My debt to Wittgenstein is large and longstanding. When I was an undergraduate, he was my hero, so I went to Oxford, where he seemed to be everybody's hero. When I saw how my fellow graduate students were (by my lights) missing the point, I gave up trying to 'be' a Wittgensteinian, and just took what I thought I had learned from the *Investigations* and tried to put it to work (Dennett, 1991, pp. 462–3).

Millikan and Dennett display the influence of the therapeutic elements in Wittgenstein's philosophy.[4] Dennett, in particular, has espoused a conception of philosophy, when done properly, as therapy against the speculative, phantasmic constructions of the intellect; he regards the philosopher as a curer of diseases (Wittgenstein, 1953, §255) rather than someone engaged in the discovery of truth. More than once, Dennett (Dennett, 1987 and Dennett, 1991) has attempted to demonstrate the futility of working with a substantial conception of meaning and consciousness.[5]

In this respect Millikan and Dennett share Wittgenstein's methodological inhibitions. But whereas Wittgenstein tried to combine his exposition of the deceptions of theoretical thinking with an approach that 'leaves everything as it is' (§124), they promote a conception of philosophy as a theoretical superstructure in dialogue with science. With some (doubtless rather important) qualifications, perhaps Brandom would agree; but this conception would probably have struck Wittgenstein as a case of reason running heedlessly over the borders of language (§119).

The philosophical landscape has, as I say, changed. Even twenty years ago it looked very different from the way it does now. This change might well lead one to conclude that the private language argument is no longer important, but this inference would be too fast. Private language arguments were never solely about private languages. They raised much wider questions about meaning and mind. Throughout the twentieth century, private language arguments threatened to take many philosophers where they did not want to go, and I think this is still the case today. Today, most philosophers are wary of embracing the positions of some of the most radical naturalists in philosophy of mind and language – Millikan and Dennett, and normative rationalists like Brandom. This reluctance can be put down, in part, to an unwillingness to embrace the lessons these philosophers have learned from Wittgenstein's profound investigations into the possibility of private language.

---

[4]   Another philosopher influenced by this methodological doctrine in Wittgenstein's philosophy is John McDowell; see his (1994).

[5]   Although I would argue, with Hutto (2003) Ch. 6, that there are important differences between Wittgenstein's and Dennett's therapeutic inhibitions.

Appendices

Arguments Examined in Chapter 2

Carnap's Private Language Argument

Initial Assumption: Suppose the sensational and physical domains are not shared between subjects.

Premise: If a sentence A is uttered by S1 referring to her sensational or physical domain, then another speaker S2 cannot determine whether A is true.

Premise: A sentence means nothing more to a speaker than what can be tested about it (verificationism).

Intermediate Conclusion: Sentence A is meaningless to S2; S1 cannot communicate anything by uttering A. (Referential privacy leads to incommunicability).

Premise: Intersubjective communicability is a fact; sentences about the sensational and the physical are intelligible (as is shown by the objectivity of scientific discourse).

Conclusion: Given this inconsistency, we should reject our initial assumption with regard to both the sensational and the physical domain.

Neurath's Private Language Argument

Protocol sentences are revisable. This follows from the fact that they are scientific claims, for scientific claims are capable of evaluation and hence can in principle be overturned.

Initial Assumption: Suppose that at t2 we want to evaluate a protocol sentence P used by S at t1.

Premise: Protocol sentences, indeed all sentences, are physically instantiated strings of symbols.

Intermediate conclusion: The only way to evaluate P at t2 is to compare it with the set of physically instantiated strings of symbols which one holds to be true.

Premise: A sentence means nothing more to a speaker than what can be tested about it (verificationism).

Conclusion: The meaning of P cannot be a particular sensation, because we would not check P by comparing it to an immediately 'given' or sensational domain. Indeed since the evaluation of P occurs by comparing sets of physical strings of symbols, S has no privileged way of evaluating P.

The intermediate conclusion would not be accepted by Carnap. Carnap would ask: Why not say that the only way to evaluate P is by checking whether it correctly describes what S experienced on the relevant occasion (repeat the experiment)?

However, this question assumes that the sentence has (or had) determinate meaning. More precisely, it assumes that the semantics of the sentence can be determined by examining its syntax.

These assumptions conflict with the message of **Neurath's boat simile** – that is, with Neurath's semantic holism. So we have no guarantee, other than its fitness to remain in our body of scientific discourse, that P is true.

Argument Examined in Chapter 3

The Phenomenological Language Argument

Initial Assumption: Suppose I have a phenomenological language. This would be a language that describes visual space (*Gesichtsraum*) without invoking notions applying outside that space, i.e. a language whose terms express concepts wholly derived, directly, from visual space.

Premise: In visual space there is no distinction between 'being' and 'seeming to be' (epistemic infallibility).

Premise: In visual space the following is possible: it seems to be the case, and therefore it is the case, that

$$|a| = |b|, \quad |c| = |d|, \quad |24c| = |a|, \quad |25d| = |b|$$

Premise: The identity-relation in visual space is transitive.

Intermediate Conclusion: Therefore one can conclude, about the visual image of $|d|$, that,

$$|d| = |c| = 24/25\,|d|$$

Premise: The concept of length is a function linking an entity to a value; it cannot assume two values.

Conclusion: The concept of length cannot be expressed in the phenomenological language (conceptual unintelligibility).

Argument Examined in Chapter 4

The 1941 Private Object Argument

The motivation for introducing private objects

Premise: A person who knows the meaning of 'I am in pain' should be able to distinguish cases where its assertion is warranted from cases in which it is not.

Premise: If assertion is warranted, some form of justification must support it.

Premise: Among the cases where 'I am in pain' can be asserted, there are some in which there is no public evidence available.

Conclusion: So, in these cases, a private object must warrant the assertion of 'I am in pain'.

The irrelevance of private objects

Question: 'How does he who utters "I am in pain" know that the private object is present?'

Answer 1: The person experiencing pain asserts 'I am in pain' in cases where the object is present.

Rejection: This leads to a circle which makes the object irrelevant: that is, the use of the word justifies the presence of the private object, which justifies the use of the word.

Answer 2: Perhaps the speaker does not, strictly speaking, know, but only thinks that he knows, that the private object is present.

Rejection: But this situation would only make sense if it is *possible* for the speaker to know that the private object is present. Since the relevant knowledge, on this proposal, is unachievable, the speaker does not know what he thinks. Perhaps we ought to say 'He thinks, that he thinks, that he knows…' and so on, ad infinitum.

Conclusion: The private object has no explanatory value; it could be anything or nothing. It does not follow from a claim being warranted that there must be justification available.

Arguments Examined in Chapter 5

The Reductio Argument

Initial Assumption: Suppose I attempt to establish a private definition by fixing my attention on a pain as I pronounce the word 'pain' (private ostensive definition).

Premise: My private definition will have been a success, and will have introduced the word into a language, only if it led me to use the word correctly in the future. Here 'correctly' means *in accordance with a rule* (language as a set of rules).

Premise: A word can, by the definition of 'rule', be used in accordance with a rule only if one can distinguish between being under the impression that one is following a rule and actually following a rule (the essence of a rule).

Premise: I can make this distinction only if I can appeal to something independent of my impressions capable of proving that I am, or am not, following a rule (no proof, no difference).

Premise: But there is nothing independent of my impressions to appeal to in the considered case (excludes memory).

Conclusion: Hence my private definition cannot have been successful.

The Solitary Language Argument

Premise: A solitary speaker cannot learn his language, so he must invent it himself.

Premise: In a language invented by a solitary speaker, the meaning of the words will not be independent of the speaker's use of those words.

Premise: If there is no independence of meaning, the words cannot be misunderstood.

Conclusion: If the words cannot be misunderstood, there is no possibility of distinguishing 'seems correct' from 'correct' (Negation of the equivalent of the consequent in the second premise of the Reductio Argument).

The External Private Language Argument

Premise: The Argument from Analogy presupposes that it makes sense to attribute thoughts and feelings to another human figure.

Premise: A sentence can mean something to a speaker, only if he has a criterion for deciding whether it can be warrantedly asserted.

Intermediate Conclusion: So 'that human figure has thoughts and feelings' (where the figure in question is another person) has criteria of assertion.

Premise: It is in the nature of criteria that their satisfaction, in a certain situation, entitles one to a knowledge-claim about what the sentence asserts.

Premise: It is also in the nature of criteria that their satisfaction or non-satisfaction can be recognized.

Premise: So a speaker has access to a situation in which he can know whether another human figure has thought and feelings – namely, the one in which the above-mentioned criteria are satisfied.

Conclusion: Hence analogical reasoning is unnecessary.

Arguments Examined in Chapter 8

Kenny's Argument Against Fixing the Use of a Word in Private

Suppose I fix my attention on a sensation while I write down 'E'. Some time afterwards, I say 'this is E again.' What can 'E' mean here?

Rejection of the first reply

Suppose I answer the above question by saying: 'By "E" I mean *this*', while gesturing (as it were) at my current sensation.

The Principle of Bipolarity: for a statement to be capable of being true, it must also be capable of being false (Candlish (1998); factual assertions presuppose a distinction between truth and falsity.

This presupposes that what gives a statement its content cannot at the same time give it its truth (Candlish (1998): the distinction between truth and falsity presupposes a distinction between origin of meaning and origin of truth).

But in the present case I assert, of my present sensation, that it is E, while at the same time explaining the meaning of 'E' by reference to that sensation; so the origin of meaning is conflated with the origin of truth.

My explanation of what I mean by 'E' is therefore unsuccessful.

Rejection of the second reply

Suppose I say instead: 'By "E" I mean the sensation I named "E" in the past.'

Since no ostensive definition would have been effected by this, all I can refer to by '...the sensation I named "E" in the past' is the memory of naming a sensation 'E' in the past. (This is a crucial, but well-hidden, premise in Kenny's text.)

In other words, 'E' means the sensation I remember naming 'E' in the initial setting.

Hence 'this is E again' means that the present sensation is the sensation I remember naming 'E' in the past.

Once again, however, this means that the origins of truth and meaning have been conflated, because 'this is E again' will be true only if the present sensation is E, i.e. the sensation I *remember* naming 'E' in the past.

To see this, consider the possibility that 'this is E again' is false. 'This is E again' will be false only if the present sensation is not the one I remember naming 'E' in the past.

This is only possible if the sensation I remember naming 'E' in the past is not the one I remember naming 'E' in the past. But this is absurd, so there is no real possibility of falsehood.

Rejection of the third reply

Suppose I try saying: 'By "E" I mean the sensation correlated with a rise in blood pressure.'

On this suggestion, 'this is E again' will be false only if my present sensation is not the one correlated with a rise in blood pressure.

But since 'E' does not mean the sensation associated with a rise in blood pressure, it remains possible that the present sensation is not E even though my blood pressure has risen.

But then my present sensation is correlated with a rise in blood pressure, which means that 'this is E again' is true.

Arguments Examined in Chapter 9

The Memory-Criteria Argument

In what follows I begin (with one exception) by numbering sentences from each of the relevant sections of *Philosophical Investigations*. These numbers are repeated in parenthesis as the following explication proceeds, in order to indicate the progress being made through Wittgenstein's text. Where no number appears, the relevant step in the argument is an expansion of Wittgenstein's own argumentation.

Philosophical Investigations §258

1 Let us 2 I want 3 To this end 4 I will remark first 5 But I can 6 How? 7 Not in 8 But I speak 9 But what is 10 A definition 11 Well, that 12 But 'I 13 But in the 14 One would like 15 And that

Suppose I, a speaker of a shared language, wish to keep a diary about the recurrence of a certain sensation. For this purpose I associate a sign 'E' with the sensation. In the circumstances, this sign will be a descriptive, one-word sentence and whose meaning is private (1–3).

By the privacy requirement 'E' cannot be given a verbal definition, since this would make it a word in the shared, public language (4).

By the privacy requirement 'E' cannot be defined by ordinary ostension, for although 'E' would then be independent of the shared language, this definition would also make it public (5–7).

Hence I will have to employ a kind of ostension in which I speak out, or write down 'E', while focusing my attention on the relevant sensation, thereby impressing on myself the connection between sign and sensation (8).

If this is supposed to fix the meaning of 'E' (and this is indeed the purpose of a definition), then the meaning of 'E' will be the connection I have impressed on myself (9–11).

But this can only mean that my criterion for 'E' referring to x is that I remember correctly that 'E' refers to x (12). (Perhaps it is better to say that my criterion for understanding 'E' is the fact that I remember correctly the impressed connection, and this is my understanding of 'E'.)

But in the present case I have no criterion for remembering correctly, since that presupposes that I understand what I am supposed to remember, and so it does not make sense to say that I remember correctly (or wrongly) that 'E' refers to x (13).

So I can only have a criterion to the extent that I seem to remember correctly. But then 'E' will refer to x whenever I have the impression that 'E' refers to x (14–15).

Philosophical Investigations §265

§265 argues by analogy, and a sentence-by-sentence treatment would, I think, be unnecessarily lengthy. Just as he invokes an analogy with a table for translation, Wittgenstein also considers a table for train departures.

From §258, 13: Can I not find a criterion in memory?

My criterion would then be: I remember that 'E' refers to x when and only when my memory is supported by a clear memory that 'E' refers to x.

By analogy: Can I not appeal to a *clear* memory in order to justify my dim recollection that 'E' refers to x, just as I can appeal to a table, in my memory, to justify my translation of the word W with W*?

If the table in my memory exists independently of my memory, the clear memory of the table in which W is translated into W* can justify my translation of W with W*.

But if the table exists only in my imagination, my clear memory of it can justify only my imaginative belief that W should be translated using W*.

The second of these is analogous to the situation with 'E': my clear memory that 'E' refers to x can justify at most my belief that I remember that 'E' refers to x, not that I do so remember.

We are still left with the problem that one cannot remember something one does not understand, and this goes for both a clear memory and a dim one.

The Manometer-Beetle Argument

Philosophical Investigations §270

1 Let us 2 I discover 3 So I 4 This is 5 And now it seems 6 Let us suppose 7 And that alone 8 (We as it 9 And What 10 Perhaps 11 And why 12 Well, aren't

Suppose I have the following experience: whenever I have a particular sensation my blood pressure rises (2).

Using 'E' as sign for that experience, I might have a use for writing 'E' in my diary (3–4).

So 'E' describes a certain (genuinely) private sensation correlated with a rise in blood pressure.

Or we might say: 'E' describes the impression that my blood pressure is rising.

Suppose the concept of identification plays a role here; then misidentification should make sense (6).

Since 'E' does not designate the rise in blood pressure, the misidentification would not arise merely when no rise in blood pressure occurs.

So a mistake will have to occur whenever I have the impression that my blood pressure is rising but do not notice it. But here, if I do not notice, I do not have the impression. Likewise I can not lack the impression that my blood pressure rises, and at the same time think I have the impression; then I have it (6).

So a mistake is not possible here, and consequently the concept of identification plays no role. Every sensation I describe using 'E' is E (5, 7).

Philosophical Investigations §293

1 If I say 2 And how 3 Now someone 4 Suppose 5 No one can 6 Here it 7 One might 8 But suppose 9 If so 10 The thing 11 No, one 12 That is to say

Suppose I know only from my own case what pain means (1).

If everyone speaks about the same thing when talking about pain, it will follow that everyone knows only from his own case what pain is (1).

But why would I now think that everyone speaks about the same (2)?

Suppose each of us knows what pain is only from his own case (3 and the second part of 1).

By analogy: suppose everyone has a box into which no one else can look, and that everyone refers the content of the box as 'beetle' (4, 5).

Then it might be that each of us has something different in his box (6), or even that whatever is in my box constantly changes (7) or that my box is empty (10). The answer, then, to the question posed in (2), is that we should not think that everyone is speaking about the same thing.

Hence, so far as common use is concerned, it would be irrelevant whether there is anything at all in the box, let alone a private object (11).

Conversely, if each of us identified the presence of a beetle by reference to his own box, we would not arrive at a common use for the word 'beetle' (8, 9).

Thus, if sensations are conceived of as private objects, they become irrelevant to our public language (12).

Translated Passages

This appendix provides the original German text of passages that have been translated by the author in the text.

Page 11:
'... abgeschwächter Restbestand idealistischer Metaphysik ...' (Neurath, 1932a, 540).

Page 27:
'... Carnap ist gewissenhaft, wo es sich um Zitate in seinen eigenen Werken handelt, und nur seine Hauptquelle hat er verschwiegen.
2. Dass ich mich nicht mit der Frage des "Physikalismus" befasst hätte, ist unwahr ...
3. Ich glaube nicht, dass Carnap sich nicht mehr an das Gespräch mit Waismann erinnert, worin diesem ihm meine Auffassung der hinweisenden Definitionen mitgeteilt hat.
4. Seine Auffassung der Hypothesen hat Carnap von mir ...' (Nedo/Ranchetti (eds), 1983, 254–5).

Page 29:
'Wenn man aber sagt: Der Philosoph muss aber eben in diesen Kessel hinuntersteigen und die reine Realität selbst erfassen und ans Tageslicht ziehen so lautet die Antwort dass er dabei die Sprache hinten lassen müsste und daher unverrichteter Dinge wieder heraufkommt.
Und doch kann es eine phänomenologische Sprache geben.(Wo muss diese Halt machen?)' (Wittgenstein, 1994, 3).

Page 30:
'Die Annahme dass eine phänomenologische Sprache möglich wäre und die eigentlich erst das sagen würde was wir in der Philosophie ausdrücken müssen/ wollen ist – glaube ich – absurd. Wir müssen mit unserer gewöhnlichen Sprache auskommen und sie nur richtig verstehen. D.h. wir dürfen uns nicht von ihr verleiten lassen Unsinn zu reden.' (Wittgenstein, 1994, 102).

Page 31:
'Die Verification ist nicht e i n Anzeihen der Wahrheit, sondern d e r Sinn des Satzes.' (Wittgenstein, 1994, 84).

Page 32:

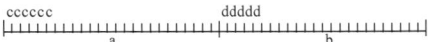

'Es ist offenbar möglich dass mir die Strecken a und b gleichlang erscheinen dass mir auch die Stücke c und d gleichlang erscheinen dass aber ihre Zählung ergibt dass ich 25 c und 24 d habe. Hier haben wir die Frage: Wie kann das möglich sein? Ist es hier richtig zu sagen: Es ist eben so, und wir sehen nur dass der Gesichtsraum nicht den Regeln – etwa – des euklidischen Raumes folgt. Das würde heissen, dass die Frage "wie kann es möglich sein?" unsinnig und also unberechtigt wäre. Hier läge also gar nichts Paradoxes sondern wir hatten dass nur einfach hinzunehmen.' (Wittgenstein, 1994, 18).

Page 32:
'Wenn man aber nicht sagen kan, dass in a und b eine bestimmte Anzahl von Teilen ist, wie soll ich dass Gesichtsbild dann beschreiben? Es zeigt sich – glaube ich – hier, dass das Gesichtsbild viel komplizierter ist als es auf den ersten blick scheint. Was es so viel komplizierter macht ist z.B. der faktor den die Bewegung des Auges erzeugen.' (Wittgenstein, 1994, 19).

Page 33:
'Oder soll ich nun sagen dass eben doch auch im Gesichtsraum etwas anders *scheinen* kann als es *ist*? Gewiss nicht!
... Es sei denn, dass es überhaupt keinen Sinn hat von Strecken im *Gesichtsraum* auszusagen, dass sie gleich *sind* ... Dass es also ein *absolutes* Scheinen gäbe.' (Wittgenstein, 1994, 18).

Page 34:
'Die phänomenologische Sprache oder "primäre Sprache" wie ich sie nannte schwebt mir jetzt nicht mehr als Ziel vor; ich halte sie jetzt nicht mehr für möglich.' (Wittgenstein, 1994, 118).

Page 38:
'Das Phänomen ist nicht Symptom für etwas anderes sondern ist die realität.
Das Phänomen ist nicht Symptom für etwas anderes was den Satz erst wahr oder falsch macht sondern ist selbst das was ihn verifiziert.' (Wittgenstein, 1994, 128).

Page 42:
'Wie ein Satz verifiziert wird, das sagt er. Vergleiche die Allgemeinheit der eigentlichen Sätze, mit der allgemeinheit in der Arithmetik. Sie wird anders verifiziert und ist darum eine andere.' (Wittgenstein, 1994, 84).

Page 160:
'Was meine ich bei der zweiten Gelegenheit mit "E"?' (Candlish, 1998, 153).

Page 160:
'..., dass mit "E" nichts anderes gemeint ist als dieselbe (Art von) Empfindung, wie ich sie jetzt habe.' (Candlish, 1998, 153).

Page 165:
'In PU 270 wird für "E" ein bestimmter Gebrauch als Empfindungsäusserung beschrieben und gezeigt, *dass innerhalb dieses Gebrauchs die identifizierung*

keine Rolle spielt. Hier[§293] wird mit dem Ziel der Widerlegung Vorausgesetzt, "Käfer" werde auf Grund der identifizierung des Schachtelinhalts verwendet, und daraus geschlossen, *dass diese Rolle der Identifizierung den vorgeblichen Gebrauch ausschliesst.*' (von Savigny, 1988, 344)

Page 165:
'Das deutet auf eine weitere Chance für den Befürworter des Privatsprachengedankens hin: Könnte der Privatsprachler seinem Zeichen "E" nicht vielleicht eine Bedeutung verleihen, indem er den privaten Zeichengebrauch mit einem öffentlichem Phänomen verknüpft?' (Candlish, 1998, 159).

Page 169:
'Dass jemand mit einer Äusserung, mit einer Handlung, mit einem Bild usw. etwas meint (etwas darunter versteht), betrifft ihn nicht isoliert. Vielmehr besteht die Tatsache darin, dass die Muster seines individuellen Verhaltens in bestimmter Weise in Muster des sozialen Verhaltens in der Gemeinschaft, zu der er gerechnet wird, eingebettet sind.' (von Savigny, 1988, 7).

Bibliography

Albritton, R., 'On Wittgenstein's use of the Term "Criterion"', *The Journal of Philosophy*, 56 (1959): 845–57.

Ambrose, A., 'Review of *Philosophical Investigations*', *Philosophy and Phenomenological Research*, 15 (1954): 111–15.

Ambrose, A. and Lazerowitz, M. (eds), *Ludwig Wittgenstein: Philosophy and Language* (London: George Allen and Unwin, 1972).

Armstrong, B. F., 'Wittgenstein on Private Languages: It Takes Two to Talk', *Philosophical Investigations*, 7 (1984): 46–62.

Ayer, A. J., 'Can There Be a Private Language?', (1954). Reprinted with additional notes in (Jones (ed.), 1971): 50–61.

Ayer, A. J., *The Problem of Knowledge* (Harmondsworth: Penguin, 1956).

Ayer, A. J. (ed.), *Logical Positivism* (Glencoe, Illinois: The Free Press, 1959).

Baker, G., 'Criteria: A New Foundation for Semantics', *Ratio*, 16 (1974). Reprinted in (Shanker (ed.), 1986): 194–226.

Baker, G., 'Following Wittgenstein: Some Signposts for *Philosophical Investigations* §§143–242', in (Holtzman and Leich (eds), 1981): 31–71.

Baker, G. P. and Hacker, P. M. S., *Wittgenstein: Understanding and Meaning* (Oxford: Basil Blackwell, 1980).

Baker, G. P. and Hacker, P. M. S., *Scepticism, Rules & Language* (Oxford: Basil Blackwell, 1984).

Baker, G. P. and Hacker, P. M. S., *Wittgenstein: Rules, Grammar and Necessity* (Oxford: Basil Blackwell, 1985).

Block, I. (ed.), *Perspectives on the Philosophy of Wittgenstein* (Oxford: Basil Blackwell, 1981).

Bloor, D., *Wittgenstein: A Social theory of Knowledge* (New York: Columbia University Press, 1983).

Bloor, D., *Wittgenstein, Rules and Institutions* (London: Routledge, 1997).

Boghossian, P. A., 'The Rule–Following Considerations', *Mind*, 98 (1989): 507–49.

Brandom, R. B, *Making it Explicit: Reasoning, Representing and Discursive Commitment* (Cambridge, MA: Harvard University Press, 1994).

Buck, R., 'Non-other Minds', in R. J. Butler (ed.), *Analytical Philosophy* (Oxford: Basil Blackwell, 1962): 187–210.

Burge, T., 'Philosophy of Language and Mind: 1950–1990', *The Philosophical Review*, 101 (1992): 3–51.

Candlish, S., 'The Real Private Language Argument', *Philosophy*, 55 (1980): 85–94.

Candlish, S., 'Wittgenstein's Privatsprachenargumentation', in (von Savigny (ed.), 1998): 143–66.

Canfield, J. V. (ed.), *The Philosophy of Wittgenstein. A Fifteen Volume Collection* (New York: Garland, 1986).

Canfield, J. V., 'The Community View', *The Philosophical Review*, 105 (1996): 469–88.

Canfield, J. V., 'Private Language: The Diary Case', *Australasian Journal of Philosophy*, 79 (2001): 377–94.

Carnap, R., *The Logical Structure of the World* (1928). Reprinted in his (2003): 1–300.

Carnap, R., 'Pseudoproblems in Philosophy', (1929). Reprinted in his (2003): 301–43.

Carnap, R., *The Unity of Science* (1932a). Reprinted in his, *The Unity of Science – Translated with an Introduction by M. Black* (Bristol: Thoemmes Press, 1995).

Carnap, R., 'Psychology in Physical Language' (1932b). Translated. (Ayer (ed.), 1959): 165–97.

Carnap, R., 'On Protocol Sentences' (1932c). Translated by R. Creath and R. Nollan, *Noûs*, 21 (1987): 457–70.

Carnap, R., *The Logical Structure of the World and Pseudoproblems in Philosophy*, translated by R. A. George (Chicago: Open Court, 2003).

Carnap, R.; Hahn, H.; Neurath, O. et al. [Official author: Verein Ernst Mach], 'Scientific World Conception: The Vienna Circle' (1929). Translated. (Neurath, 1973): 299–318.

Carney, J. D., 'Private Language: The Logic of Wittgenstein's Argument', *Mind*, 69 (1960): 560–5.

Cartwright, N. et al, *Otto Neurath: Philosophy between Science and Politics* (Cambridge: Cambridge University Press, 1996).

Castañeda, H.–N., 'The Private Language Argument as a *reductio ad absurdum*' (1962), Reprinted in (Jones (ed.), 1971): 132–54 and 173–82.

Castañeda, H.–N., 'Consciousness and Behaviour: Their Basic Connections', in his, *Intentionality, Minds, and Perception* (Detroit: Wayne State University Press, 1967a): 121–75.

Castañeda, H.–N., 'The Private Language Problem', in P. Edwards et al (eds), *Encyclopedia of Philosophy* (New York: Macmillan and Free Press, 1967b).

Cavell, S., *The Claim of Reason: Wittgenstein, Skepticism, Morality, and Tragedy* (New York: Oxford University Press, 1979).

Chappell, V. C. (ed.), *Ordinary Language* (Englewood Cliffs, New Jersey: Prentice–Hall, 1964).

Chihara, C.S. and Fodor, J.A., 'Operationalism and ordinary language: A critique of Wittgenstein' (1965). Reprinted in (Pitcher (ed.), 1966): 384–419.

Cirera, R., *Carnap and the Vienna Circle – Empiricism and Logical Syntax*, (Studien zur österreichischen Philosophie, Band XXIII) (Amsterdam, NL: Rodopi, 1994).

Collins, J., 'Review of *Philosophical Investigations*', *Thought*, XXIX (1954): 287–92.

Cook, J. W., 'Wittgenstein on Privacy', *The Philosophical Review*, 74 (1965): 281–314.

Cook, J. W., 'Human Beings', in P. Winch (ed.), *Studies in the Philosophy of Wittgenstein* (London: Routledge and Kegan Paul: 1969): 117–51.

Cook, J. W., 'Solipsism and Language', in (Ambrose and Lazerowitz, 1972): 37–73.

Cook, J. W., *Wittgenstein, Empiricism and Language* (New York: Oxford University Press, 2000).

Craig, E., 'Meaning, Use and Privacy', *Mind*, XCI (1982): 541–64.

Dennett, D. C., *The Intentional Stance* (Cambridge, MA: MIT Press, 1987).

Dennett, D. C., *Consciousness Explained* (London: Penguin Press, 1991).

Donagan, A., 'Wittgenstein on Sensation', in (Pitcher (ed.), 1966): 324–51.

Dummett, M., 'Oxford Philosophy' (1960). Reprinted in his (1978): 431–6.

Dummett, M., 'The Philosophical Basis of Intuitionistic Logic' (1973). Reprinted in his (1978): 215–47.

Dummett, M., 'Can Analytical Philosophy be Systematic, and Ought it to be?' (1975). Reprinted in his (1978): 437–58.

Dummett, M., *Truth and Other Enigmas* (Cambridge, MA: Harvard University Press, 1978).

Feigl, H. 'Physicalism, Unity of Science and the Foundations of Psychology', in Schilpp (ed.) (1963): 227–68.

Feyerabend, P., 'Wittgenstein's Philosophical Investigations', *The Philosophical Review*, 64 (1955): 449–83.

Feyerabend, P., 'Problems of Empiricism', in R. G. Colodny (ed.), *Beyond the Edge of Certainty* (Englewood Cliffs, New Jersey: Prentice-Hall, 1965): 145–260.

Findlay, J. N., 'Review of *Philosophical Investigations*', *Philosophy*, XXX (1955): 173–9.

Fodor, J. A., *In Critical Condition: Polemical Essays on Cognitive Science and the Philosophy of Mind* (Cambridge, MA: MIT Press, 1997).

Fogelin, R. J., *Wittgenstein* (London: Routledge and Kegan Paul: 1976).

Frongia, G. and McGuinness, B., *Wittgenstein: A Bibliographical Guide* (Oxford: Basil Blackwell, 1990).

Garver, N., 'Discussion: Wittgenstein on Private Language', *Philosophy and Phenomenological Research*, XX (1959): 389–96.

Gilbert, M., 'On the question Whether Language Has a Social Nature: Some Aspects of Winch and Others on Wittgenstein', *Synthése*, 56 (1983): 301–18.

Glock, H.–J., *A Wittgenstein Dictionary* (Oxford: Basil Blackwell, 1996).

Goldberg, B., 'The Linguistic Expression of Feeling', *American Philosophical Quarterly*, 8 (1971): 86–92.

Hacker, P. M. S., *Insight and Illusion* (Oxford: Clarendon Press, 1972).

Hacker, P. M. S., *Wittgenstein: Meaning and Mind. An analytical commentary on the Philosophical Investigations, vol. 3* (Oxford: Basil Blackwell, 1990)

Hacker, P. M. S., *Wittgenstein: Mind and Will. An analytical commentary on the Philosophical Investigations, vol. 4* (Oxford: Basil Blackwell, 1996a).

Hacker, P. M. S., *Wittgenstein's Place in Twentieth–century Analytic Philosophy* (Oxford: Basil Blackwell, 1996b).

Hale, B. and Wright, C. (eds), *A Companion to the Philosophy of Language* (Oxford: Basil Blackwell, 1997).

Haller, R. and Rutte, H., 'Gespräch mit Heinrich Neider', *Conceptus* (1977): 29–30.

Hallett, G., *A Companion to Wittgenstein's "Philosophical Investigations"* (London: Cornell University Press, 1977).

Hartnack, J., *Wittgenstein og den moderne filosofi* (Copenhagen, Denmark: Gyldendal, 1960).

Heath, P. L., 'Wittgenstein Investigated', *Philosophical Quarterly*, VI (1956): 66–71.

Hervey, H., 'The Private language Problem', *Philosophical Quarterly*, VII (1957), pp. 63–75.

Hintikka, J., 'Ludwig's Apple Tree: On the Philosophical Relations between Wittgenstein and the Vienna Circle' (1993). Reprinted in his, *Selected Papers, Vol. 1: Ludwig Wittgenstein; Half-Truths and One-and-a-Half-Truths* (Dordrecht, NL: Kluwer, 1996).

Hintikka, M. B. and Hintikka, J., *Investigating Wittgenstein* (Oxford: Basil Blackwell, 1986).

Holborow, L. C., 'Wittgenstein's Kind of Behaviourism?', *Philosophical Quarterly*, XVII (1967): 345–57.

Holtzman, S. H. and Leich, C. M., *Wittgenstein: To Follow a Rule* (London: Routledge and Kegan Paul, 1981).

Hutto, D. D., *Wittgenstein and the End of Philosophy – Neither Theory nor Therapy* (Basingstoke, Hampshire: Palgrave/Macmillan, 2003).

Jones, O. R. (ed.), *The Private Language Argument* (London: Macmillan and Co, 1971).

Kenny, A., 'Cartesian Privacy', in (Pitcher (ed.), 1966): 352–70.

Kenny, A., 'The Verification Principle and the private language argument', in (Jones (ed.), 1971): 204–28.

Kenny, A., *Wittgenstein* (London: Allen Lane, 1973).

Koethe, J., *The Continuity of Wittgenstein's Thought* (New York: Cornell University Press, 1996).

Kripke, S. A., *Wittgenstein on Rules and Private Language* (Oxford: Basil Blackwell, 1982).

Lee, D. (ed.), *Wittgenstein's Lectures, Cambridge 1930–1932* (Oxford: Basil Blackwell, 1980).

Lieb, I. C., 'Wittgenstein's Investigations', *Review of Metaphysics*, VIII (1954): 125–43.

Linsky, L., 'Wittgenstein on Language and some Problems of Philosophy', *The Journal of Philosophy*, 54 (1957): 285–93.

Lycan, W. G., 'Non–Inductive Evidence: Recent Work on Wittgenstein's 'Criterion'', *American Philosophical Quarterly* 8 (1970): 109–25.

Malcolm, N., 'Moore and Ordinary Language' (1942). Reprinted in (Chappell (ed.), 1964): 5–23.

Malcolm, N., 'Wittgenstein's *Philosophical Investigations*', *Philosophical Review*, 62 (1954): 530–59.

Malcolm, N., 'Knowledge of Other Minds', *The Journal of Philosophy*, 55 (1958): 969–77.

Malcolm, N., 'George Edward Moore', in his *Knowledge and Certainty* (Englewood Cliffs, New Jersey: Prentice-Hall, 1963).

Malcolm, N., 'The Privacy of Experience', (1967). Reprinted in his *Thought and Knowledge* (New York: Cornell University Press, 1977): 104–32.

Malcolm, N., *Ludwig Wittgenstein: A Memoir*, second edn (Oxford: Oxford University Press, 1984).

Malcolm, N., *Nothing is Hidden* (Oxford: Basil Blackwell, 1986).

Marks, C. E., 'Verificationism, Scepticism, and the Private Language Argument', *Philosophical Studies*, 28 (1975): 151–71.

McDowell, J., 'Wittgenstein on Following a Rule', (1984). Reprinted in his *Mind, Value & Reality* (Cambridge, MA: Harvard University Press, 1998): 221–62.

McDowell, J., *Mind and World* (Cambridge, MA: Harvard University Press, 1994).

McGinn, C., *Wittgenstein on Meaning* (London: Basil Blackwell, 1984).

McGinn, M., *Wittgenstein and the Philosophical Investigations* (London, Routledge, 1997).

Mill, J. S., *An examination of Sir William Hamilton's Philosophy*, third edn (London: Longmans, 1867).

Millikan, R. G., *White Queen Psychology and Other Essays for Alice* (Cambridge, MA: MIT Press, 1993).

Millikan, R. G., *Language: A Biological Model* (Oxford: Clarendon Press, 2005).

Moore, G. E., 'Wittgenstein's Lectures in 1930–33', (1954). Reprinted in (Wittgenstein, 1993): 46–114.

Mundle, C. W. K., '"Private Language" and Wittgenstein's Kind of Behaviourism', (1960). Reprinted in (Jones (ed.), 1971): 103–17.

Nedo, M. and Ranchetti, M. (eds), *Wittgenstein: Sein Leben in Bildern und Texten* (Frankfurt am Main, Suhrkamp, 1983).

Neurath, O., 'Physikalismus', (1931). Reprinted in his (1981): 417–21.

Neurath, O., 'Soziologie im Physikalismus', *Erkenntnis*, 2 (1932a): 393–431.

Neurath, O., 'Das Fremdpsychische in der Soziologie', *Erkenntnis*, 3 (1932b): 105–6.

Neurath, O., 'Protocol Sentences', (1932c). Translated in (Ayer (ed,), 1959): 199–208.

Neurath, O., 'Radical Physicalism and 'the Real World' ', (1934). Translated in his (1983): pp. 100–114.

Neurath, O., *Empiricism and Sociology*, M. Neurath and R. S. Cohen (eds) (Dordrecht, NL: Reidel, 1973).

Neurath, O., *Gesammelte philosophische und methodologische Schriften*, R. Haller and H. Rutte (eds) (Wien: Hölder–Pichler–Tempsky, 1981).

Neurath, O, *Philosophical Papers 1913–1946*, R.S. Cohen and M. Neurath (editors and translators.) (Dordrecht, NL: Reidel, 1983).

Paul, G. A., 'Wittgenstein', in A. J. Ayer et al (eds), *The Revolution in Philosophy* (London: Macmillan, 1956): 88–96.

Pears, D., *Ludwig Wittgenstein* (New York: The Viking Press, 1970).

Perkins, M., 'Two Arguments Against a Private Language', *The Journal of Philosophy*, 62 (1965): 443–59.

Pitcher, G., *The Philosophy of Wittgenstein* (Englewood Cliffs, New Jersey: Prentice-Hall, 1964).

Pitcher, G. (ed.), *Wittgenstein: The Philosophical Investigations* (New York: Anchor Books, 1966).

Price, H. H., 'Our Evidence for the Existence of Other Minds', *Philosophy*, 13 (1938): 425–56.

Putnam, H., 'Brains and Behaviour', in R.J. Butler (ed.), *Analytical Philosophy (Second Series)* (Oxford: Basil Blackwell, 1965): 1–19.

Quine, W. V. O., 'Two Dogmas of Empiricism', *The Philosophical Review*, 60 (1951): 20–43.

Quine, W. V. O., 'On Mental Entities', in his *The Ways of Paradox* (New York: Random House, 1966): 208–14.

Rhees, R., 'Can There Be a Private Language?', (1954). Reprinted in (Jones (ed.), 1971): 61–75.

Rorty, R., 'Mind-Body Identity, Privacy, and Categories', *Review of Metaphysics*, 19 (1965): 41–8.

Rorty, R. (ed.), *The Linguistic Turn* (Chicago: The University of Chicago Press, 1967).

Rorty, R., 'Wittgenstein, Privileged Access, and Incommunicability' (1970). Reprinted in (Shanker (ed.), 1986): 279–302.

Russell, B., *An Inquiry Into Meaning and Truth* (London: Allen and Unwin, 1970).

Ryle, G., *The Concept of Mind* (London: Hutchinson House, 1949).

Ryle, G., 'Ludwig Wittgenstein', (1951). Reprinted in his *Collected Papers, Vol. 1* (London: Hutchinson of London, 1971): 249–58.

Ryle, G., 'Ordinary Language', (1953). Reprinted in (Chappell (ed.), 1964): 24–40.

Ryle, G., 'Autobiographical', in O.P Wood and G. Pitcher (eds), *Ryle: A Collection of Critical Essays* (New York: Doubleday, 1970).

Sartorelli, J., 'Review of Baker and Hacker(1984)', *Philosophical Review*, 100 (1991): 660–62.

Savigny, E. von, *Die Philosophie der normalen Sprache* (Frankfurt: Suhrkamp Verlag, 1969).

Savigny, E. von, *Analytische Philosophie* (Freiburg: Verlag Karl Alber, 1970).

Savigny, E. von, *Wittgensteins "Philosophische Untersuchungen" – Ein Kommentar für Leser. Band I und II* (Frankfurt am Main: Vittorio Klostermann, 1988).

Savigny, E. von (ed.), *Ludwig Wittgenstein, Philosophische Untersuchungen* (Berlin: Akademischer Verlag, 1998).

Schilpp, P. A. (ed.), *The Philosophy of Rudolf Carnap*, (La Salle, Illinois: Open Court, 1963).

Schlick, M., 'The Turning Point in Philosophy', (1930). Translated in his (1979): 154–60.

Schlick, M., 'Form and Content. An Introduction to Philosophical Thinking', (1932). Reprinted in his (1938): 151–250.

Schlick, M., 'On the Relation between Psychological and Physical concepts', (1935). Reprinted in his (1979): 420–36.

Schlick, M., 'Meaning and Verification', (1936). Reprinted in his (1938): 337–69.

Schlick, M., *Gesammelte Aufsätze: 1926–1936* (Wien: Gerold & Co, 1938).

Schlick, M., *Philosophical Papers Vol. 2 (1925–1936)*, eds H. L. Mulder and B. van de Velde-Schlick (Dordrecht, NL: Reidel, 1979).

Sellars, W., 'Empiricism and the Philosophy of Mind', (1956). Reprinted in his *Science, Perception and Reality* (New York: Routledge and Kegan Paul, 1963): 127–96.

Shanker, S., 'Introduction: Approaching the *Investigations*', in (Shanker (ed.), 1986): 1–23.

Shanker, S. (ed.), *Ludwig Wittgenstein: Critical Assessments, Vol. II* (London: Routledge, 1986).

Shoemaker, S., *Self–Knowledge and Self–Identity* (Ithaca: Cornell University Press, 1963).

Smerud, W. B., *Can There Be a Private Language?* (Paris: Mouton, 1970).

Stace, W.T., *The Theory of Knowledge and Existence* (Oxford: Clarendon Press, 1932).

Stern, D. G., 'Review Essay: Recent work on Wittgenstein 1980–1990', *Synthése*, 98 (1994): 415–58.

Stern, D. G., 'A new exposition of the 'private language argument': Wittgenstein's 'Notes for the "Philosophical Lecture"', *Philosophical Investigations*, 17 (1994): 552–65.

Stern, D. G., *Wittgenstein on Mind and Language* (New York: Oxford University Press, 1995).

Strawson, P. F., 'Critical Notice: Philosophical Investigations', in *Mind*, LXIII (1954): 70–99.

Strawson, P. F., 'Persons', *Minnesota Studies in the Philosophy of Science*, II (1958): 330–53.

Strawson, P. F., *Individuals – An Essay in Descriptive Metaphysics* (London: Methuen, 1959).

Strawson, P. F., '"Scruton and Wright on Anti-Realism Etc."', *Aristotelian Society Proceedings* LXXVII (1976): 15–21.

Thomson, J. J., 'Private Languages', (1964). Reprinted in (Jones (ed.), 1971): 183–204.

Uebel, T. E., *Overcoming Logical Positivism from Within. The Emergence of Neurath's Naturalism in the Vienna Circle's Protocol Sentence Debate* (Amsterdam, NL: Rodopi, 1992).

Uebel, T. E., 'Physicalism in Wittgenstein and the Vienna Circle', in K. Gavroglu et al (eds), *Physics, Philosophy and the Scientific Community* (Dordrecht, NL: Kluwer, 1995).

Walton, D.; Strongman, K. T., 'Neonate Crusoes, the private language argument and psychology', *Philosophical Psychology*, 11 (1998): 443–65.

Warnock, G. J., 'Gilbert Ryle's Editorship', *Mind*, 85 (1976): 47–56.

Williams, M., 'Blind obedience: rules, community and the individual', (1991). Reprinted in her *Wittgenstein, Mind and Meaning* (London: Routledge, 1999): 157–87.

Winch, P., *The Idea of a Social Science* (London: Routledge and Kegan Paul: 1959).

Wisdom, J., 'Wittgenstein on "Private Language"', in (Ambrose and Lazerowitz, 1972): 13–26.

Wittgenstein, L., *Tractatus Logico–Philosophicus*, (1921). Translated. (London: Routledge and Kegan Paul, 1961).

Wittgenstein, L., 'Some Remarks on Logical Form', (1929). Reprinted in his (1993): 29–35.

Wittgenstein, L., *Philosophical Investigations*, (1953). Translated. (Oxford: Basil Blackwell, 1974).

Wittgenstein, L., *Remarks on the Foundations of Mathematics*, Translated. (Oxford: Basil Blackwell, 1956).

Wittgenstein, L., *The Blue and Brown Books.* (Oxford: Oxford University Press, 1958).

Wittgenstein, L., *Notebooks 1914–1916.* Translated. (Oxford: Basil Blackwell, 1961).

Wittgenstein, L., *Philosophical Remarks*, (1964). Translated. (New York: Barnes and Noble, 1975).

Wittgenstein, L., *Ludwig Wittgenstein and the Vienna Circle – conversations recorded by Friedrich Waismann*, (1967a). Translated. (Oxford: Basil Blackwell, 1979).

Wittgenstein, L., *Zettel* (Oxford: Basil Blackwell, 1967b).

Wittgenstein, L., 'Notes for Lectures on 'Private Experience' and 'Sense Data' ', R. Rhees (ed.), (1968). Reprinted in (Jones (ed.), 1971): 229–76.

Wittgenstein, L., *Philosophical Occasions 1912–1951*, J. Klagge and A. Nordmann (eds) (Indianapolis: Hackett, 1993).

Wittgenstein, L., *Wiener Ausgabe, vol. 2*, M. Nedo (ed.) (Vienna: Springer Verlag, 1994).

Wittgenstein, L., *Philosophische Untersuchungen: Kritisch-genetische Edition.* J. Schulte (ed.) in co-operation with H. Nyman, E. von Savigny and G. H. von Wright (Frankfurt am Main: Suhrkamp Verlag, 2001).

Wittgenstein, L., *The Big Typescript: TS 213 – German–English Scholars' Edition*, C. G. Luckhardt and M. Aue (eds) (Oxford: Blackwell Publishers, 2005).

Wright, C., 'Anti–realist Semantics: the Role of Criteria', (1978). Reprinted in his (1987): 241–66.

Wright, C., *Wittgenstein on the Foundations of Mathematics* (Cambridge, MA: Harvard University Press, 1980).

Wright, C., 'Second Thoughts about Criteria', (1984). Reprinted in his (1987): 267–87.

Wright, C., *Realism, Meaning and Truth* (Oxford: Basil Blackwell, 1987).

Wright, C., *Truth and Objectivity* (Cambridge, MA: Harvard University Press, 1992).

Wright, G.H. von, 'The Origin and Composition of the *Investigations*', in C.G. Luckhardt (ed.), *Wittgenstein: Sources and Perspectives* (Hassocks: Harvester Press, 1979).

Index